**BSA**

# SERVICE  SHEETS

# *1958 to 1967*
# *C15-C15T-C15S-C15SS*
# *B40-SS90-B40E*

*A Floyd Clymer Publication*
*Published in 2021 by VelocePress.com*

# INTRODUCTION

Welcome to the world of digital publishing ~ the book you now hold in your hand was printed using the latest state of the art digital technology. The advent of print-on-demand has forever changed the publishing process, never has information been so accessible and it is our hope that this book serves your informational needs for years to come. If this is your first exposure to digital publishing, we hope that you are pleased with the results. Many more titles of interest to the classic automobile and motorcycle enthusiast, collector and restorer are available via our website at www.VelocePress.com. We hope that you find this title as interesting as we do.

# NOTE FROM THE PUBLISHER

The information presented is true and complete to the best of our knowledge. All recommendations are made without any guarantees on the part of the author or the publisher, who also disclaim all liability incurred with the use of this information.

# TRADEMARKS

We recognize that some words, model names and designations, for example, mentioned herein are the property of the trademark holder. We use them for identification purposes only. This is not an official publication.

# INFORMATION ON THE USE OF THIS PUBLICATION

This manual is an invaluable resource for those interested in performing their own maintenance. However, in today's information age we are constantly subject to changes in common practice, new technology, availability of improved materials and increased awareness of chemical toxicity. As such, it is advised that the user consult with an experienced professional prior to undertaking any procedure described herein. While every care has been taken to ensure correctness of information, it is obviously not possible to guarantee complete freedom from errors or omissions or to accept liability arising from such errors or omissions. Therefore, any individual that uses the information contained within, or elects to perform or participate in do-it-yourself repairs or modifications acknowledges that there is a risk factor involved and that the publisher or its associates cannot be held responsible for personal injury or property damage resulting from the use of the information or the outcome of such procedures.

# WARNING!

One final word of advice, this publication is intended to be used as a reference guide, and when in doubt the reader should consult with a qualified technician.

# BSA 'SERVICE SHEETS'

## UNDERSTANDING AND INTERPRETING THE 1945 AND ONWARDS PUBLICATIONS

In 1945, after the war had ended, BSA resumed production of their civilian line of motorcycles. However, they continued their pre-war practice of publishing repair, overhaul and technical information in the form of individual 'Service Sheets'. It should be noted that BSA never intended that these service sheets would be distributed to the general public, they were 'dealer only' publications and, as such, the print quality was at times somewhat questionable. It was not until the early 1960's that BSA eventually started publishing model specific workshop manuals that were available to the general public. Consequently, these 'Service Sheets' were the only publications available for the maintenance and repair of BSA models that were manufactured through the early 1960's.

At some point in the 1930's, BSA adopted the practice of identifying their various model types by 'groups' and the models manufactured from 1945 through the mid 1960's were in Groups A, B, C, D and M. The service sheets that were associated to a particular group were identified numerically and, while there were some exceptions due to overlapping data between models, in general terms the numbers relate to a particular model group. They are as follows: The 200 series of service sheets were applicable to Group A models, the 300 series to Group B, the 400 series to Group C, the 500 series to Group D and the 600 series to Group M. In addition, there were a 700 series applicable to mechanical maintenance and an 800 series for electronic service and wiring diagrams. Both the 700 and 800 series of service sheets contained information that was <u>not</u> model specific but was applicable across multiple model groups. Finally, there were a 900 series for the BSA Dandy and a 1000 series for the BSA Sunbeam and Triumph Tigress scooter.

Unfortunately, as these service sheets were issued individually and at random times, the numbering sequence within any group is, at times, illogical and not necessarily consecutive. Consequently, assembling those individual sheets into a publication that serves as a model specific workshop manual is a somewhat difficult task and owners of BSA motor cycles are subjected to considerable confusion surrounding the appropriate selection from the multitude of reprints that have recently flooded the on-line marketplace. Many of the reprints found on internet websites are from 'bedroom sellers' at enticingly low prices by individuals that really have no idea what they are selling. Many are nothing more than poor quality comb-bound photocopies that are scanned and printed complete with greasy pages and thumbprints and, as such, are deceptively described as 'pre-owned', 'used' or even 'refurbished'! In addition, they are often advertised for the incorrect series and/or model years of motorcycles.

The most complete compilation of the 1945 and onwards service sheets was issued by BSA in the form of a 'dealer only' ring binder that contained all of the individual service sheets totaling to almost 500 pages, it is extremely scarce and difficult to find. It is this ring bound publication that was used to create this 'Service Sheet' manual'.

# 'C' GROUP SERVICE SHEET MANUALS 1958-1967

This manual includes the 21 service sheets (87 pages) published by BSA under part number 00-4082. However, an additional 13 service sheets have been added from that 'dealer only' publication, to produce a single manual containing 34 service sheets (148 pages) that cover the 1958 to 1967 unit construction, swing arm C15, C15T, C15S, C15SS and B40 models. Please note that service sheets other than those in the 400 series that are included in this publication may also contain data that is applicable to 'other' model groups, as that was the original intention.

For additional information the reader is directed to **'The Book of the BSA OHV & SV singles 250cc 1954 to 1970'** (ISBN 9781588501585) which covers the C10L, C11G, C12, C15, C15SS, C15T. C15S, SS80, Sportsman, C15G, C25 Barracuda & B25 Starfire.

## GENERAL INDEX

# BSA SERVICE SHEET No. 412C

## D3, D5, D7, C12, C15 and B40 SWINGING ARM MODELS
### REAR SUSPENSION

**FRAME**

The silent bloc bushes fitted to the rear suspension swinging arm are unlikely to need replacement for some considerable time. If it is found necessary to renew them, first remove the suspension units by detaching the top pivot bolts and the bottom retaining nuts.

Remove the rear wheel and chainguard. Undo the fork spindle nut and tap out the spindle, using a suitable drift.

Lift the rear fork until it is clear of the side plates; it can then be turned and pulled away from the rear.

After the central distance piece has been displaced the bushes can be removed with a suitable drift.

**DISMANTLING THE SUSPENSION UNITS**

Early C12 models were fitted with a damper spring of 100 lb./inch rate, this was later increased to 124 lb./inch.

The 124 lb./inch spring, part number 29–4570 can be fitted to early machines where it is considered necessary.

The spring is retained by circlips fitted at its base and a service tool, part number 61–5064 has been introduced to facilitate removal.

The tool is assembled as shown in Fig. C46 and when the nut is screwed down sufficiently the spring is compressed thus releasing the circlips. The circlips can be extracted through the apertures in the tool and the spring comes away when the tool is removed.

Reassembly is in the reverse order.

Fig. C46.

B.S.A. MOTOR CYCLES LTD., Service Department, Armoury Road, Birmingham 11.
Printed in England at the B.S.A. Press

## MODELS C15 AND B40
## ENGINE DISMANTLING FOR DECARBONISING

It will facilitate this work if the dual seat and petrol tank are removed. Take off the seat which is attached to the frame by the top bolts of the rear suspension units and clipped to a cross tube at the front.

Turn off the petrol tap and detach the petrol pipe by unscrewing the union nut. The tank is mounted on rubber pads and secured by a single bolt which passes through a rubber sleeve in the centre of the tank. Remove the rubber cap on the tank top, unscrew the nut, and withdraw the tank leaving the bolt in the frame.

Disconnect the engine steady bracket from the frame and the rubber connection between the air cleaner and carburetter.

The exhaust pipe is a push on fit and can be removed after the finned collar has been slackened and the bolts securing the pipe to the frame released.

Disconnect the exhaust lifter from the lever on top of the rocker box.

### Removing the Cylinder Head and Valves

Take off the oil feed pipe to the rocker spindles and remove the sparking plug.

Remove the two 5/16 in. nuts holding the engine steady bracket to the rocker box, revolve the engine to set the piston at T.D.C. on the compression stroke, i.e., with both valves closed, and take off the four nuts *H* (Fig. C1A) holding the cylinder head and barrel.

Late model B40 machines have an extra nut each side of push rod tower.

With the rocker box in position on the head raise the head until it clears the fixing studs, rotate the whole assembly about the push rods to clear the frame tube, and lift off.

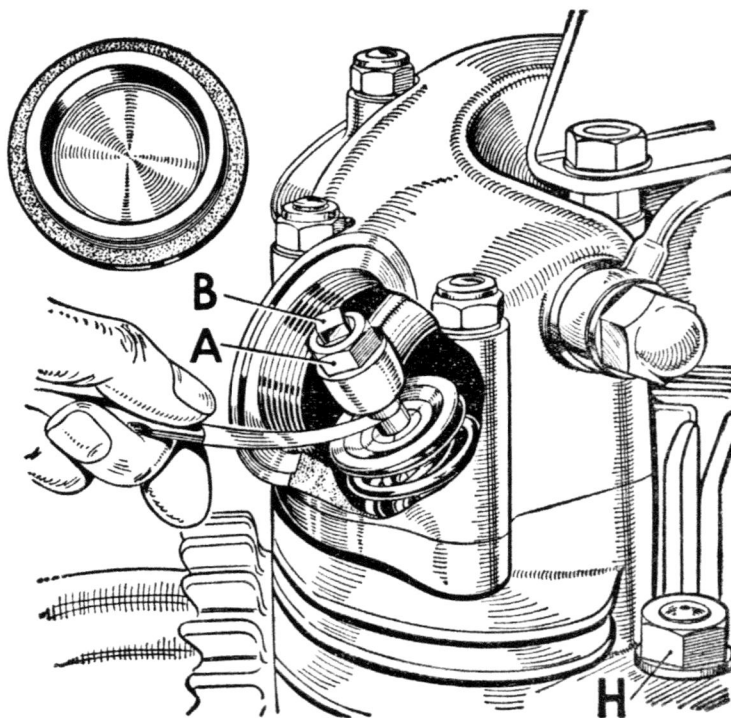

Fig. C1A. Tappet Adjustment.

Take the push rods out of the tube and on 250c.c. models remove the tube. There are sealing rings at each end, and if there has been any sign of leakage the seals should be replaced.

Now take off the two thin nuts on the steady stay studs and the seven 1/4 in. nuts holding the rocker box to the head, unscrew the two circular inspection covers, remove the cover above the push rod tube by unscrewing the centre bolt, and lift the rocker box from the head.

There should be no need to disturb the rockers unless it is known that they require attention. Carefully remove the head gasket.

It is not necessary or desirable to remove the cylinder barrel unless it is suspected that the piston or its rings are the cause of some trouble.

Compress the valve springs with Service Tool 84061–3340 and remove the split cotters and springs. Take out the valves.

Scrape all carbon from cylinder head and ports and from the top of the piston, finally polishing with fine emery cloth. Take care not to damage the valve seats. Remove all traces of loose carbon and dust. Rotate the engine so that the piston descends to allow removal of dust from the upper cylinder walls.

## Valve Springs

After a period of several thousand miles, valve springs tend to lose their efficiency due to heat, and as their cost is relatively low, it is good policy to renew them at this stage rather than dismantle specially for this purpose at a later date. The correct free length is, inner 1-5/8 in., outer 2-1/32 in. for C15, C15T and B40. Note: The high performance scrambles engine uses different valve springs their free lengths being :– inner 1.500″ outer 1.670″. The fitted length must be 1-5/16″.

## Grinding in Valves

Valve grinding should only be carried out where the pitting is not deep. If deep pit marks are evident the valve should be refaced on a machine, as grinding in would only cause wear of the seats and the valve may become pocketed.

Clean all carbon off the valve and from the stem underneath the head, being careful not to damage the face or the portion of the stem which moves in the valve guide.

Smear a small quantity of grinding compound—obtainable from any garage, over the valve face and return it to its seat.

Using Tool number 11465–9240 rotate the valve backwards and forwards maintaining a steady pressure, every few strokes lifting the valve from its seat and turning to a new position.

Continue until the face shows a smooth surface all round with no dark spots.

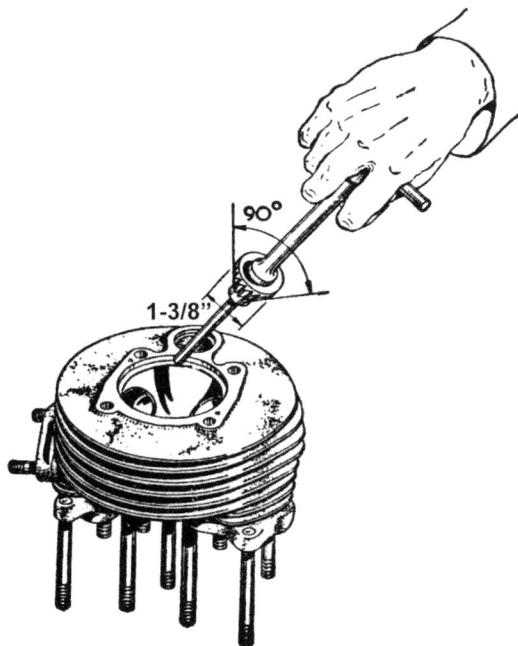

**Fig. C2A.** Cutting the Valve Seats.

It is most important that valves are ground in on their correct seats, for this reason both valves are marked, one "IN" and the other "EX."

After grinding remove all traces of compound from both valve face and seating, and smear the stems with clean engine oil.

If the valve seats in the head require re-cutting, use Service Tools number 61–3293 Pilot, 61–3298 Cutter (Fig. C2A).

## Fitting New Guides

When new guides are to be fitted, the old ones can be driven out with Service Tool number 61–3265 from inside the combustion chamber and new ones fitted with the same punch from above.

Before driving in the new guides make sure that the circlips are a good fit. Valve seats in the head must always be re-cut when new guides are fitted to ensure that the seat is concentric with the guide bore.

## Removing the Cylinder Barrel

Slacken off the two nuts on the crankcase at the base of the cylinder and slide the cylinder off, steadying the piston as it emerges from the barrel. Cover the crankcase mouth with clean rag to prevent dust and grit falling in.

Fig. C3A. Checking Piston Ring Gap

## Piston Rings

The gudgeon pin is located by means of wire circlips which must be removed with the tang of a file or similar tool. Warm the piston and withdraw the gudgeon pin, thus freeing the piston, and immediately after its removal mark the inside of the piston so that it may be reassembled in its original position.

If inspection of the piston rings shows that they are stuck, prise them out very carefully, and clean them. Remove any carbon from the grooves and rings, but before replacing, check them in the cylinder for gap. (Fig. C3A). If the gaps are excessive, new rings having gaps of between .009 in and .013 in. when in position must be fitted.

## B.S.A. Service Sheet No. 421 (contd.)

At this stage it is advisable to check the big end bearing for wear. Turn the engine until the piston is at the top of its stroke, and resting both hands on the sides of the crankcase mouth, hold the connecting rod between fingers and thumbs, and feel for up and down play. It should be remembered that, even though there may be a little play present it will not necessarily mean sudden failure of the bearing, though it will inevitably become worse. Where play seems excessive, and big end noise has been noticed with the engine running, the engine should be completely dismantled, and a new big end assembly fitted.


### Assembly after Decarbonising

Replace the valves and springs in the cylinder head, making sure that the valves are assembled on the seats from which they were removed, and take care to see that the split collets are seated correctly in their grooves in the valve stems—a dab of grease on the stem will assist this operation.

Pour a little oil into the crankcase, and smear the cylinder walls liberally with oil. See that the cylinder base washer is in good condition—if damaged, replace, otherwise oil leaks will develop. Turn the engine until the crankshaft is a little past bottom dead centre, then compressing the top piston ring with the fingers, slide the cylinder barrel over the piston and top ring. Compress each ring in turn as the barrel is refitted, and take care to avoid breaking the rings. It is essential to see that the mouth of the crankcase is completely covered with rag before commencing to replace the cylinder as if it is uncovered, and a ring is broken, the pieces may drop into the crankcase and will be difficult to recover. Return the piston to top dead centre on the compression stroke, ready for the cylinder head to be fitted.

Replace the push rod tube in position alongside the cylinder barrel, apply a little grease to the lower ends of the push rods and place the rods in position on the tappets. Replace the head gasket.

Refit the rocker box to the cylinder head leaving off the inspection covers, and slacken off the rocker adjusting screws.

Place the head in position over the studs, locate the outer push rod in the inlet rocker (rear) and the inner push rod on exhaust rocker (front) as in Fig. C4A.

Screw on the four cylinder head nuts and washers and tighten down firmly and evenly. Check that the push rods are correctly fitted and replace the inspection covers and washers.

Securely tighten the two nuts on the crankcase immediately below the cylinder base and check over the rocker box nuts.

Replace the engine steady stay over the two thin 5/16 in. nuts screw on the thick 5/16 in. nuts and spring washers and tighten securely, re-connect the steady stay to the frame.

**B.S.A. Service Sheet No. 421** (contd.)

## Tappet Adjustment

Rotate the engine forward until the inlet valve is just closed and the push rod is free to rotate and set the exhaust valve clearance by screwing the adjuster pin *B* (Fig. C1A) in or out and tighten the locknut *A* (Fig. C1A) securely.

Rotate the engine forward again until the exhaust valve clearance is just taken up but before the valve starts to open, and set the inlet valve clearance. Check both settings after the locknuts have been tightened to make sure that they have not altered.

Finally replace the tappet inspection covers, sparking plug, H.T. lead, carburetter, air cleaner connection, petrol tank, petrol pipe and dual seat.

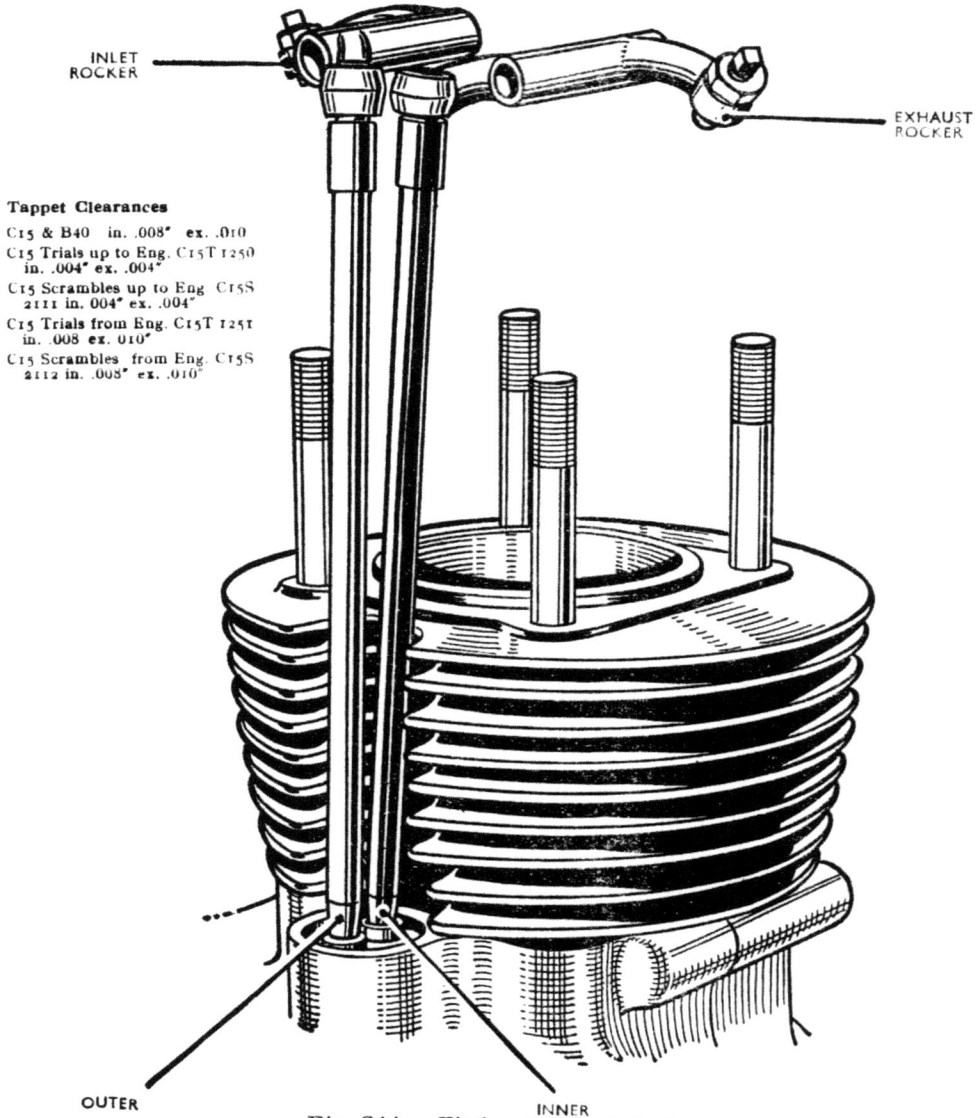

INLET ROCKER

EXHAUST ROCKER

**Tappet Clearances**

C15 & B40   in. .008″ ex. .010

C15 Trials up to Eng. C15T 1250
in. .004″ ex. .004″

C15 Scrambles up to Eng. C15S
2111 in. 004″ ex. .004″

C15 Trials from Eng. C15T 1251
in. .008 ex. 010″

C15 Scrambles from Eng. C15S
2112 in. .008″ ex. .010″

OUTER

INNER

Fig. C4A.   Fitting the Push Rods.

B.S.A. MOTOR CYCLES LTD., Service Dept., Armoury Road, Birmingham **11**.

Printed in England — B.S.A. Press

8

# ~~BSA~~ SERVICE SHEET No. 422

### MODELS C15 AND B40
#### (Except those with Engine Nos. prefixed C15F or B40F)
### DISMANTLING AND REASSEMBLING THE CLUTCH, GEARBOX AND GEARCHANGE

The gears are contained in a separate housing formed in the rear portion of the crankcase and become accessible after the inner and outer timing covers have been removed from the R/H side of the unit, so that the valve timing pinions are uncovered at the same time.

Parts such as the kickstart spring and pawl, cam plate and spring, selector forks and footchange return spring, can be replaced without removing any other parts but if the gears are to be removed then the whole of the primary drive must be dismantled first.

**Primary Drive**

Disconnect the alternator lead by pulling out the three connectors. Remove the left hand footrest, it is fitted to a taper shaft and will require a sharp blow with a mallet to release it after the nut which has a L/H thread, has been removed.

Place a large flat tin under the primary chain case to catch the oil, and take out the 10 screws holding the cover. The screws are of three different lengths and careful note should be taken of their respective positions to facilitate refitting, screw M (Fig. C5A) also serves as the level plug.

Depress the rear brake pedal and take off the primary chain case cover.

To remove the stator take off the three nuts and washers E (Fig. C6A) and pull the alternator lead through the rubber grommet in the back of the chain case.

Note carefully that the stator plate is fitted with the lead on the outside.

Bend back the tab of the lock washer B (Fig. C6A) under the engine main shaft nut and remove the nut C which has a R/H thread.

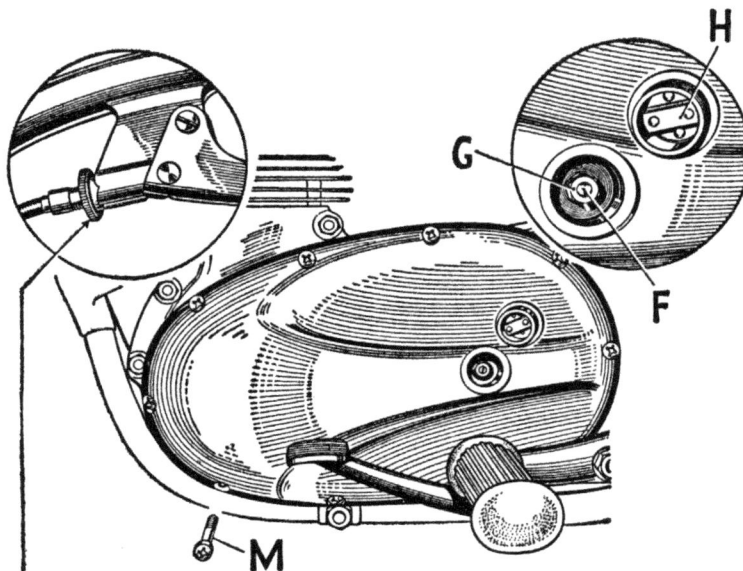

Fig. C5A.   Clutch Adjustment

It will facilitate the removal of the nut if top gear is engaged and the rear brake applied.

**B.S.A. Service Sheet No. 422 (contd.)**

Pull off the rotor and take out the Woodruff key to avoid it being lost.

Remove the four spring retaining nuts P (Fig. C6A) on the clutch, and withdraw the springs and cups. The pressure plate L (Fig. C6A) and the remaining clutch plates can now be removed but note should be made of the order in which they are fitted.

Bend back the tab of the lock washer and unscrew the gearbox main shaft nut. The lock washer has a special tongue which engages in the hub of the clutch and it must be refitted in the same way.

The thrust washer which will now be exposed is recessed on one side and must be fitted with the recess outwards.

Pull out the clutch push rod, engage top gear, apply the rear brake, and unscrew the gearbox main shaft nut.

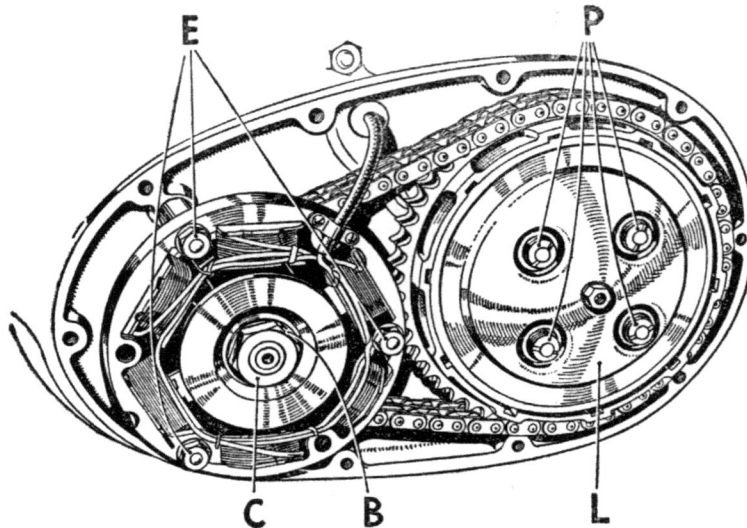

Fig. C6A.   Clutch and Generator Removal.

With extractor number 82561-3583 (Fig. C7A) the clutch sleeve can be freed from the tapered main shaft and the chainwheel, chain and engine sprocket withdrawn together and laid face down on the bench with the spring studs uppermost.

The clutch centre B (Fig. C8A) can be lifted out leaving the sleeve C and rollers in the chainwheel.

To examine the cush drive rubbers take out the four counter sunk head screws and lift off the front cover plate, unless wear or damage is suspected however the rubbers should not be disturbed.

New rubber inserts E (Fig. C8A) should be fitted as shown with the thicker segment being inserted first on the pressure or driven side of the vane and compressed by slightly rotating the vane, when the thinner segments can be pressed into position. A special tool No. 83161-3689 is necessary for the B40 as the rubbers are much stronger and of equal thickness.

Later model C15 and B40 machines with eight rubbers of equal thickness now use eight round rubbers of equal thickness. Neither the wedge or the round rubbers of equal thickness can be used on the early models unless the clutch centre and spider are changed for the latest type, but, the old type rubbers will continue to be available as spares.

When reassembling the clutch, note that the plates are alternately plain and segmented, the first plate next to the chainwheel being plain.

10

With the clutch removed the detachable plate registered in the rear half of the chain case is now exposed.

Take out the six counter sunk head screws and remove the plate complete with the oil seal.

If the oil seal is suspected of being faulty or leakage has occurred it should be replaced, care being taken not to damage the outer surface of the bush on which the seal bears.

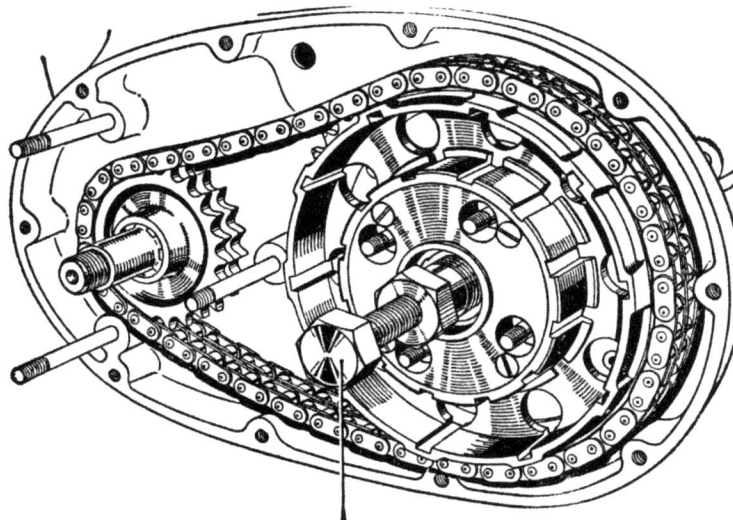

Fig. C7A. Removing the Clutch.

Between the circular plate and the end of the pinion sleeve is a felt washer, the purpose of this washer is to prevent grit damaging the oil seal.

At this stage the gearbox can be dismantled providing the main shaft high gear (or pinion sleeve) is not being disturbed, but if complete dismantling is required the tab washer under the sprocket nut should be turned back and the nut slackened off while it is still possible to engage the gears.

It is now necessary to turn to the other side of the engine unit to remove the inner and outer timing covers.

Take off the exhaust system by slackening the pinch bolt in the finned collar and removing the bolts securing the pipe and silencer to the frame.

Scribe a pencil mark across the body of the distributor and the top of the crankcase to assist in resetting the ignition timing.

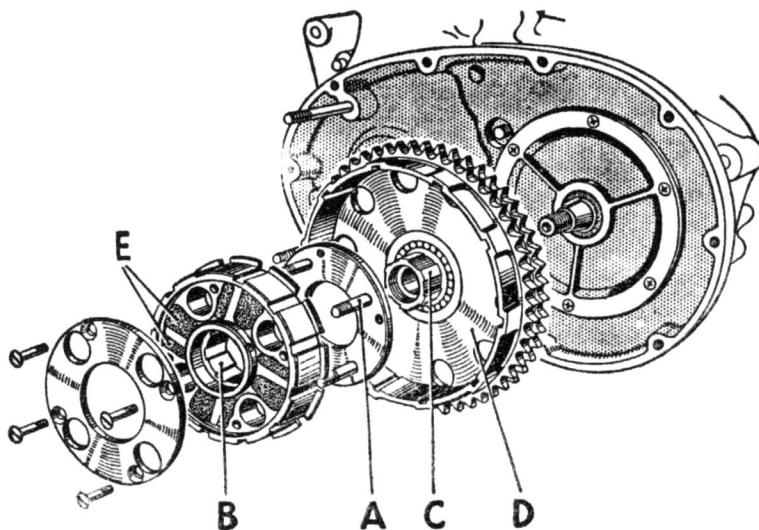

Fig. C8A. Cush Drive Unit.

Release the pinch bolts in the kickstart and foot change levers and remove the levers, slacken the R/H footrest nut and tap the footrest down out of the way.

Unscrew the seven outer cover retaining screws, noting their respective locations, particularly the long small headed screw which also clamps the contact breaker unit.

With the outer cover removed disconnect the clutch cable and withdraw it through the back of the inner cover, being careful not to lose the ball located in the thrust button on the clutch actuating lever.

Prise the kickstart return spring anchor plate (Fig. C9A) off the two flats on the spindle and remove the plate and spring.

Turn back the tab on the lock washer under the cam shaft nut and remove the nut, lock washer, thrust washer and the small locating peg for the thrust washer.

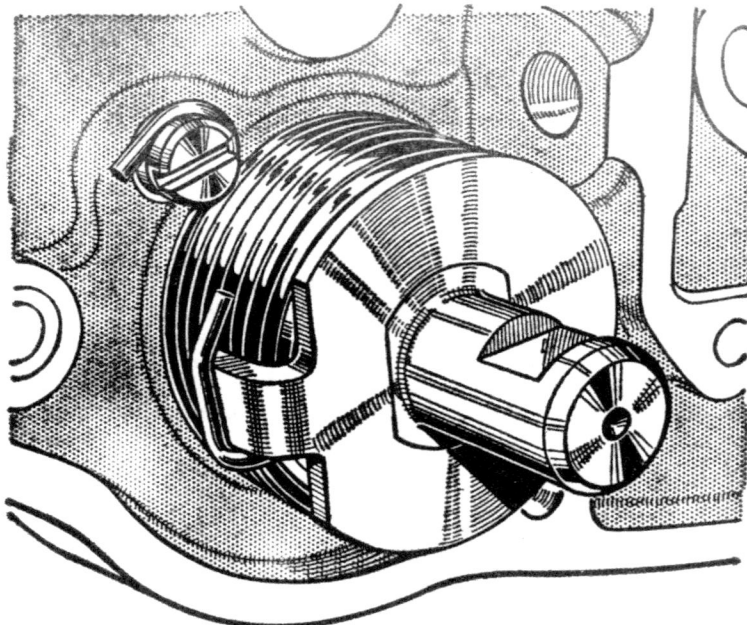

Fig. C9A.   Fitting the Kickstarter Spring.

Take off the cover plate adjacent to the gear change spindle by removing the two screws and remove the split pin from the cam plate pivot.

The pivot pin can now be withdrawn towards the L/H side leaving the cam plate in the gearbox.

After removing the eight recessed screws the inner cover joint can be broken by tapping the kickstart spindle boss with a mallet.   Ease the cover off gently, applying finger pressure to the spindle ends to avoid displacing other components.

The gear cluster, shafts and actuating parts are now exposed together with the valve timing gears and dismantling on the R/H side is therefore the same as for exposing the valve timing pinions.

Unscrew the fulcrum bolt E (Fig. C10A) carrying the return spring when the plunger quadrant, shaft and spring can be removed.   The cam plate can now be taken away from the selector forks.

If the cam plate spring blade B (Fig. C11A) attached to the rear wall of the gearbox is satisfactory it need not be disturbed.

The gear cluster together with the main shaft, lay shaft and selector forks can now be withdrawn leaving the selector fork shaft and pinion sleeve in position in the box.

Note :- If the only attention required is renewal of the kickstart pawl and spring it is only necessary to pull the kickstart spindle away from the layshaft first gear.   Make sure that the ratchet in the first gear is fit for further use.

While the gears can be removed from the shafts it should be noted that the smallest gear on the mainshaft is a press fit, thus retaining the adjacent gear, similarly the innermost gear on the lay shaft is a press fit also retaining the adjacent gear.

Note position of thrust washers.

Do not disturb the high gear (or pinion sleeve unless it is known that the bearing or oil seal is faulty, but if it ts to be removed, fake off the rear chain, sprocket, locknut and tab washer.

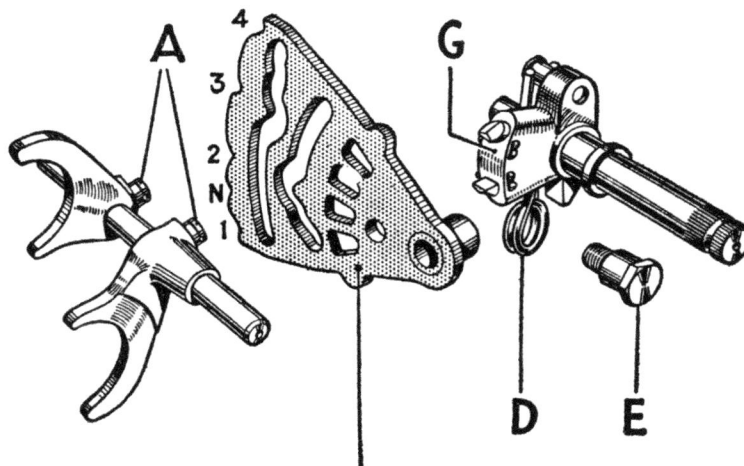

Fig. C10A.   Gearchange Mechanism.

Heat the portion of the gearbox round the pinion sleeve by applying rag dipped in boiling water and tap the bearing and pinion into the gearbox shell.  The replacement should be inserted and driven well home while the gearbox is still warm.

**Reassembly**

Pick up the main shaft and lay shaft complete with the gear cluster and the selector forks as shown in Fig. C11A.

The selector forks are interchangeable but it is advisable to replace them in their spective positions.

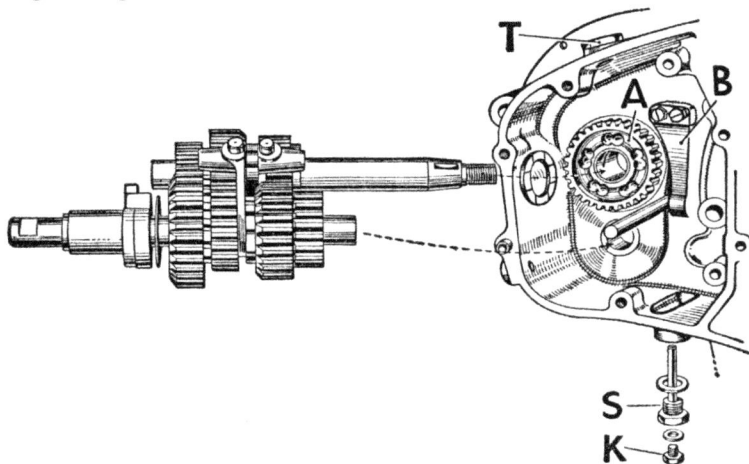

Fig. C11A.   The Gearbox and Gears.

Now slide the whole assembly carefully into position locating the selector forks over the spindle as the assembly enters. Engage the cam plate in the 2nd gear notch (Fig. C10A) on the leaf spring at the back of the box and over the rollers on the selector fork pegs.

**Replacing the Footchange Return Spring**

Hold the shaft in a vice using soft clamps, with the short end and the peg uppermost, then with two substantial tools such

13

as screwdrivers, one through the loop and the other between the prongs twixt the spring *D* (Fig. C10A) and force it over the short end of the shaft so that the prongs lie in the position shown in Fig. C12A. The spring will be squared up when the pivot bolt *E* is screwed home.

Insert the footchange lever quadrant shaft into the box and start the bolt *E* (Fig. C10A) with the fingers, twisting the spring slightly at the same time, finally locking the bolt securely.

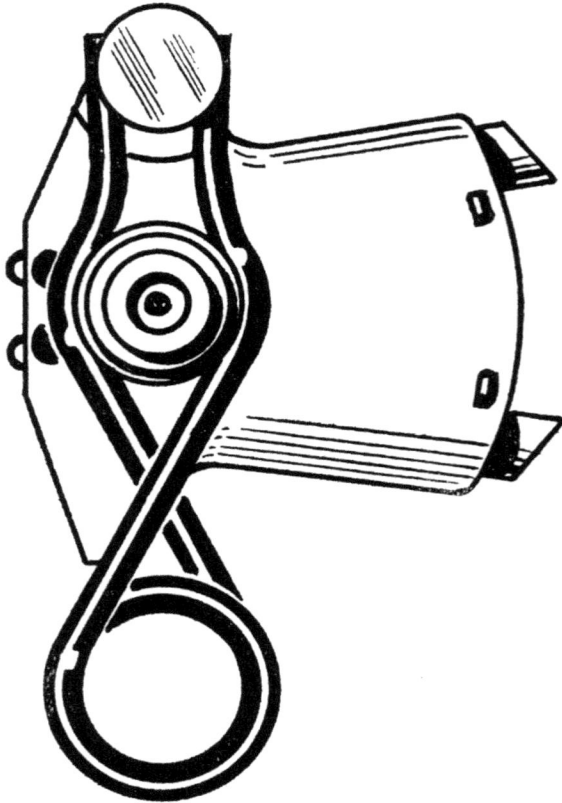

Fig. C12A. Fitting Footchange Return Spring.

See that the crankcase and inner cover joint faces are clean, apply a thin film of jointing compound and slide the inner cover over the various spindles at the same time carefully guiding the cam plate into the slot in the inner cover. Make sure that the cover is close up to the crankcase, replace the eight screws, the cam plate pivot pin, split pin, the washer and cover over the pivot and the two screws.

Before proceeding further check the gear selection.

Place the kickstart spring in position with hook over the stop plate screw, engage the tag on the anchor plate in the outer end of the spring and turn the plate anti-clockwise approximately 180° to engage the plate over the two flats on the spindle as shown in (Fig. C9A).

Pass the clutch cable through the back of the inner cover, apply a dab of grease to the pad on the clutch thrust arm and insert the small steel ball, then connect the cable to the arm.

Replace the thrust washer on the cam shaft with counter sunk face inwards and insert the small peg in the shaft, fit the tab washer and nut, tighten securely and turn the tab over.

Now replace the outer cover being careful to screw the small headed screw into the distributor clip.

Fit the remaining screws and the kickstart and foot change levers.


**Primary Case**

If the gearbox sprocket has been removed it must now be replaced with the boss inwards, then the tab washer and nut.

Thread the rear chain over the sprocket and couple up the ends, select top gear, apply the rear brake then tighten the sprocket nut securely, finally turning over the tab washer.

Where the oil seal is being replaced in the chain case back, it should be pressed in from the gearbox side flush with the cover and the lip inwards.

Place the felt grit protection washer in position over the bronze bush and against the end of the pinion sleeve.

Refit the cover with a paper gasket which need only be jointed on one side and screw in the six counter sunk head screws. Place the felt washer over the gearbox main shaft next to the cover. Replace clutch push rod.

Smear the clutch sleeve C (Fig. C8A) with grease and place the 24 rollers in position. Next slide the chain wheel over the rollers and the clutch centre B (Fig. C8A) over the splines of the clutch sleeve. Place the engine sprocket on the bench alongside with the boss upwards and thread the primary chain over both the sprocket and chain wheel pulling the chain taunt.

The engine main shaft distance piece should not have been disturbed but if it was removed for any reason it must now be replaced with the chamfered side inwards.

See that the Woodruff keys are fitted to both main shafts and that they are a good fit in the keyways.

Pick up the engine sprocket, chain and chain wheel in both hands and slide them over their respective shafts. Place the thick washer with the recess outwards in position against the clutch sleeve then the tab washer which has a special tongue fitting into the clutch centre, then the lock nut. Turn the tab washer over the nut after tightening.

Now place the clutch plates in position starting with one plain plate then one segmented plate and so on alternately, there being five plain plates and four segmented plates.

Place the pressure plate in position then the four spring cups and springs which should be of equal length. If there is any doubt about the condition of the springs, replace them since they are quite cheap to buy.

Screw on the four spring nuts until the underside of each head is approximately 1/8 in. from the face of each cup.

If the springs are compressed excessively, the handlebar lever will be stiff to operate, alternatively, if the spring pressure is insufficient the clutch will tend to slip. Adjust for true running of the plates by declutching and depressing the kickstart lever, when it will be seen if the plates are running true or not. If necessary, adjust the nuts individually to correct any run out.

Replace the rotor with the recessed face outwards, fit the tab washer and nut, turning the tab over the nut after tightening securely.

Place the three distance pieces on the stator plate studs and replace the stator with the lead wires on the outside and at the top.

Screw on the three nuts and spring washers and tighten evenly.

The air gap between the rotor and stator should be equal all round, when correct thread the lead wires through the rubber grommet in the back of the case.

Refit the primary case and the 10 screws, shortest at the rear and longest at the front.

Connect up the lead wires, check the ignition timing, and finally tighten the distributor clamp screw and replace the exhaust system.

Note :- C15 scrambles and sports star models are fitted with a primary chain tensioner. This tensioner can be fitted to C15 Star models the parts required being 13741-0143. 10641-0146 (2) and 10641-0148.

Service Bulletin No 83 (Sept. 1961) gives full instructions for fitting.

B.S.A. MOTOR CYCLES LTD.,
Service Dept., Armoury Road, Birmingham 11.
Printed in England. — B.S.A. Press

# *BSA* SERVICE SHEET No. 422A

**MODELS C15 AND B40 WITH ENGINE NUMBERS
PREFIXED C15F OR B40F**

**DISMANTLING AND REASSEMBLING THE CLUTCH,
GEARBOX AND GEARCHANGE**

The gears are contained in a separate housing formed in the rear portion of the crankcase and become accessible after the inner and outer timing covers have been removed from the right-hand side of the unit, so that the valve timing pinions are uncovered at the same time.

If the gears are to be removed then the whole of the primary drive must be dismantled first.

## PRIMARY DRIVE

Disconnect the alternator lead by pulling out the three connectors. Remove the left-hand footrest, it is fitted to a taper shaft and will require a sharp blow with a mallet to release it after the nut which has a left-hand thread, has been removed.

Place a large flat tin under the primary chaincase to catch the oil, and take out the 10 screws holding the cover. The screws are of three different lengths and careful note should be taken of their respective positions to facilitate refitting, screw (M) Fig. C5A also serves as the level plug.

Depress the rear brake pedal and take off the primary chaincase cover.

To remove the stator take off the three nuts and washers (E) Fig. C6A, and pull the alternator lead through the rubber grommet in the back of the chaincase.

Note carefully that the stator plate is fitted with the lead on the outside.

Bend back the tab of the lockwasher (B) Fig. C6A under the engine crankshaft nut and remove the nut (C) which has a right-hand thread.

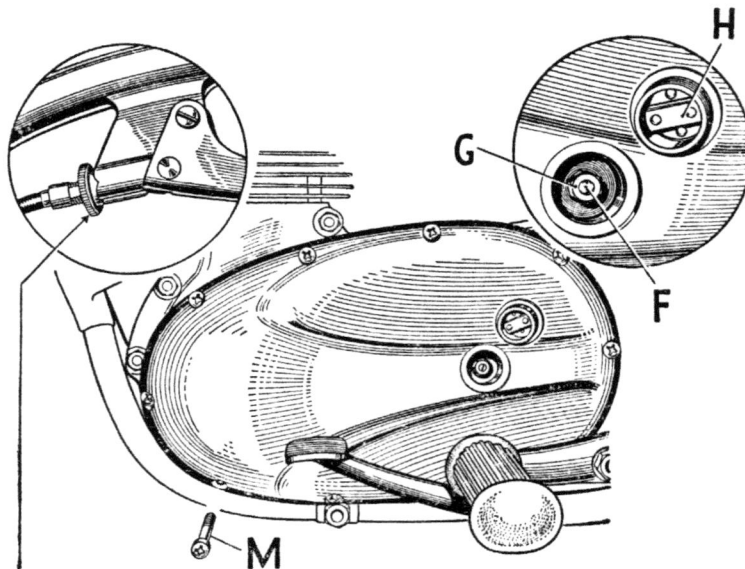

FIG. C5A. *Clutch adjustment.*

It will facilitate the removal of the nut if top gear is engaged and the rear brake applied.

16

Pull off the rotor and take out the Woodruff key to avoid it being lost.

Remove the four spring retaining nuts (P) Fig. C6A on the clutch, and withdraw the springs and cups. The pressure plate (L) Fig. C6A and the remaining clutch plates can now be removed but note should be made of the order in which they are fitted.

Bend back the tab of the lockwasher, pull out the clutch push rod, engage top gear, apply the rear brake, and unscrew the gearbox main shaft nut. The lockwasher has a special tongue which engages in the hub of the clutch and it must be refitted in the same way.

The thrust washer which will now be exposed is recessed on one side and must be refitted with the recess outwards.

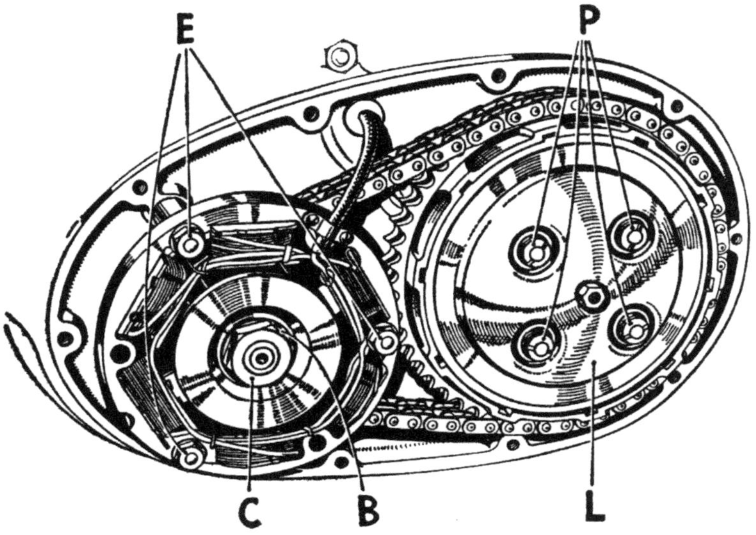

FIG. C6A. *Clutch and generator removal.*

With extractor number 61–3583 (Fig. C7A) the clutch sleeve can be freed from the tapered main shaft and the chainwheel, chain and engine sprocket withdrawn together and laid face down on the bench with the spring studs uppermost.

The clutch centre (B) Fig. C8A can be lifted out leaving the sleeve (C) and rollers in the chainwheel.

To examine the cush drive rubbers take out the four countersunk head screws and lift off the front cover plate, unless wear or damage is suspected the rubbers should not be disturbed.

New rubber inserts (E) Fig. C8A should be fitted as shown with the thicker segment being inserted first on the pressure or driven side of the vane and compressed by slightly rotating the vane, when the thinner segments can be pressed into position. A special tool numbered 61–3689 is necessary for the B40F as the rubbers are much stronger and of equal thickness.

When reassembling the clutch, note that the plates are alternately plain and segmented, the first plate next to the chainwheel being plain.

With the clutch removed the detachable plate registered in the rear half of the chaincase is now exposed.

Take out the six countersunk head screws and remove the plate complete with the oil seal.

If the oil seal is suspected of being faulty or leakage has occured it should be replaced, care being taken not to damage the outer surface of the bush on which the seal bears.

FIG. C7A. *Removing the clutch.*

Between the circular plate and the end of the pinion sleeve is a felt washer, the purpose of this washer is to prevent grit damaging the oil seal.

At this stage the gearbox can be dismantled providing the main shaft high gear (or pinion sleeve) is not being disturbed, but if complete dismantling is required the tab washer under the sprocket nut should be turned back and the nut slackened off while it is still possible to engage the gears.

It is now necessary to turn to the other side of the engine unit to remove the inner and outer timing covers.

Take off the exhaust system by slackening the pinch bolt in the finned collar and remove the bolts securing the pipe and silencer to the frame.

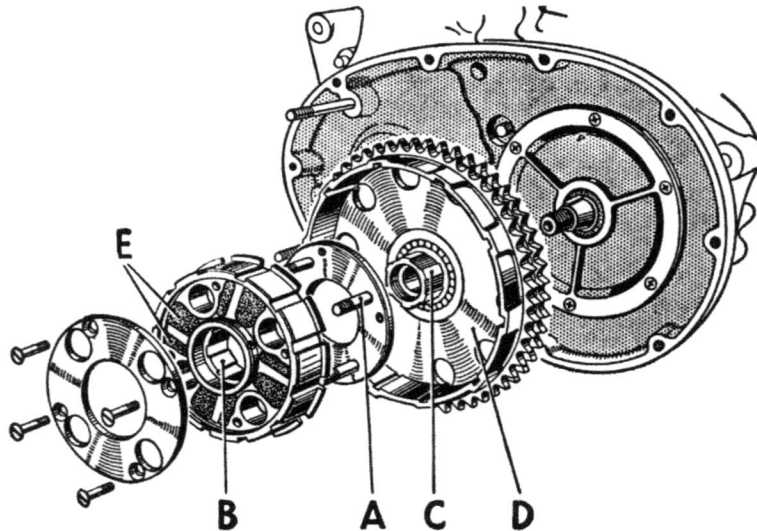

FIG. C8A. *Cush drive unit.*

Release the pinch bolts in the kickstart crank (with carrier) and the footchange lever, and take off both.

Slacken the right-hand footrest nut and tap the footrest out of the way.

Disconnect the clutch cable, unscrew the seven cover retaining screws, noting their respective locations and remove cover.

If the clutch actuating lever is to be withdrawn, care must be taken to avoid losing the operating rack and ball which are loosely located on the inside of the outer cover.

Take out the two contact breaker securing bolts and the central fixing bolt that secures the spindle to the camshaft. Disconnect the low-tension lead and withdraw contact breaker. If necessary the cam can be removed with Service Tool No. 61-3761.

Release the spring from the kickstart spindle and take off spindle with bush. After removing the eight recessed fixing screws, the inner cover joint can be broken by tapping gently around the edges with a mallet.

The cover, complete with the gear cluster and footchange mechanism can then be eased away, leaving only the valve timing gear and oil pump exposed.

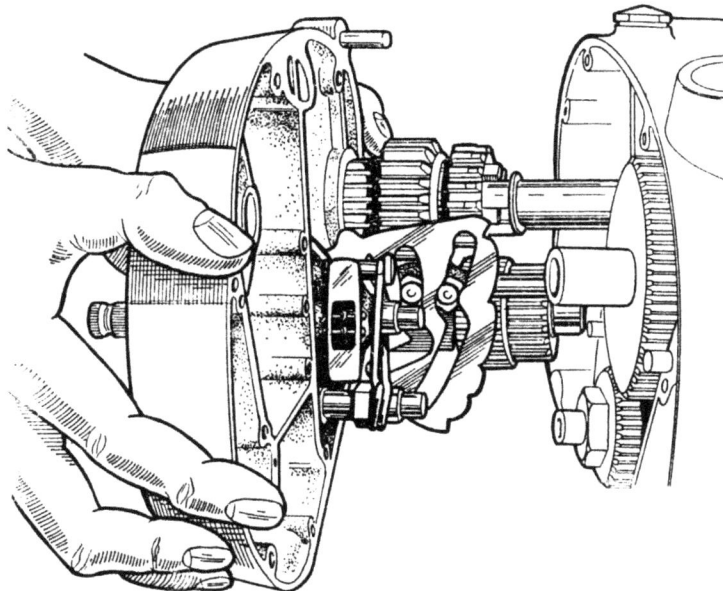

FIG. C9A. *Removing the inner timing cover.*

Withdraw the plunger quadrant and return spring from the inner cover, leaving the fulcrum bolt in position. After extracting the split pin from the cam plate pivot, the pivot and the cam plate can be drawn away from the cover.

The mainshaft is secured to the inner cover by a locking washer and nut (also retaining the kickstart mechanism) and may be left in place while the layshaft, gears and selector forks are removed.

It should be noted that the smallest gear on the mainshaft is a press fit, thus retaining the adjacent gear; similarly, the innermost gear on the layshaft is a press fit also retaining the adjacent gear.

Note position of each thrust washer and ensure that they are replaced correctly.

Do not disturb the high gear (or pinion sleeve) unless it is known that the bearing or oil seal is faulty. First heat the portion of the gearbox around the pinion sleeve by applying rag dipped in hot water, then tap the bearing and sleeve into the gearbox shell. The replacement bearing should be inserted and driven right home while the case is still warm.

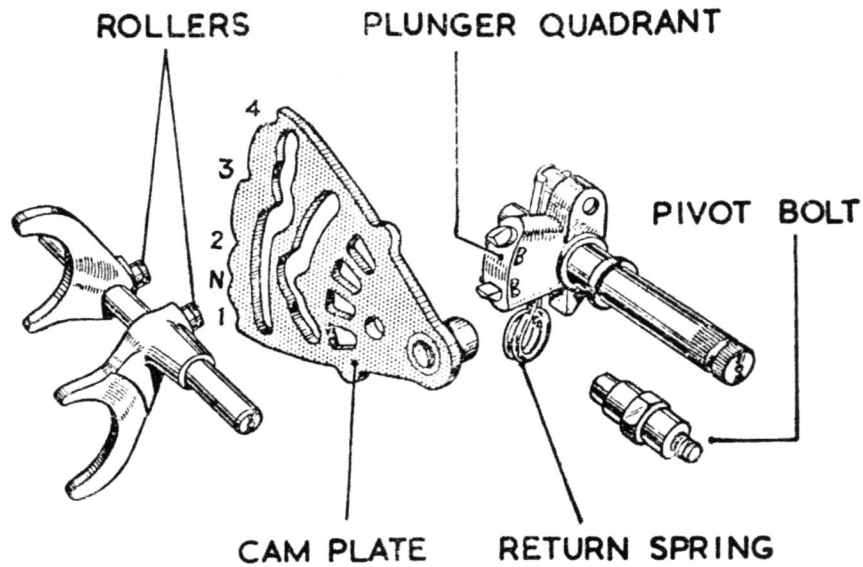

Fig. C10A. *Gearchange Mechanism.*

**REASSEMBLY**

Reassemble the layshaft, gear cluster and selector forks to the mainshaft. The selector forks are interchangeable on all models (except the C15 Trials machine which has wide ratio gears) but it is advisable to replace them in their respective positions.

Insert the selector spindle through the forks and into its location in the cover.

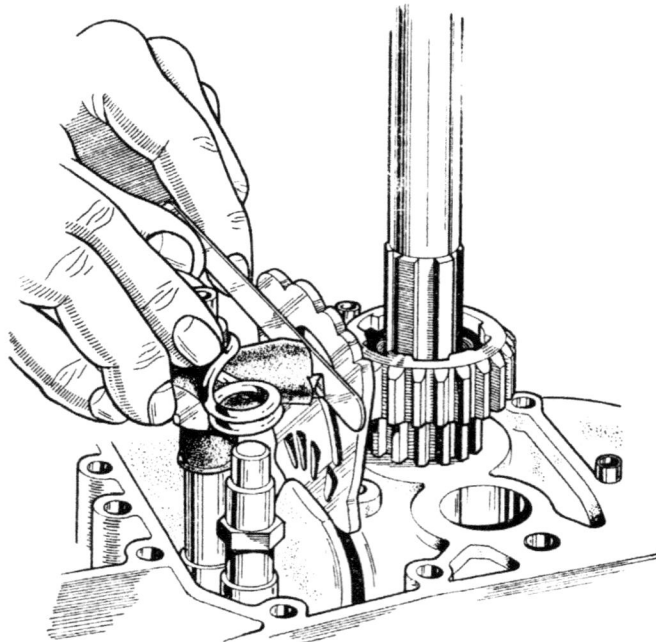

Fig. C11A. *Fitting Gearchange Plunger Quadrant.*

Carefully guide the cam plate into the slot in the inner cover, replace the pivot and secure with the split pin. Engage the cam plate over the selector fork rollers and set the plate so that the second gear notch will locate with the leaf springs in the crankcase.

Hold the quadrant shaft in a vice using soft clamps, with the short end and the peg uppermost. With two substantial tools such as screwdrivers, one through the loop and the other between the prongs, twist the spring and force it over the short end of the shaft. Square the spring up, replace the plunger quadrant in the inner cover and locate the spring over the pivot bolt (see Fig. C11A).

See that the crankcase and inner cover joint faces are clean, apply a thin film of jointing compound and carefully refit the cover (with gear cluster and footchange mechanism) to the crankcase. After checking that the gear cluster and selector fork spindle are correctly located, and that the cover is close up to the crankcase the eight securing screws can be replaced and tightened.

Before proceeding further, check the gear selection.

Insert the contact breaker into the camshaft spindle, replace central fixing bolt and securing bolts loosely, and reconnect the low-tension lead.

Replace the kickstart spindle, spring and spindle bush.

Locate the clutch operating rack and ball in the outer cover, insert the clutch actuating lever into its aperture in top of cover and mesh the pinion with the operating rack.

Refit the outer cover with the seven screws in their respective locations.

Reconnect the clutch cable and replace the kickstart and footchange levers.

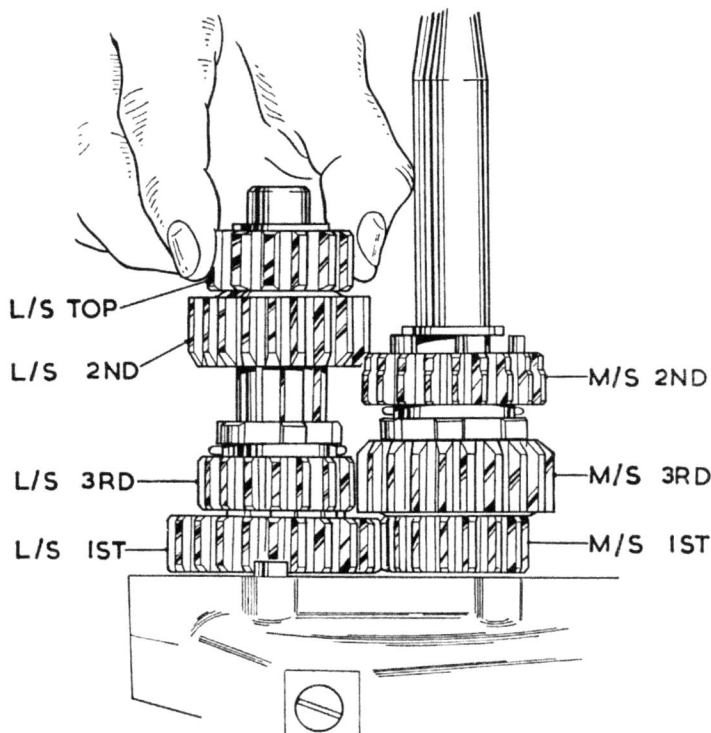

FIG. C12A. *Gearbox assembly.*

## PRIMARY CASE

If the gearbox sprocket has been removed it must now be replaced with the boss inwards, then the tab washer and nut.

Thread the rear chain over the sprocket and couple up the ends, select top gear, apply the rear brake then tighten the sprocket nut securely, finally turning over the tab washer.

Where the oil seal is being replaced in the chaincase back, it should be pressed in from the gearbox side flush with the cover and the lip inwards.

Place the felt grit protection washer in position over the bronze bush and against the end of the pinion sleeve.

Refit the cover with a paper gasket which need only be jointed on one side and screw in the six countersunk head screws. Place the felt washer over the gearbox mainshaft next to the cover. Replace clutch push rod.

Smear the clutch sleeve (C) Fig. C8A with grease and replace the 25 rollers in position. Next slide the chainwheel over the rollers and the clutch centre (B) Fig. C8A over the splines of the clutch sleeve. Place the engine sprocket on the bench alongside with the boss upwards and thread the primary chain over both the sprocket and chainwheel pulling the chain taut.

The crankshaft distance piece should not have been disturbed but if it was removed for any reason it must now be replaced with the chamfered side inwards.

See that the Woodruff keys are fitted to both mainshafts and that they are a good fit in the keyways.

Pick up the engine sprocket, chain and chainwheel in both hands and slide them over their respective shafts. Place the thick washer with the recess outwards in position against the clutch sleeve then the tab washer which has a special tongue fitting into the clutch centre, then the locknut. Turn the tab washer over the nut after tightening.

Now place the clutch plates in position starting with one plain plate then one segmented plate and so on alternately, there being five plain plates and four segmented plates.

Place the pressure plate in position then the four spring cups and springs which should be of equal length. If there is any doubt about the condition of the springs, replace them since they are quite cheap to buy.

Screw on the four spring nuts until the underside of each head is approximately $\frac{1}{8}$ in. from the face of each cup.

If the springs are compressed excessively, the handlebar lever will be stiff to operate, alternatively, if the spring pressure is insufficient the clutch will tend to slip. Adjust for true running of the plates by declutching and depressing the kickstart lever, when it will be seen if the plates are running true or not. If necessary, adjust the nuts individually to correct any run out.

Replace the rotor with the recessed face outwards, fit the tab washer and nut, turning the tab over the nut after tightening securely.

Place the three distance pieces on the stator plate studs and replace the stator with the lead wires on the outside and at the top.

Screw on the three nuts and spring washers and tighten evenly.

The air gap between the rotor and stator should be equal all round, when correct thread the lead wires through the rubber grommet in the back of the case.

Refit the primary case and the 10 screws, shortest at the rear and longest at the front.

Replace the exhaust system, remembering to tighten the pinch bolt in the finned collar.

Note:—C15 Scrambles and Sports Star models are fitted with a primary chain tensioner. This tensioner can be fitted to C15 Star models the parts required being 41–0143, 41–0146 (2) and 41–0148.

Service Bulletin No. 83 (September 1961) gives full instructions for fitting.

**B.S.A. MOTOR CYCLES LTD.**, Service Department, Armoury Road, Birmingham 11.
Printed in England                                           B.S.A. PRESS

MODELS C15 AND B40
(except those with Engine Nos. prefixed C15F or B40F)
COMPLETE DISMANTLING OF THE ENGINE/GEARBOX UNIT

The procedure for complete dismantling of the engine and gearbox unit will be described from the point reached in the section on decarbonising (Service Sheet No. 421), continuing with dismantling of the gearbox (Service Sheet No. 422). Further dismantling will be assumed to commence at this point.

Pull out the distributor noting the way the clip is fitted (see Fig. C13A) inset.

Lift the tappets to the highest position and take out the camshaft, the tappets can now be withdrawn downwards into the timing chest. Note that the lubrication holes are facing towards the gearbox.

Take off the sump cover and filter.

Remove the three screws marked (A) Fig. C14A, holding the oil pump and draw the pump down and out of the crankcase.

It is not advisable to attempt dismantling of the oil pump, should a fault be suspected a serviced unit can be obtained through your dealer.

Using a brass or copper drift ⅜ in. dia. through the pump drive aperture, tap the distributor drive shaft and bush upwards clear of the mainshaft worm wheel after removing the drive bush grub screw.

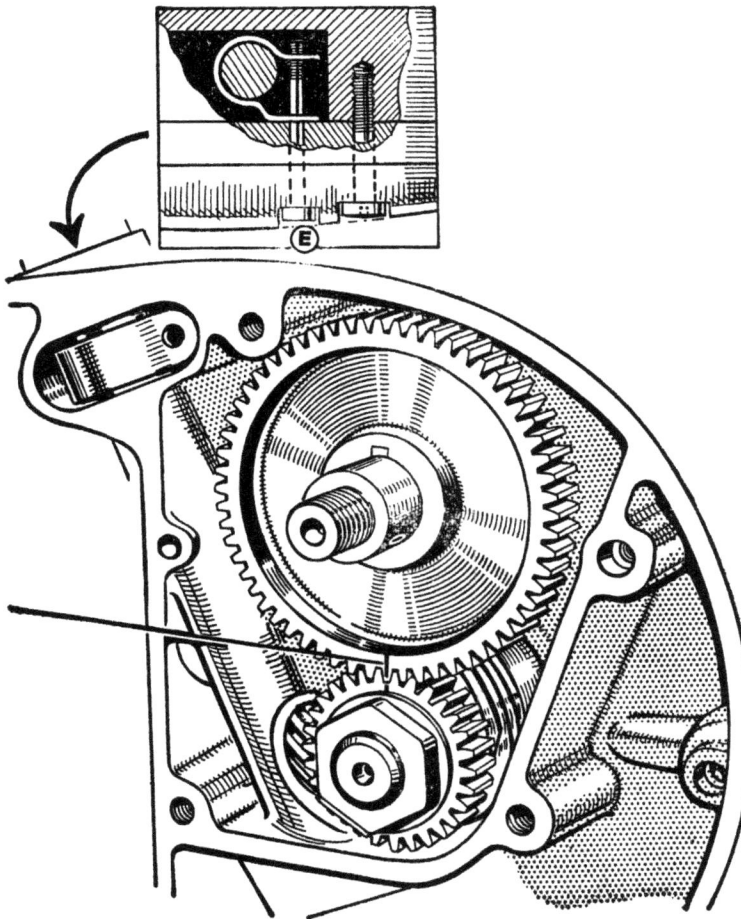

FIG. C13A. *Valve timing marks.*

Flatten the tab washer on the mainshaft, unscrew the nut (right-hand thread) and with extractor 61–3681, fitted with legs 61–3588, pull off the mainshaft pinion.

The same extractor now fitted with legs number 61–3585 can be used to draw off the mainshaft worm wheel. If the Woodruff key is loose in the shaft it should be replaced, also take careful note of the way in which the wormwheel is fitted.

On later model C15 machines and B40 models, the distributor drive bush is secured by a grub screw which must be removed before the bush is driven out.

Unscrew the four $\frac{5}{16}$ in. nuts (two in the primary case and two at the base of the cylinder) and take out the three bolts at the front of the crankcase to split the case.

Part the case by drawing off the drive side together with the flywheel assembly.

Carefully tap out the flywheel assembly from the drive side half noting the position of the main-shaft distance piece which has the chamfer facing inwards.

The spacer on the drive side shaft can be drawn off with tool number 61–3593 if necessary.

If any of the bushes in the crankcase are to be replaced the case should be heated in hot water and each replacement bush fitted immediately the old bush has been extracted and while the case is still hot.

**Parting the Flywheels**

The flywheels are a press-fit on the crankpin and no attempt should be made to part them unless the services of an expert mechanic and fully equipped workshop are available.

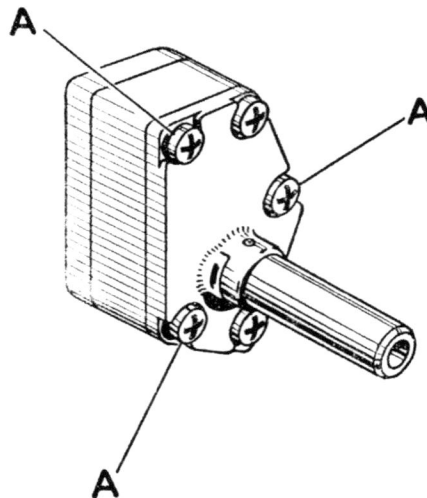

FIG. C14A. *Oil pump.*

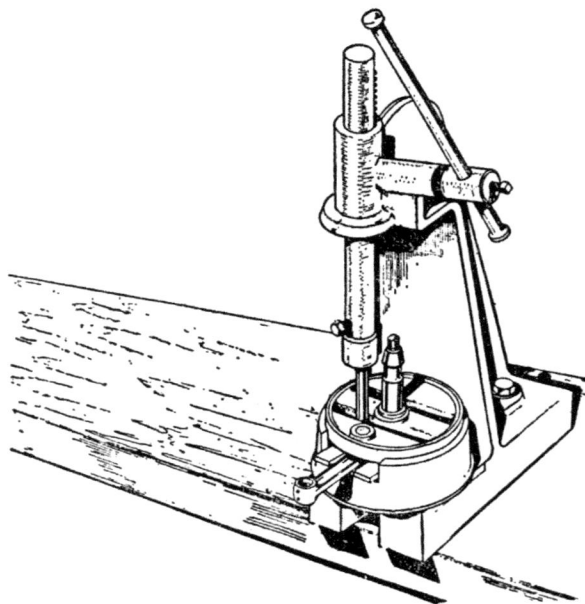

FIG. C15A. *Parting the flywheels with service tool 61–3589 for C15 or 61–3686 for B40.*

Should the big-end assembly require replacement it is advisable to obtain a works reconditioned unit through the medium of your dealer.

If it has been decided that the big-end bearing must be replaced the flywheels should now be parted, using service tool number 61–3589 (Fig. C15A). Place the flywheels in the bolster and position the stripping bars, service tool number 61–3590. Use the punch, service tool number 61–3601 to drive out the crankpin. Take off the uppermost flywheel and reverse the lower one in the bolster. Again using service tool number 61–3601 drive out the crankpin.

Reassembly of the unit is described on Service Sheet No. 424.

**B.S.A. MOTOR CYCLES LTD.,** Service Department, Armoury Road, Birmingham 11

B.S.A. PRESS

## MODELS C15 AND B40 WITH ENGINE NUMBERS
## PREFIXED C15F OR B40F

### COMPLETE DISMANTLING OF THE ENGINE/GEARBOX UNIT

The procedure for complete dismantling of the engine and gearbox unit will be described from the point reached in the section on decarbonising (Service Sheet No. 421), continuing with dismantling of the gearbox (Service Sheet No. 422A). Further dismantling will be assumed to commence at this point.

Raise the tappets as high as possible and take out the camshaft. The tappets can now be withdrawn downwards into the timing chest. Note that the lubrication holes in the tappets are facing towards the gearbox.

Take off the sump cover (secured by four nuts) and remove the filter.

Take out the three screws marked (A) Fig. C14A securing the oil pump and draw the pump down and out of the crankcase.

It is not advisable to attempt dismantling the oil pump. Should a fault be suspected, a service unit can be obtained through your dealer.

Take out the plug and washer from the top of the crankcase and note that the oil pump drive spindle is held in position by a bush, which is itself retained by a grub screw passing through the housing.

Remove the grub screw and, using a soft metal drift $\frac{3}{8}$ in. diameter through the pump drive aperture, tap the drive shaft and bush upwards clear of the worm wheel.

Examination of the timing gears will show that there are marks on the faces of the gears. These marks are to assist in correct reassembly, so ensuring precise valve timing. It is good practice to familiarise oneself with them before removing the gears (see Fig. C13A).

Flatten the tab washer on the crankshaft, unscrew the nut (right-hand thread) and with extractor 61–6381, fitted with legs 61–3588, pull off the crankshaft pinion. The same extractor, now fitted with legs 61–3585, can be used to withdraw the worm wheel.

If the Woodruff key is loose in the shaft it should be replaced; also take careful note of the way in which the worm wheel is fitted.

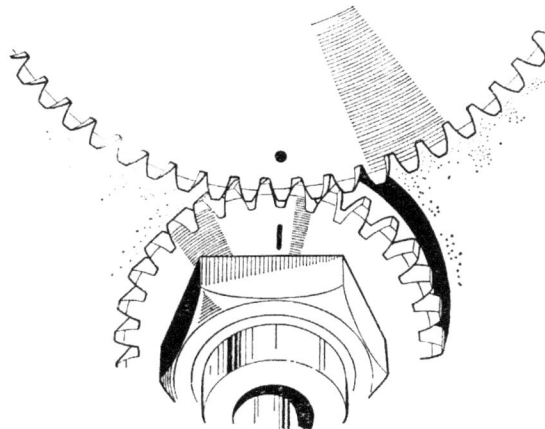

Fig. C13A. *Valve timing marks.*

Unscrew the four $\frac{5}{16}$ in. nuts (two in the primary case and two at the base of the cylinder) and take out the three bolts at the front of the crankcase to split the case.

Part the case by drawing off the driveside together with the flywheel assembly.

Carefully tap out the flywheel assembly from the driveside half noting the position of the mainshaft distance piece which has the chamfer facing inwards.

The spacer on the timing-side shaft can be drawn off with tool number 61–3593 if necessary.

If any of the bushes in the crankcase are to be replaced the case should be heated in hot water and each replacement bush fitted immediately the old bush has been extracted and while the case is still hot.

## PARTING THE FLYWHEELS

The flywheels are a press-fit on the crankpin and no attempt should be made to part them unless the services of an expert mechanic and fully equipped workshop are available.

Should the big-end assembly require replacement it is advisable to obtain a works reconditioned unit through the medium of your dealer.

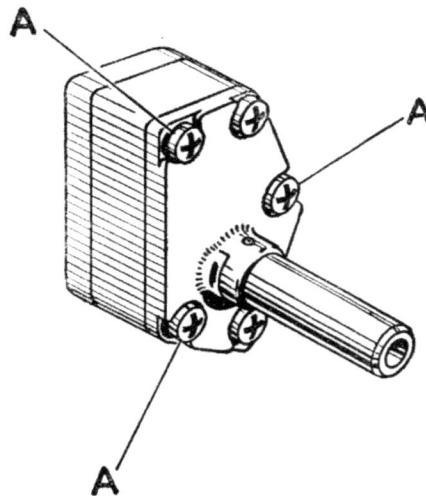

FIG. C14A. *Oil pump.*

If it has been decided that the big-end bearing must be replaced the flywheels should now be parted, using Service Tool No. 61–3589 (Fig. C15A). Place the flywheels in the bolster and position the stripping bars Service Tool No. 61–3590. Use the punch Service Tool No. 61–3601 to drive out the crankpin. Take off the uppermost flywheel and reverse the lower one in the bolster. Again using Service Tool No. 61–3601 drive out the crankpin.

Reassembly of the unit is described on Service Sheet No. 424A.

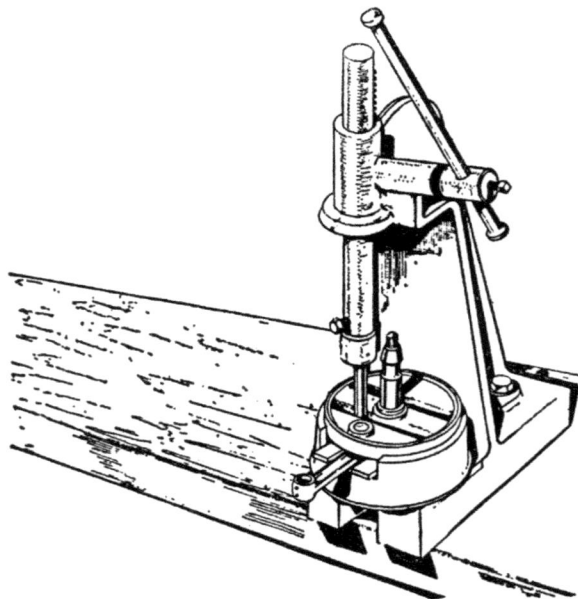

FIG. C15A. *Parting the flywheels with Service Tool 61–3589 for C15 or 61–3686 for B40.*

B.S.A. MOTOR CYCLES LTD., Service Department, Armoury Road, Birmingham 11.

# BSA SERVICE SHEET No. 424

## MODELS C15 AND B40
## REASSEMBY OF THE ENGINE – GEARBOX UNIT
### (EXCEPT MODELS WITH ENGINE NUMBERS PREFIXED C15F OR B40F

Before commencing to assemble it is important to see that all parts are quite clean and free from road grit and dust both inside and outside as some of the grit may get transferred to vital bearing surfaces during handling.

### CRANKCASE
Clean off all the old jointing compound being careful not to damage the joint faces.

If new bushes or ball races are to be inserted, warm the crankcase halves, extract the old part and press in the new part while the case is still hot.

Where oil-ways are drilled in bushes it is essential that the holes are correctly positioned so that the oil-ways are not blocked.

On the drive-side the bearings are fitted from inside the case and the oil seals from the outside. When fitting a replacement seal note that the lip must be facing inwards.

### FLYWHEEL ASSEMBLY
To fit a new connecting rod and big-end assembly, place the gear-side flywheel in the bolster, locate the crankpin over the hole in the flywheel using the gauge so that the oil hole is in line with the oil-way in the flywheel and press right home. Check the oil-ways for clearance, now place the connecting rod and the drive-side flywheel in position and using the bridge piece, Service Tool number 8 44 61–3591 over the crankpin hole press the crankpin fully "home" into the drive-side flywheel (Fig. C16A).

The flywheels will now be only approximately aligned and must be trued.

As the flywheels on the model B40 are larger diameter, different Service Tools are required, these are:—

> Model C15 Bolster 8 73 61–3589
> Model B40 Bolster 8 73 61–3686
> Model C15 Gauge 8 28 61–3597
> Model B40 Gauge 8 28 61–3687

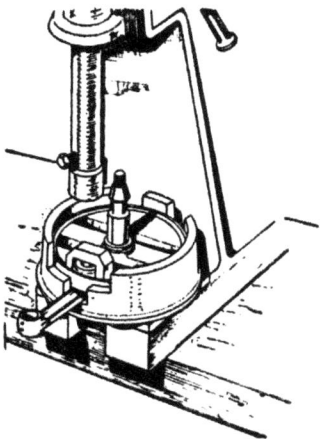

Fig. C16A.
*Reassembly of the Flywheels.*

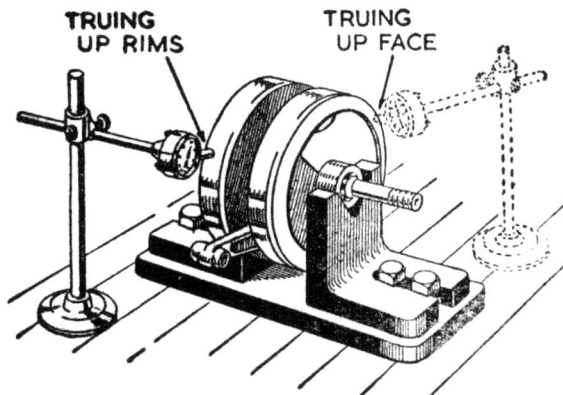

Fig. C17A.
*Checking Flywheel Alignment.*

Mount the assembly in vee blocks with the mainshaft bearing on the drive-side shaft and Service Tool number 8 **33** 61–3592 on the gear-side shaft over the drilled bush. True up as indicated in Fig. C18A using a dial indicator gauge for checking.

True the wheels to within 005 in., the drive-side shaft to within .002 in. and the gear-side shaft to within .0005 in.

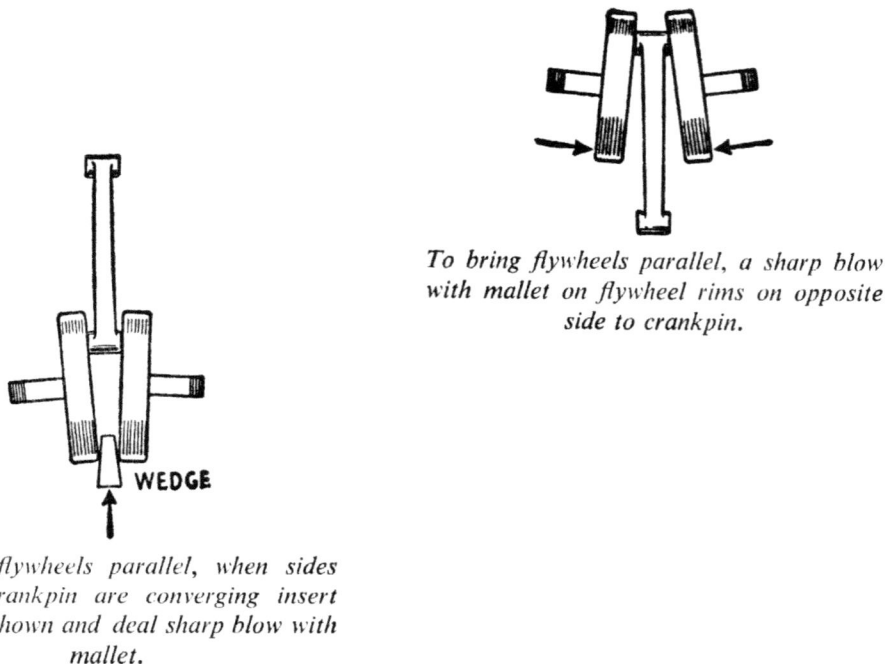

*To bring flywheels parallel, a sharp blow with mallet on flywheel rims on opposite side to crankpin.*

WEDGE

*To bring flywheels parallel, when sides opposite crankpin are converging insert wedge as shown and deal sharp blow with mallet.*

**Fig. C18A.**

Having renewed the big-end assembly and checked for concentricity, replace the left-hand side half crankcase over the flywheel assembly. This operation will be simplified if a block of wood is used, it should be deep enough to keep the end of the shaft clear of the bench and wide enough to support the flywheels.

Apply a coating of jointing compound to the joint faces, fit the right-hand half case and replace the three bolts at the front of the case and the four nuts (two at the base of the cylinder and two in the primary case). Tighten the bolts and nuts evenly to avoid distorting the joint faces.

Replace the Woodruff key on the right-hand side mainshaft and refit the worm gear and timing pinion with the extension inwards, fit the tab washer and nut, turning over the tab on to the nut after tightening securely.

In order to ensure correct positioning of the distributor, pick up the drive and holding it with the slot in line with the crankshaft, mesh the teeth with those on the mainshaft worm wheel.

Place the distributors drive bush in position on top of the drive and tap gently down until the circular groove is in line with the screw hole in the housing.

Replace the oil pump using a new paper gasket.

The oil pressure release valve is situated on the front right-hand half of the crankcase and may not have been disturbed, but it is as well, at this stage, to make sure that it is clean and free from grit.

After thoroughly cleaning the sump filter replace the filter and cover using a new gasket, which need only be "jointed" on one side, tighten the four nuts on to shakeproof washers. Turn the crankshaft to T.D.C.

Now pick up the tappets and insert them into the holes from inside the timing chest and with lubrication holes in the tappets towards the gearbox. Holding the tappets up insert the camshaft with the screwed end outwards and mesh the timing mark with the mark on the mainshaft pinion.

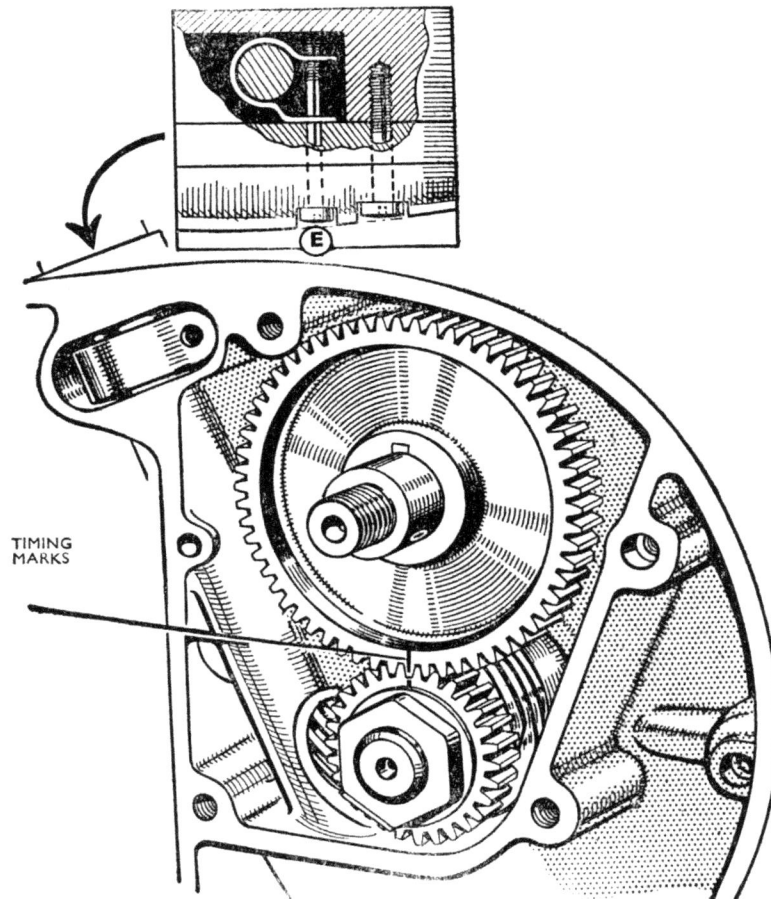

TIMING MARKS

Fig. C19A. *Valve Timing Marks.*

Insert the distributor clip into the aperture in the crankcase as shown in Fig. C19A, and fit the distributor loosely in position with the wire clip away from the cylinder.

On later model C15 machines and the B40, the cover is retained by a single centre screw.

**B.S.A. Service Sheet No. 424 (contd.)**

Assembly from this point is described in Service Sheet number 422 continuing with Service Sheet number 421.

After assembly of the engine and gearbox it is only necessary to retime the ignition. Expose the contact breaker by taking off the cover (A) as shown in Fig. C20A and with the sparking plug out, insert a thin rod through the plug hole, rotate the crankshaft until the piston is at top dead centre on the compression stroke with both valves closed.

Now keeping the rod as vertical as possible rotate the engine backwards until the piston is 1/16 in. for C15 or 1/32 in. for B40 from the top of the stroke when the contacts should be just about to open. This is best determined by inserting a piece of cigarette paper between the points which are about to open when the paper can be withdrawn by a gentle pull.

If the setting is incorrect with the piston set as above, rotate the distributor gently until the points are about to open then tighten the clip screw and re-check the setting. The fully open gap (B), should be .015 in.

Finally reconnect the distributor and alternator leads and replace the spark plug and high tension lead.

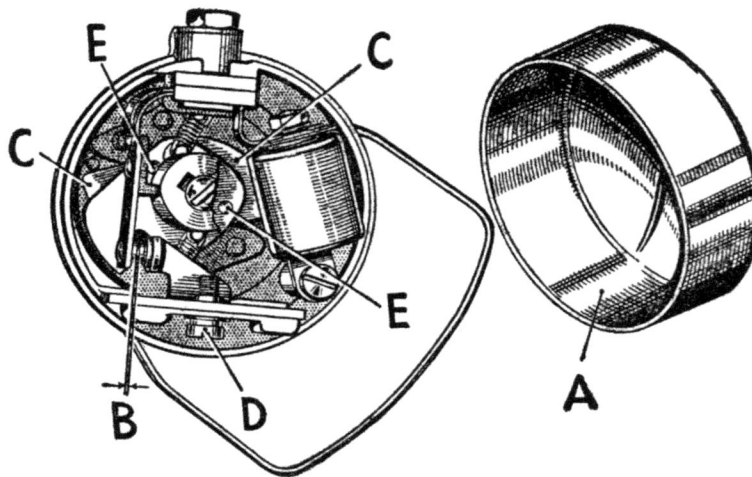

Fig. C20A.   *Contact Beaker and Auto-advance Mechanism.*

**Ignition Timing, models C15T and C15S**

The two models are timed by a different method due to the "energy transfer" system. This system is sensitive in operation and the following instructions must be strictly followed for best results.

Set the contact breaker to .015 in. Bring the piston to the top of the bore on the compression stroke. Rotate the engine backwards so that the piston descends about ½ in. then bring the rotor into the position shown, in this position the contact breaker points should be just about to open, if necessary, adjust by turning the contact breaker housing.

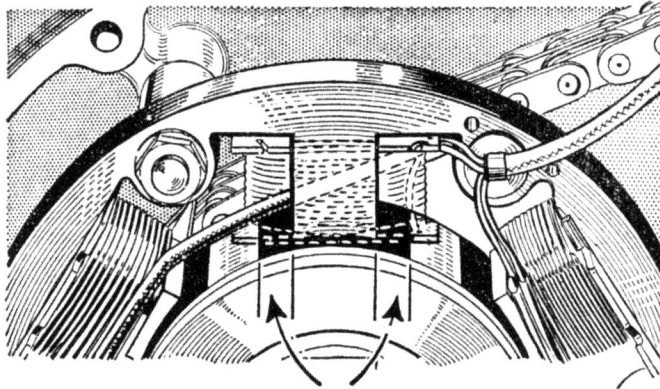

OVERLAP
MUST BE EQUAL ON BOTH
SIDES WHEN POINTS ARE
BREAKING

**Special Note**

The above remarks apply to Standard and Competition models fitted with contact breaker units having a 15 degree advance.

Later models are fitted with a unit which is limited to 10 deg. advance. These can be identified by the 10 deg. stamped on auto-advance bob-weight visible just below the contact breaker. On these models the ignition setting is 5 deg. B.T.D.C. for both Standard and Competition models.

**B.S.A. MOTOR CYCLES LTD.,** Service Department, Armoury Road, Birmingham 11.

**MODELS C15 AND B40 WITH ENGINE NUMBERS
PREFIXED C15F OR B40F**

## REASSEMBLY OF THE ENGINE/GEARBOX UNIT

Before commencing to assemble it is important to see that all parts are quite clean and free from road grit and dust both inside and outside as some of the grit may get transferred to vital bearing surfaces during handling.

### CRANKCASE

Clean off all the old jointing compound being careful not to damage the joint faces.

If new bushes or ballraces are to be inserted, warm the crankcase halves, extract the old part and press in the new part while the case is still hot.

Where oil-ways are drilled in bushes it is essential that the holes are correctly positioned so that the oil-ways are not blocked.

On the driveside the bearings are fitted from inside the case and the oil seals from the outside. When fitting a replacement seal note that the lip must be facing inwards.

### FLYWHEEL ASSEMBLY

To fit a new connecting rod and big-end assembly, place the gearside flywheel in the bolster, locate the crankpin over the hole in the flywheel using the gauge so that the oil hole is in line with the oil-way in the flywheel and press right home. Check the oil-ways for clearance, now place the connecting rod and the driveside flywheel in position and using the bridge piece, Service Tool number 61–3591 over the crankpin hole press the crankpin fully "home" into the driveside flywheel (Fig. C16A).

The flywheels will now be only approximately aligned and must be trued.

As the flywheels on the model B40 are larger diameter, different Service Tools are required, these are:—

Model C15 Bolster 61–3589
Model B40 Bolster 61–3686
Model C15 Gauge 61–3597
Model B40 Gauge 61–3687

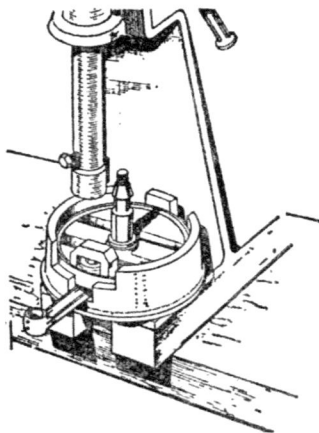

FIG. C16A.
*Reassembly of the flywheels.*

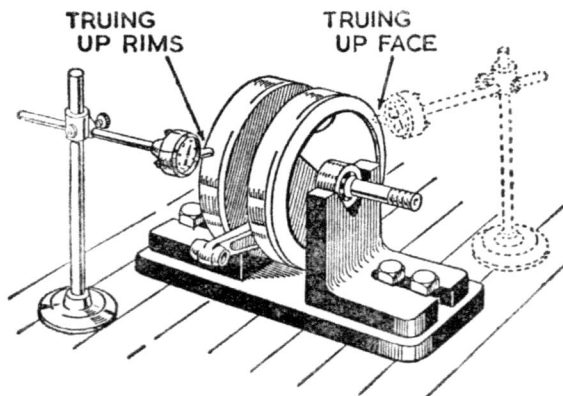

TRUING
UP RIMS

TRUING
UP FACE

FIG. C17A.
*Checking flywheel alignment.*

Mount the assembly in vee-blocks with the mainshaft bearing on the driveside shaft and Service Tool number 61–3592 on the gearside shaft over the drilled bush. True up as indicated in Fig. C18A using a dial indicator gauge for checking.

True the wheels to within .005 in., the driveside shaft to within .002 in. and the gearside shaft to within .0005 in.

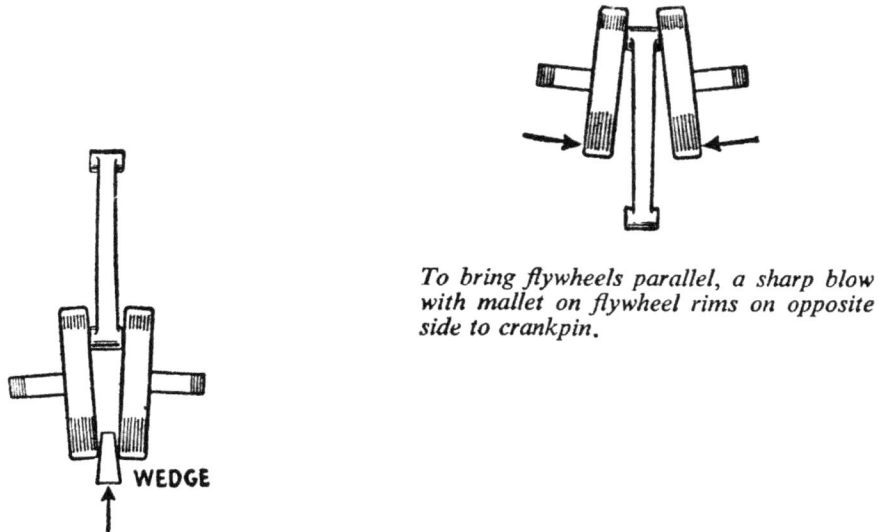

*To bring flywheels parallel, a sharp blow with mallet on flywheel rims on opposite side to crankpin.*

*To bring flywheels parallel, when sides opposite crankpin are converging insert wedge as shown and deal sharp blow with mallet.*

FIG. C18A.

Having renewed the big-end assembly and checked for concentricity, replace the left-hand side half crankcase over the flywheel assembly. This operation will be simplified if a block of wood is used, it should be deep enough to keep the end of the shaft clear of the bench and wide enough to support the flywheels.

Apply a coating of jointing compound to the joint faces, fit the right-hand half case and replace the three bolts at the front of the case and the four nuts (two at the base of the cylinder and two in the primary case). Tighten the bolts and nuts evenly to avoid distorting the joint faces.

Replace the Woodruff key on the right-hand side mainshaft and refit the worm gear and timing pinion with the extension inwards, fit the tab washer and nut, turning over the tab on to the nut after tightening securely.

Replace the oil pump drive in the shaft aperture and mesh the teeth with those on the mainshaft worm wheel.

Place the oil pump drive bush into position on top of the drive and tap gently down until the circular groove is in line with the screw hole in the housing.

Replace the grub screw to secure the bush and drive and refit **plug and washer.**

Fit the oil pump, using a new paper gasket.

The oil pressure release valve is situated on the front right-hand half of the crankcase and may not have been disturbed, but it is as well, at this stage, to make sure that it is clean and free from dirt. If the valve has been removed ensure that, on reassembly, the spring is refitted with its larger end inside the screwed plug.

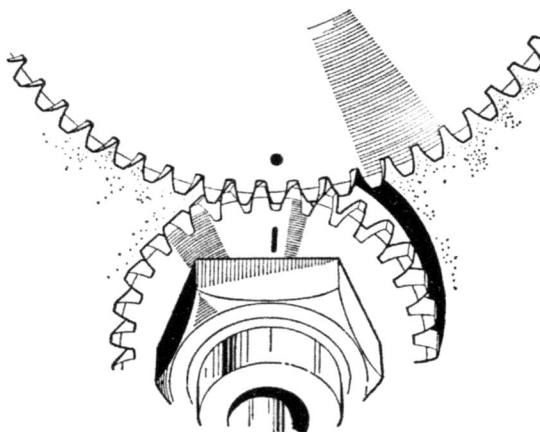

FIG. C19A.   *Valve timing marks.*

After thoroughly cleaning the sump filter, replace the filter and cover using a new gasket, which need only be "jointed" on one side. Tighten the four nuts on to shakeproof washers.

Turn the crankshaft to top dead centre and insert the tappets into the holes from inside the timing chest, with the lubrication holes in the tappets towards the gearbox. Holding the tappets up, insert the camshaft and mesh the timing mark with the mark on the crankshaft pinion (see Fig. C19A).

Assembly from this point is described in Service Sheet No. 422A continuing with Service Sheet No. 421.

After assembly of the engine and gearbox it is only necessary to retime the ignition.

Expose the contact breaker by taking off the cover and with the sparking plug out, insert a thin rod through the plug hole, rotate the crankshaft until the piston is at top dead centre on the compression stroke with both valves closed.

Now, keeping the rod as vertical as possible, rotate the crankshaft backwards until the piston is .280 in. or 33½ degrees from the top of the stroke. Take out the central fixing bolt and free contact breaker from its location in the camshaft. Rotate the spindle until the points are just about to open, ease the contact breaker back into the camshaft and secure in position with the fixing bolt.

The ignition timing is now set in the full retard position but this is not ideal because whilst the timing will be set for engine tick-over speeds, the firing at wide throttle openings will vary due to the differences in the amount of automatic-advance.

Since exact timing accuracy is required at operating speeds, it is better to time the engine in the fully advanced position, so transferring any variations in the firing to the tick-over or low engine speeds when it can least affect the performance.

Whilst setting the ignition timing, therefore, the contact breaker cam must be held in the fully advanced position.

**B.S.A. Service Sheet No. 424A (contd.)**

With the piston at the recommended position before top dead centre, rotate the cam in an anticlockwise direction until the bob-weights are fully expanded and hold in position. Loosen the contact breaker plate bolts and rotate the plate either backwards or forwards until the contact points are just opening. Tighten the bolts, release the cam and re-check the setting. There should be no change in the fully-open contacts gap setting.

Finally, reconnect the contact breaker and stator leads and replace the spark plug.

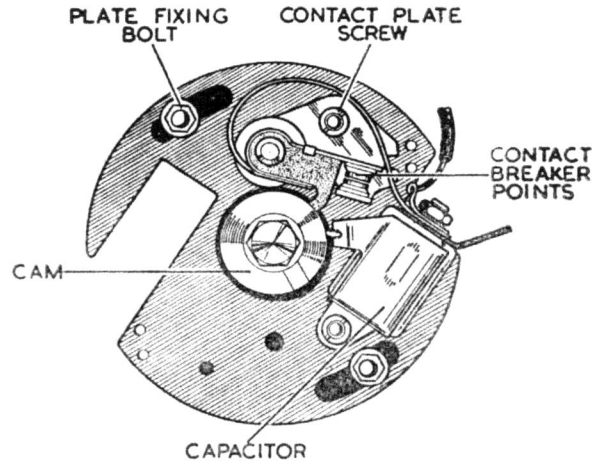

FIG. C20A. *Contact breaker*

**IGNITION TIMING (models C15T and C15S)**

The two models are timed by a different method due to the "energy transfer" system. This system is sensitive in operation and the following instructions must be strictly followed for best results.

Set the contact breaker to .015 in. Bring the piston to the top of the bore on the compression stroke. Rotate the engine backwards so that the piston descends about ½ in. then bring the rotor into the position shown, in this position the contact breaker points should be just about to open, if necessary, adjust by turning the contact breaker housing.

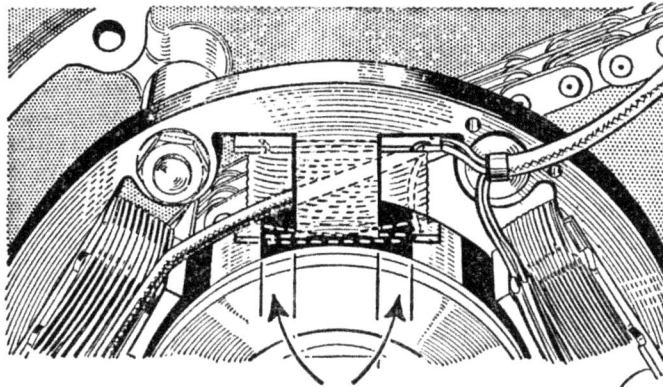

OVERLAP
MUST BE EQUAL ON BOTH
SIDES WHEN POINTS ARE
BREAKING

**B.S.A. MOTOR CYCLES LTD.,** Service Department, Armoury Road, Birmingham 11.

Printed in England                B.S.A. PRESS

# *BSA* SERVICE SHEET No. 425

### MODELS C15 AND B40
### DISMANTLING AND REASSEMBLY OF HUBS AND BRAKES

Both wheels are fitted with ball journal bearings which do not require adjustment. The bearings are packed with grease during assembly and this should last until the machine is in need of a major overhaul.

**Front Wheel Removal**

With the machine on its centre stand place a box or small wooden trestle underneath the crankcase so that the front wheel is clear of the ground.

Disconnect the brake cable by removing the split pin *A* and the clevis pin *B*, Fig. C21A at the brake drum end, and withdraw the cable from the lug on the lower fork end. Remove the end caps *D* by unscrewing the four bolts (two in each cap) and as the last bolt is removed support the wheel to avoid damage to the threads on the bolts or the screwed sockets. The wheel will now be free.

**Front Hub Dismantling**

This should only be necessary when the bearings require replacement or greasing.

Unscrew the large nut on the spindle *F*, Fig. C21A this will be facilitated if the brake is applied using a short length of tubing, such as a box spanner, over the brake lever.

Take off the brake cover plate complete with shoes, cam and fulcrum pin.

The bearing retainer which is now exposed has a left-hand thread and can be removed by unscrewing in a clockwise direction with a suitable peg spanner. (Service Tool No. 82661-3694)

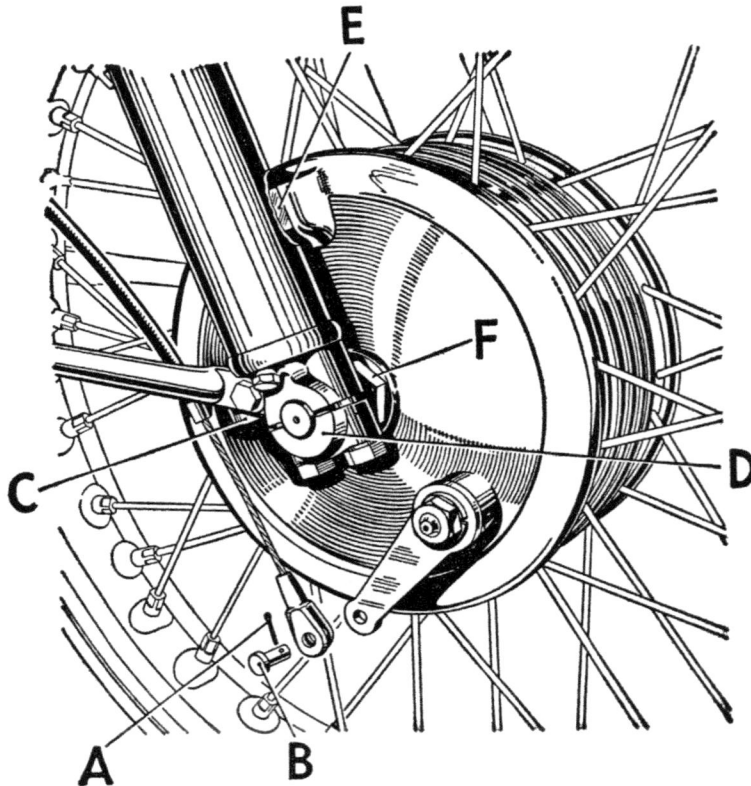

Fig. C21A.   Removing the Front Wheel.

**B.S.A. Service Sheet No. 425 (contd.)**

Now drive out the R/H or brake side bearing by striking the L/H side of the spindle with a mallet or copper hammer, if neither of these is available use a piece of hard wood placed against the end of the spindle to protect it.

To remove the L/H side bearing prise out the circlip and using a suitable drift, drive out the bearing and dust cover from the R/H side. If a suitable drift or punch is not available the spindle can be used but care should be taken to avoid damage.

### Fitting New Bearings

Place the bearing squarely in position on the R/H side and drive in using a piece of tubing on the outer ring of the bearing. When it is resting on the abutment face in the hub, screw in the lock ring using a peg spanner and turning anti-clockwise (L/H thread).

Insert the spindle, screwed end first from the L/H side, and tap it gently home so that the bearing inner ring is seated against the shoulder on the spindle.

Place the L/H bearing over the spindle and drive it into the housing until the dust cap just clears the circlip groove and replace the circlip.

### Brake Shoes

Before replacing the cover plate make sure that the brake linings are fit for further use and that the cam spindle is quite free in the cover plate.

Replacement shoes can be fitted either by springing the old ones off the fulcrum and cam spindles, or the shoes complete with spindles can be removed from the cover plate by taking off the domed nut on the fulcrum pin and the nut and lever on the cam spindle

### Replacing the Wheel

Make sure that the cover plate nut *F* (Fig. C21A) is securely tightened, engage the tongue *E* in the slot in the cover plate, replace the two caps and four bolts in the fork ends, but before final tightening pull the wheel to the R/H side so that the cover plate nut is resting against the R/H fork end.

Replace the brake cable, clevis pin and split pin and check over the fork end bolts for tightness.

### Rear Wheel Removal

With the machine on its stand disconnect the rear chain at the spring link, place a sheet of paper on the ground under the run of the chain and wind the chain off the sprocket onto the paper but leaving it on the gearbox sprocket.

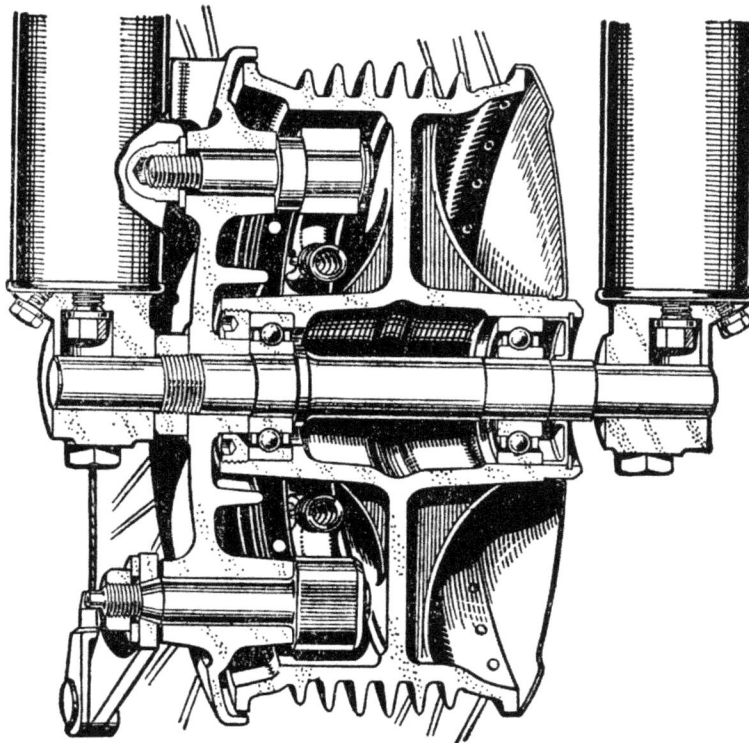

Fig. C22A. Front Hub Arrangement.

Take off the brake rod adjusting nut *A* (Fig. C23A) and the anchor arm *D* and disconnect the speedometer drive by unscrewing the union nut at the end of the cable.

Unscrew the spindle nuts *B* (Fig. C23A) and pull the wheel out of the fork ends at the same time freeing the brake rod from the swivel pin in the lever. Cant the machine over slightly towards the L/H side and remove the wheel from the R/H side.

**Rear Wheel Dismantling**

Unscrew the large central nuts on the spindle locking the spindle in the same way as described for the front wheel, and remove the brake cover plate complete with shoes and the speedometer drive gearbox from the R/H side. (Note the distance piece and driving dogs).

Next unscrew the bearing retainer which has a R/H thread and is therefore removed by using the peg spanner in an anticlockwise direction.

Now drive the spindle through the bearing on the brake side so driving out the R/H bearing together with the felt washer, housing, and plain washer.

The brake side bearing can now be driven out from the opposite side using a suitable drift or the spindle, but care must be taken not to damage the spindle threads if the spindle is used.

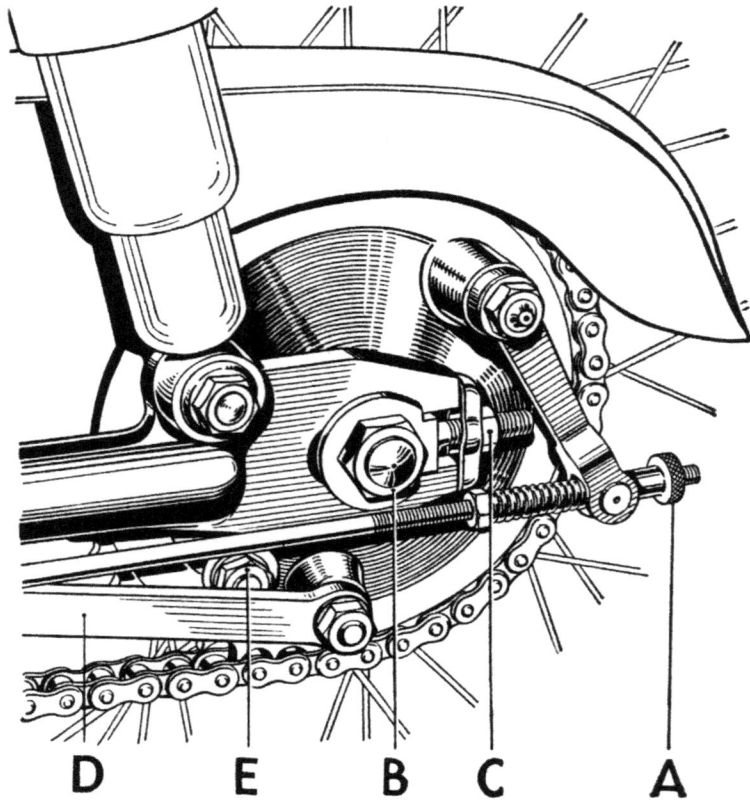

Fig. C23A. Rear Chain Adjustment.

**Fitting New Bearings**

New bearings can be fitted in the reverse order but care must be taken to see that the drive side bearing, which is the larger of the two, is close up to the abutment in the hub shell and the shoulder on the spindle.

After fitting the drive side bearing and its retainer, insert the spindle from the R/H side, drive in the R/H bearing until it is seated against the shoulder on the spindle, insert the plain washer, felt washer and housing and press down into the recess. Slide the distance piece over the R/H side spindle end, then the speedometer drive gearbox, taking care to mesh the driving dogs, and screw on the spindle lock nut, this nut can be finally tightened after the brake cover plate is fitted.

**Brake Shoes**

These are dealt with in the same manner as described for the front wheel and are interchangeable with the front shoes, the only difference being that there is the normal type of nut used on the fulcrum pin.

After replacing the cover plate and nut, tighten the lock nut on the speedometer drive.

**Brake Drum and Chainwheel**

This is registered onto the hub shell and retained by six bolts and three tab plates and should not be disturbed except for replacement purposes of either the drum or spokes on that side.

The C15 Star uses a 45T chainwheel and the B40 a 46T, both being integral with the brake drum, but, as the chain line is different on the two models, the chainwheels are not interchangeable.

C15 Competition models use the same chain line as the B40 and alternative chain rings are available in 52T, 56T and 60T sizes which can be used on the B40 if desired in conjunction with the brake drum.

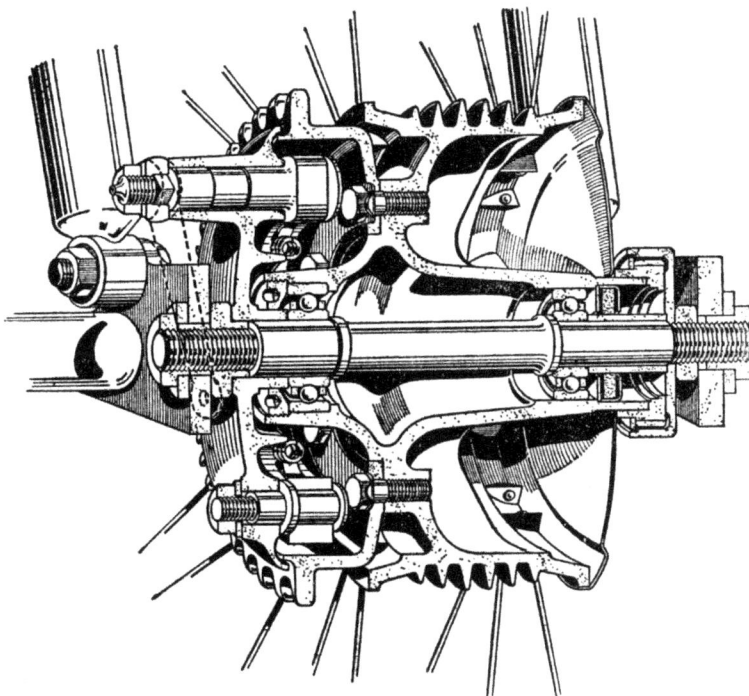

Fig. C24A. Rear Hub Arrangement.

**Rear Wheel Replacement**

Procedure is the reverse of that for removal but care should be taken to see that the wheel is in alignment with the front. This is done by applying a straight edge against the wheels which must touch the front and rear of both tyres. Also the spring on the chain connecting link must be fitted with the open end towards the rear on the top run.

It is most important to see that all nuts are securely tightened particularly those on the brake anchor strap.

B.S.A. MOTOR CYCLES LTD., Service Dept., Armoury Road, Birmingham 11.

# Model C15

### FRONT FORK AND STEERING HEAD

Under normal conditions the only servicing which the front forks will require is occasional renewal of the oil. The need for this may be indicated by excessive movement, but it should only be necessary after considerable mileage.

**Changing the Oil**
First remove the plugs marked (A) Fig. C25A, and take out the drain plugs shown at (B) Fig. C26A. After allowing the oil to drain out, apply the front brake and depress the forks a few times to drive out any oil remaining.

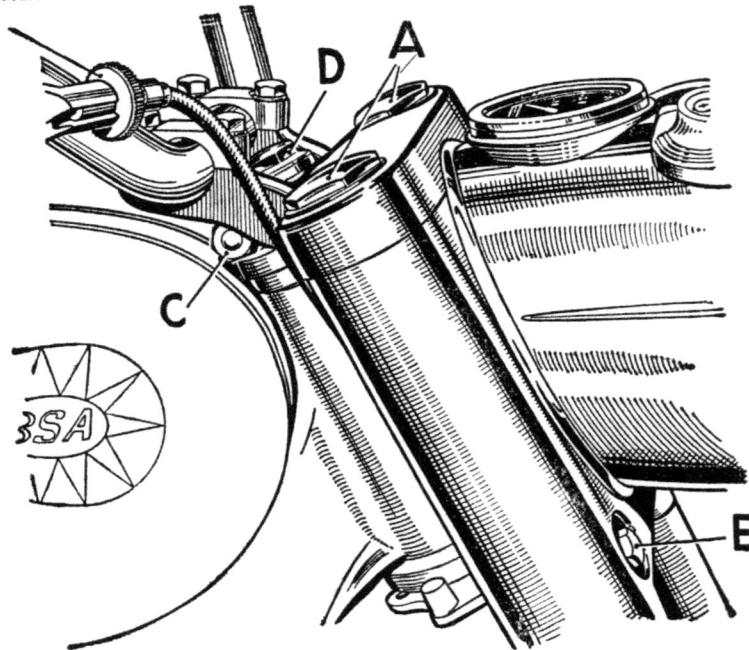

Fig. C25A. *Front fork and steering head.*

Replace the drain plugs after ensuring that the fibre washers are in good condition and refill each leg with 3½ fluid ounces of an S.A.E. 20 oil, replace the top plugs and tighten securely.

### Steering Head Adjustment

To test the head for play support the crankcase on a box so that the front wheel is clear of the ground, then standing in front of the machine with the legs together against the front tyre, push and pull alternately on the handlebars.

If any play is apparent the steering should be adjusted.

Slacken the clamping nut (C) Fig. C25A, and tighten the cap nut (D) until the adjustment is correct. The handlebars should turn freely, if the movement is "lumpy" it indicates that the top nut is too tight or the ballraces are damaged.

When the adjustment is correct, tighten the clamp nut (C) securely.

### Dismantling the Forks

It should only be necessary to dismantle the forks after a very large mileage has been covered and special Service Tools will be required.

Drain off the oil as previously described on this sheet and remove the front wheel, followed by the front mudguard complete with the stays which are retained by four nuts and bolts on each side.

Unscrew the cap nuts (A) Fig. C25A, take out the fork springs and slacken the pinch bolts (E) in the bottom yoke.

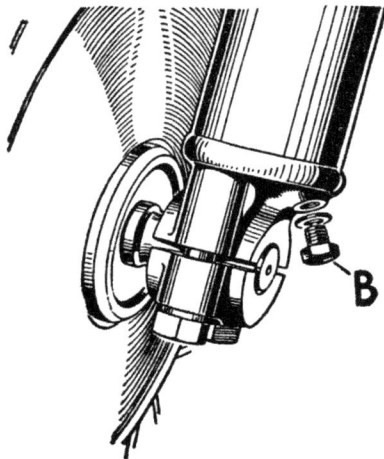

Fig. C26A. *Front fork drain plug.*

To release the legs from the top yoke screw in Service Tool number 8 41 61–3350 in place of the top cap (A), strike the end of the tool a sharp blow with a hammer and draw the leg down through the bottom yoke. Repeat the procedure for the other leg (see Fig. C27A).

The collar at the top of the sliding shaft carries an oil seal and dust shroud, on early machines only one oil seal is fitted, later models have two oil seals, one above and one below the dust shroud.

To remove the collar, hold the leg in a soft-jawed vice by gripping the wheel spindle lug and unscrew using Service Tool 8 32 61–3586. The dust shroud is a press fit into the screwed collar and retains the lower oil seal. Note that the oil seal must always be fitted with the lip downwards.

If new bushes are to be fitted the restrictor rod must now be removed. Unscrew the small-headed $\frac{5}{16}$ in. bolt which is recessed into the wheel spindle lug, a ⅛ in. Whit. socket or tubular spanner is the most suitable. When the bolt is out, turn the leg upside down when the restrictor rod will drop out of the main tube.

Note that there is a milled slot in the end of the rod. this is for drainage and the slot must be positioned over the drain screw when the rod is replaced.

Bolt the assembly into Service Tool 8 75 61–3587 using the two spindle lug bolts and draw the main tube and alloy spacer out of the sliding member. The top bush can now be lifted off and the lower bush removed ater the castellated nut has been unscrewed.

## Reassembling the Forks

After replacing the lower bush, slide on the alloy spacer tube then the top bush with the flange uppermost.

Insert the main tube into the sliding member, lower bush first and press in the distance piece and top bush.

Service Tool 8 75 61–3587 with 8 38 61–3602 can be used for this purpose or a long piece of tube having an inside diameter of $1\frac{1}{4}$ in., but great care must be exercised not to damage the top bush. Screw on the collar using Tool number 8 32 61–3586.

Now insert the restrictor rod slotted-end first, and with the aid of the spring locate the slot over the drain plug, screw in the small-headed $\frac{5}{16}$ in. diameter bolt and secure.

Take out the spring and slide the assembly up through the bottom yoke and using Service Tool 8 41 61–3350 draw the leg up tight into the top yolk tightening the pinch bolt (E) Fig. C25A before releasing the Service Tool.

The top cap (A) Fig. C25A can be used in place of the Service Tool but it must be removed again to refill with oil and to replace the spring.

After replacing both legs slacken off the top caps and the pinch bolts in the bottom yoke, replace the guard and front wheel, remove the support from underneath the engine and pump the forks up and down a few times to line up the legs, finally tightening up all nuts and bolts from the bottom upwards.

Do not forget that the front wheel must be drawn close up to the brake side before the clip bolts are tightened.

Suitable oils for the forks are Mobiloil Arctic, Shell X100–20, Castrolite, Esso 20, B.P. Energol S.A.E. 20.

## Dismantling the Steering Head

The steering can be dismantled without stripping the forks but sufficient slack must be obtained in the lighting cables and the front brake cable disconnected, to allow the column to be drawn down out of the head.

Take out the four bolts securing the handlebar and lift the bar to one side. Slacken the pinch bolt (C) Fig. C25A and take off the caps (A) and (D) Fig. C25A and the top fork cover.

Now with a rawhide or copper mallet strike the sides of the top yoke alternately to release it from the tapered legs.

Lift the top yoke to one side and draw the steering column down and out of the head but be careful to catch the bearings which will be released as the column is withdrawn. There are 24 $\frac{3}{16}$ in. diameter steel balls in each race.

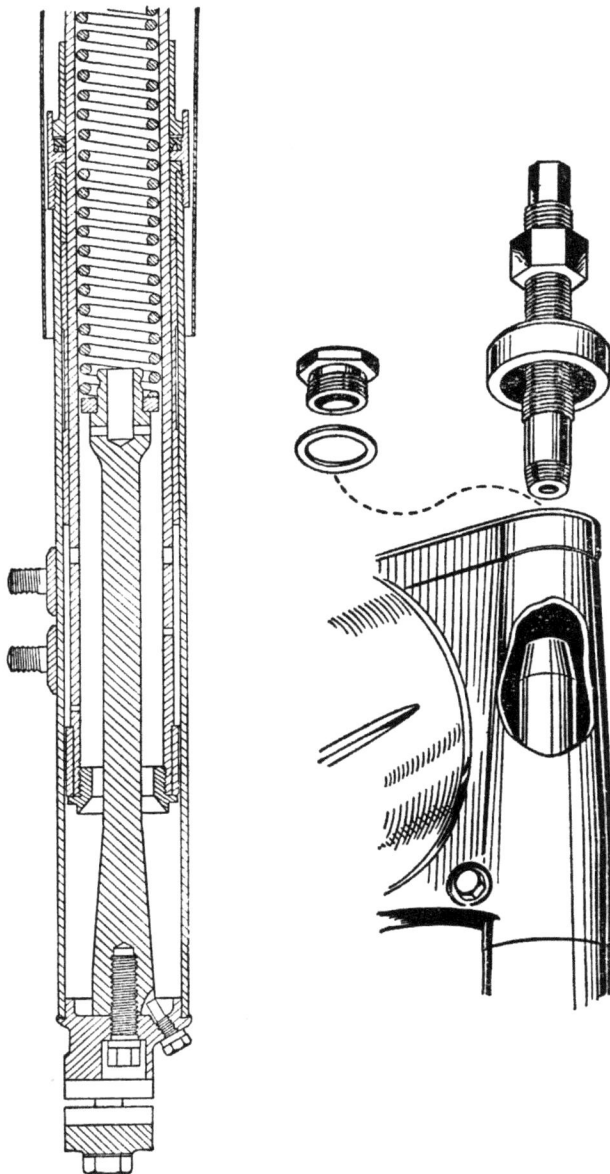

The two inner cones are the top Part number 1 19 40–5029, bottom 1 16 40–5027, and the two cups are also identical, Part number 1 17 40–4074.

The cups are a press fit into the head lug and can be driven out from opposite ends with the aid of a suitable drift.

If there are small indentations in either the cups or cones or the steel balls are pitted, they should be replaced.

**Reassembling the Steering**
Drive the new cups into the head lug using a flat plate or bar across the top of the cup and make sure that they enter the seatings squarely.

Grease the cups and press 24 balls into each. Slide the column carefully up into the head and place on the top cone and dust cover, next the top yoke and cap (D) Fig C25A. Screw in the caps (A) and replace the handlebar.

Check over the adjustment of the steering finally tightening nut (C) and replacing the brake and lighting cables.

Fig. C27A.   *Dismantling the front fork.*

**B.S.A. MOTOR CYCLES LTD.**, Service Department, Armoury Road, Birmingham 11.

Printed in England                                              THE B.S.A. PRESS

## B40 and C15 Competition Models

### FRONT FORK AND STEERING HEAD

Under normal conditions the only servicing which the front forks will require is occasional renewal of the oil. The need for this may be indicated by excessive movement, but it should only be necessary after considerable mileage.

**Changing the Oil**
First remove the plugs marked (A) Fig. C33A, and take out the drain plugs shown at (B) Fig. C34A. After allowing the oil to drain out, apply the front brake and depress the forks a few times to drive out any oil remaining.

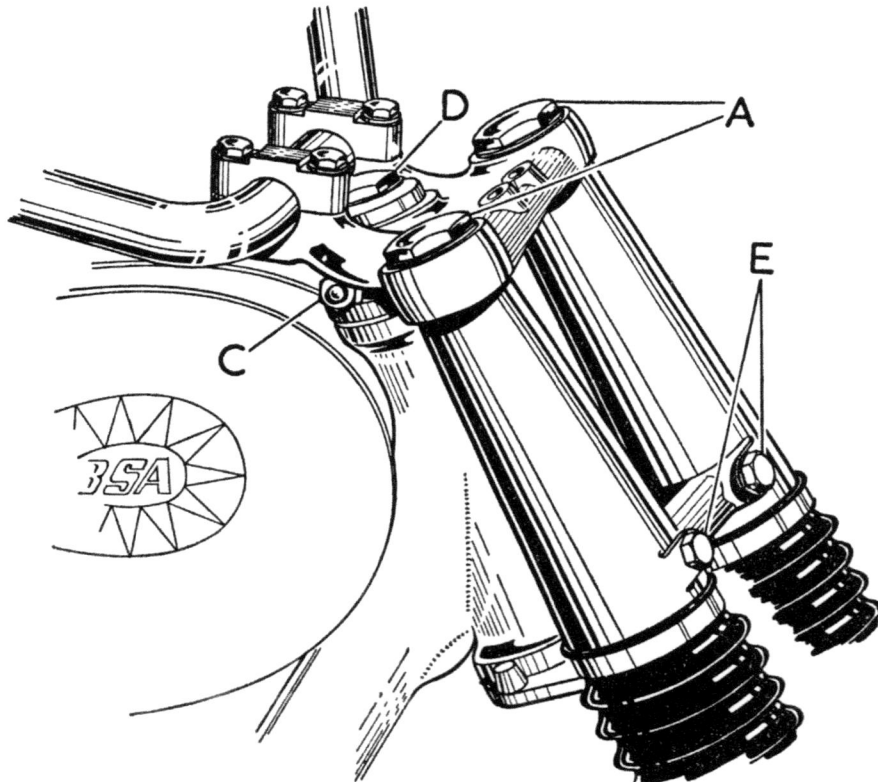

Fig. C33A. *Front fork and steering head.*

Replace the drain plugs after ensuring that the fibre washers are in good condition and refill each leg with ⅓ pint (190 c.c.) of an S.A.E. 20 oil, replace the top plugs and tighten securely.

**Steering Head Adjustment**

To test the head for play support the crankcase on a box so that the front wheel is clear of the ground, then standing in front of the machine with the legs together against the front tyre, push and pull alternately on the handlebars.

If any play is apparent the steering head bearings should be adjusted.

Slacken the clamping nut (c) Fig. C33A, and tighten the cap nut (D) until the adjustment is correct. The handlebars should turn freely, if the movement is "lumpy" it indicates that the top nut is too tight or the ballraces are damaged.

When the adjustment is correct, tighten the clamp nut (c) securely.

**Dismantling**

Before commencing work on the forks it is advisable to have the following tools and replacement parts available in case they are required:—

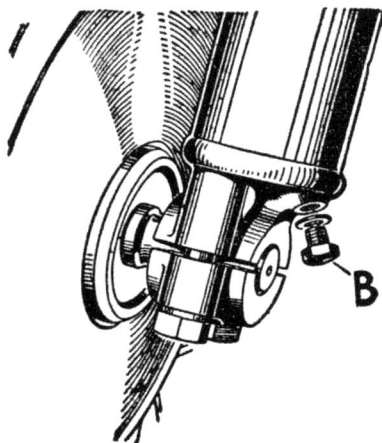

| | |
|---|---|
| SHIMS | 1 01 29–5335 (.010 in.) |
| | 1 01 29–5336 (.020 in.) |
| | 1 01 29–5337 (.030 in.) |
| OIL SEAL | 1 20 29–5313 (2) |
| TOP BUSH | 1 32 65–5424 (2) |
| LOWER BUSH | 1 29 29–5347 (2) |

A length of number five twine approx. 15 in. long.

| | |
|---|---|
| SERVICE TOOLS | 8 41 61–3350 |
| | 8 41 61–3005 |
| | 8 43 61–3006 |
| | 8 36 61–3007 |

Fig. C34A. *Front fork drain plug.*

Remove the front wheel and mudguard.

Take out the fork top cap (A) Fig. C33A, and screw tool number 8 41 61–3350 into the thread at the top of the fork shaft using the larger of the fine threads (c) Fig. C36A.

Slacken off the pinch bolt in the bottom yoke.

Remove the clip holding the rubber bellows on C15 Competition models and break the adhesion of the rubber by twisting slightly to left and right.

Take a firm grasp of the lower fork sliding member and strike the top of the tool smartly with a hammer. This will release the shaft from its taper and the complete fork leg can be drawn down and removed from the machine.

Repeat the operation on the other leg.

To dismantle the lower section of the fork hold the sliding tube by gripping the wheel spindle lug in a soft-jawed vice as in Fig. C35A, and lift off the spring followed by the rubber bellows.

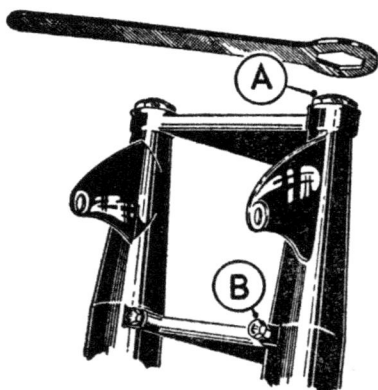

Slide Service Tool number 8 41 61–3005 over the main tube and enter the dogs in the slots at the bottom of the oil seal holder (D) Fig. C35A.

Pressing the tool down and turning at the same time unscrew the oil seal holder complete with the extension tube.

Slide the holder up the shaft until it becomes tight on the tapered section of the shaft. Do not use excessive force or the oil seal may be damaged.

The top fork bearing is retained in the sliding member by a circlip which can be prised out with a sharp tool such as the tang end of a file. There may be a number of shims fitted between the circlip and the top bush. These must be replaced if the bushes are not renewed when assembling.

Lift out the main tube complete with the oil seal holder and bushes.

Grip the tube in a vice using soft clamps on the unground portion of the shaft and unscrew the nut at the lower end of the shaft. This nut secures the lower bush and after its removal the oil seal holder, circlip, shims and bushes can be slid off the shaft.

If it is necessary to remove the oil seal place the lower edge of the holder on a soft wooden block and enter Service Tool number 8 43 61–3006 into the top of the holder (G) Fig. C39A.

Give the tool a sharp tap with a hammer and the oil seal will be driven out.

### Reassembly
Reassembly is carried out in the reverse order to dismantling. Cleanliness is essential and before attempting to reassemble clean all parts thoroughly and also clean the bench on which the forks have been dismantled.

If the oil seal is to be replaced care must be taken to see that the feather edge of the seal is not damaged. Enter the oil seal into the holder, metal part first, and drive home using Service Tool number 8 36 61–3007 (H) Fig. C39A.

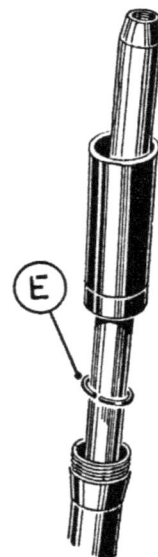

Slide the oil seal holder over the shaft until it is on the tapered section but do not use force or the seal may be damaged.

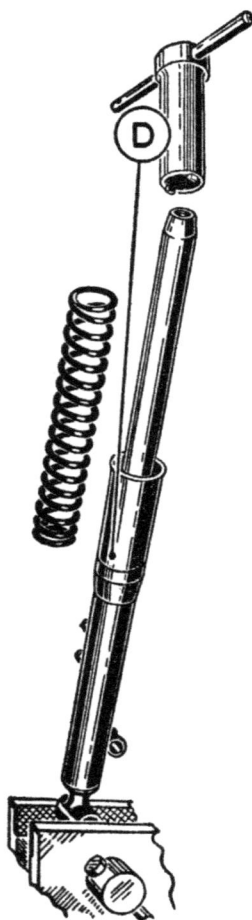

Fig. C35A.

Fig. C36A.

Fig. C38A.

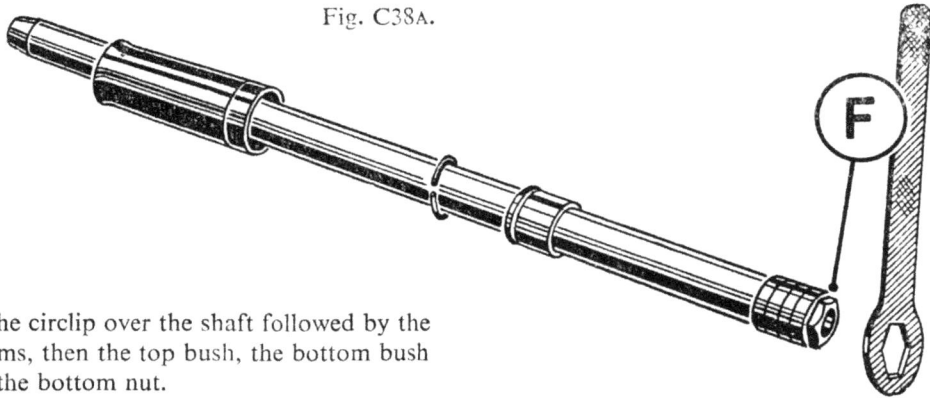

Place the circlip over the shaft followed by the packing shims, then the top bush, the bottom bush and finally the bottom nut.

Grip the sliding member in the vice and enter the mainshaft, with the assembled parts, into the sliding member. Fit the circlip over the top bush and check for up and down movement on the bush. If a new bush has been fitted it may be necessary to add to, or take from, the existing shims.

Packing shims are available in the following sizes:—
.010 in. Part number 1 01 29–5335
.020 in. Part number 1 01 29–5336
.030 in. Part number 1 01 29–5337

If the bush is not properly shimmed a tapping noise may be heard when the machine is ridden.

Having shimmed up the bush correctly and fitted the circlip firmly in position, screw down the oil seal holder on to one turn of twine round the groove at the end of the thread. This will provide an additional seal.

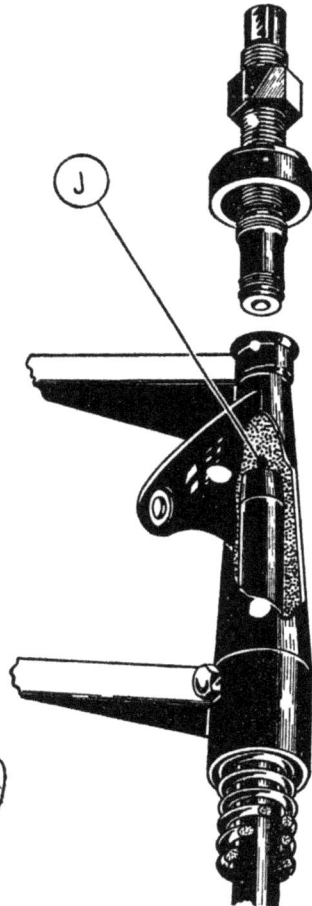

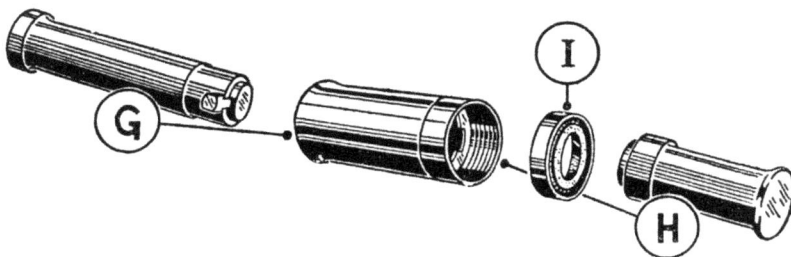

Fig. C39A.

Repeat the operation on the other leg.
Before refitting the leg to the steering head, apply a liberal coating of grease to the spring and place the spring in position and the rubber bellows if fitted over the oil seal holder, and secure with the one clip.

Now screw Service Tool number 8 41 61–3350 (minus the nut and collar) into the top of the tube and pass the tube up through the two yokes, fit the collar and nut and draw the tube firmly home into its taper (J) Fig. C37A.

Tighten the pinch bolt in the bottom yoke before removing the tool.

Repeat the operation on the other leg, replace the clips round the tops of the rubber bellows, fill the forks with the correct amount of oil (⅓ pint each leg) and replace the top fork plugs.

Finally replace the wheel and mudguard.

Do not forget that the front wheel must be drawn close up to the brake before the clip bolts are tightened.

Suitable oils for the forks are Mobiloil Arctic, Shell X100–20, Castrolite, Esso 20, B.P. Energol S.A.E. 20.

### Dismantling the Steering Head
The steering can be dismantled without stripping the forks, but when a headlamp is fitted the lighting cables and the front brake cable must be disconnected, to allow the column to be drawn down out of the head.

Take out the four bolts securing the handlebar and lift the bar to one side. Slacken the pinch bolt (C) Fig. C33A, and take off the caps (A) and (D).

Now with a rawhide or copper mallet strike the sides of the top yoke alternately to release it from the tapered legs.

Lift the top yoke to one side and draw the steering column down and out of the head but be careful to catch the bearings which will be released as the column is withdrawn. There are 24 $\frac{3}{16}$ in. diameter steel balls in each race.

The two inner cones are top, part number 1 19 40–5029, bottom 1 16 40–5027 and the two cups are identical, part number 1 17 40–4074.

The cups are a press fit into the head lug and can be driven out from opposite ends with the aid of a suitable drift.

If there are small indentations in either the cups or cones or the steel balls are pitted, they should be replaced.

### Reassembling the Steering
Drive the new cups into the head lug using a flat plate or bar across the top of the cup and make sure that they enter the seatings squarely.

Grease the cups and press 24 balls into each. Slide the column carefully up into the head and place on the top cone and dust cover, next the top yoke and cap (D) Fig. C33A. Screw in the caps (A), and replace the handlebar.

Check over the adjustment of the steering, finally tightening nut (C) and replacing the brake and lighting cables (when lamps are fitted).

**B.S.A. MOTOR CYCLES LTD.,** Service Department, Armoury Road, Birmingham 11.

# *BSA* SERVICE SHEET No. 427

## MODELS C15 AND B40
## ATTENTION WHICH CAN BE GIVEN WITHOUT DISMANTLING

**Oil Pressure Valves**

There are three ball valves in the lubrication system but only two can receive attention without complete dismantling of the engine.

The pressure release valve is situated at the front of the timing case on the right-hand side and is accessible when the plug (D) Fig. C28A is removed.

It is advisable to clean the ball, spring and ball seating every few thousand miles or when the oil is changed.

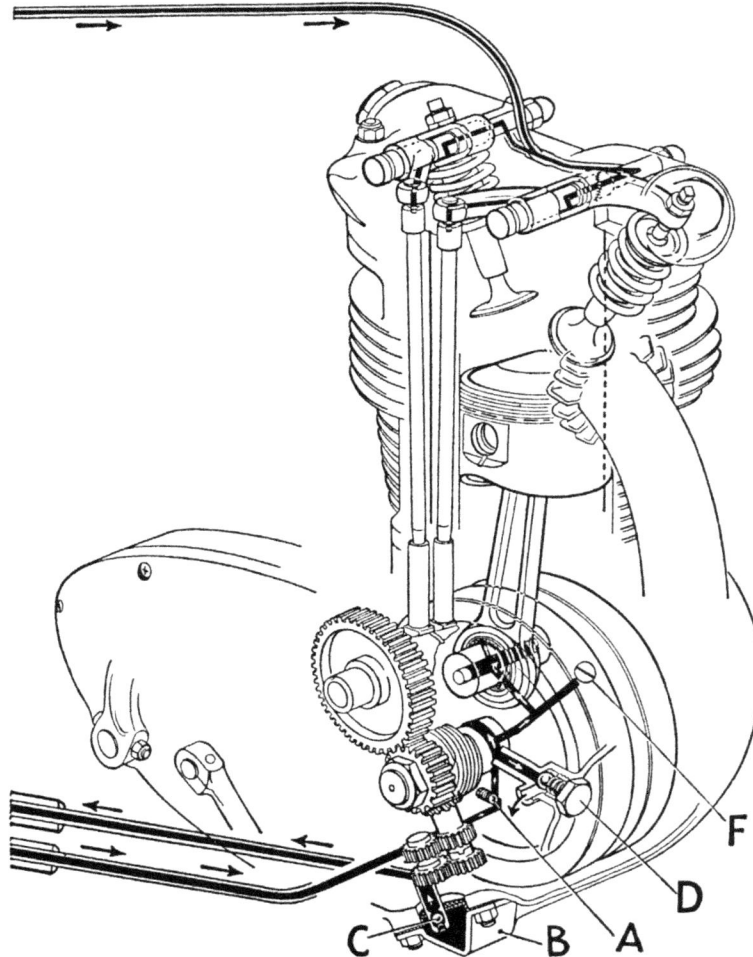

FIG. C28A. *Lubrication system.*

If the ball valve (C) Fig. C28A should be stuck on its seating it will prevent the return of oil to the tank. In this event, remove the cover plate (B) below the pump, insert a suitable piece of wire and lift the ball off its seating to free it.

**Tappet Clearance**

The engine must be quite cold whenever the tappet clearance is checked. Remove the inspection covers and take out the spark plug.

Rotate the engine forward until the INLET valve has just closed and the push rod is just free to rotate, this is the correct position for checking the EXHAUST valve.

Slide a feeler gauge between the end of the valve and the adjusting pin as shown in Fig. C29A.

If adjustment is necessary slacken the locknut (A) and adjust pin (B) until the correct gauge will just slide between the valve and the pin. Hold the pin firmly in position and tighten the locknut. Check the clearance again in case tightening the locknut has altered the setting.

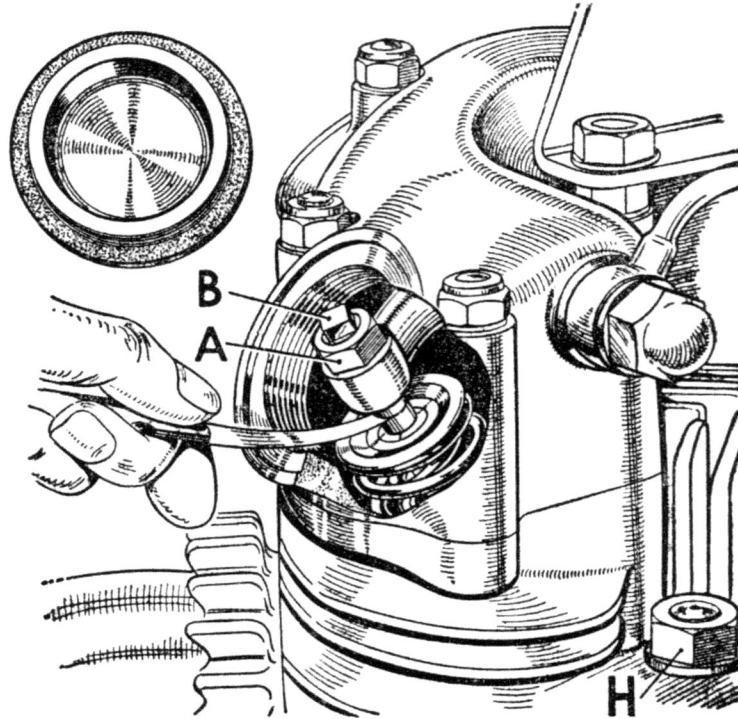

FIG. C29A. *Tappet adjustment.*

After the exhaust valve has been adjusted rotate the engine forward again until the exhaust valve clearance is just taken up, but before the valve actually starts to open.

This is the correct position for checking the inlet valve which is adjusted in a similar manner to that described for the exhaust valve.

Correct clearances are:—

C15 and B40

| | | |
|---|---|---|
| Inlet valve | .... | .008 inches |
| Exhaust valve | .... | .010 inches |

C15T prior to engine number C15T–1251.
C15S prior to engine number C15S–2112.

| | | |
|---|---|---|
| Inlet valve | .... | .004 inches |
| Exhaust valve | .... | .004 inches |

C15 Trials and Scrambles machines after the above engine numbers are fitted with camshafts having ramp cams and on these machines the tappet clearances are the same as the other models, i.e.:—

Inlet .008 inches.          Exhaust .010 inches.

These new camshafts can be fitted to earlier machines if necessary. The spares number is 1 43 40–0477.

**Contact Breaker Gap**

Remove the cover (A), Fig. C30A after pressing aside the spring clip or removing the centre screw.

The gap between the points when fully open should be .015 in. Rotate the engine slowly until the foot of the rocker arm is on the peak of the cam, then check the gap between the contacts at (B) with the feeler gauge.

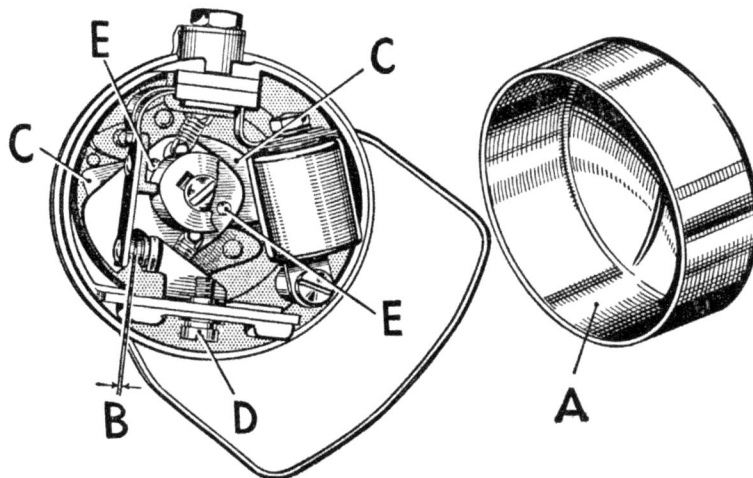

FIG. C30A. *Contact breaker and auto-advance mechanism (early type).*

If the gap requires adjusting, slacken the screw (D) and move the plate until the gap is correct, then retighten the screw and re-check the setting.

No oil or grease should be allowed to get on the contact breaker points which should always be clean and dry.

**Ignition Timing**

To check the ignition timing expose the contact breaker as previously described. As a slight variation in the contact breaker gap alters the timing (wide gap advances and narrow gap retards the timing), it is advisable to check after adjusting the points.

With the spark plug out, engage top gear and turn the engine by means of the rear wheel until the piston is at the top of its stroke with both valves closed, if either valve is open rotate the engine one complete revolution to bring the piston to the correct position, that is: top dead centre on the compression stroke.

Insert a slim rod, such as an old spoke, through the spark plug hole and keeping the rod as vertical as possible, make a mark in line with some point on the head such as one of the fins, now make a second mark $\frac{1}{32}$ in. above. Re-insert the rod and, again keeping it as vertical as possible, turn the engine back by revolving the rear wheel backwards until the piston has descended to bring the second mark on the rod in line with the point chosen on the head.

The piston should now be at the firing point (see table) and the contact breaker points should be just about to open.

If the setting is incorrect, slacken the clip screw (E) Fig. C31A, which is situated at the top of the outer timing cover and rotate the body of the distributor gently either way until the foot of the rocker arm is at the base of the cam when the points should be just about to separate. This gives a timing in the static position.

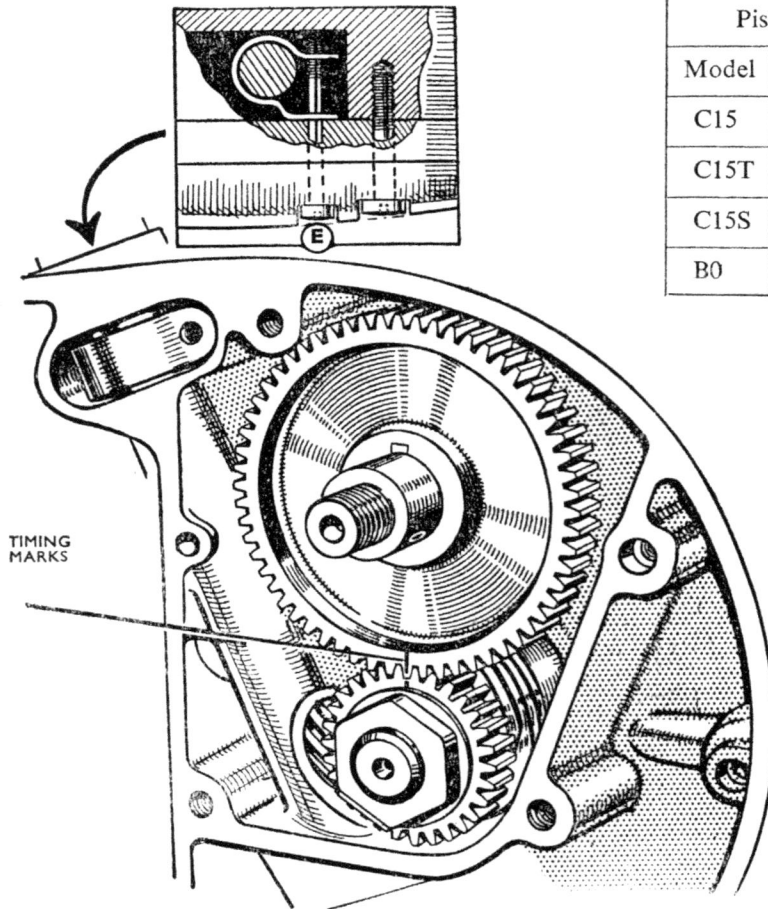

| Piston position before T.D.C. | | |
|---|---|---|
| Model | Degrees | Inches |
| C15 | | |
| C15T | 33½° F.A. | 9/32 in. F.A. |
| C15S | | |
| B0 | | |

F.A.—Fully advanced.

FIG. C31A. *Valve timing marks.*

To obtain the correct timing in the fully advanced position, reset the piston 9/32 in. B.T.D.C., now hold the auto-advance in the advanced position by turning the cam anti-clockwise and reset the body of the distributor so that the points are just about to open.

**Ignition Timing (engines prefixed C15F and B40F)**

Engines with numbers prefixed C15F or B40F have the contact breaker fitted at the side of the timing cover. On these models access to the contact breaker is obtained by removing two cover screws. Timing is adjusted by slackening two pillar bolts and moving the contact breaker plate to left or right as required.

When it is necessary to remove the auto-advance and contact breaker cam, take off the contact breaker plate, remove the centre bolt holding the cam and using tool number 8 **14** 61–5005 pull off the unit by simply screwing the extractor bolt in until the unit is released from its taper in the cam-shaft spindle.

To reset the contact breaker cam, position the piston as previously described, insert the auto-advance unit loosely in the camshaft then replace the contact breaker plate midway in the slots with the points at approximately 3 o'clock. Now turn the cam to right or left until the points are about to open and secure the cam with the centre bolt. Obtain the final setting in the fully advanced position as described for the older models except that in this case the final adjustment is made by turning the contact breaker plate whilst holding the cam in the advanced position.

### Models C15T and C15S

The C15T and C15S are timed by a different method due to their being equipped with the "energy transfer" ignition system. This system is very sensitive in operation and the following instructions should be strictly followed if the best results are to be obtained.

Set the contact breaker gap to .015 in. before commencing to time the engine.

Now bring the piston to top of the bore on the compression stroke as described previously, then rotate the engine backwards so that the piston descends about ½ in., before bringing the rotor into the position shown in Fig. C32A. The rotating of the engine backwards first, ensures that the backlash is taken up in the gears. It therefore follows that while bringing the rotor into the position illustrated, the engine should be in a state of constant forward revolution.

Now with the rotor in this position the contact breaker points should be just about to open. This can be checked and if necessary corrected as with the standard models.

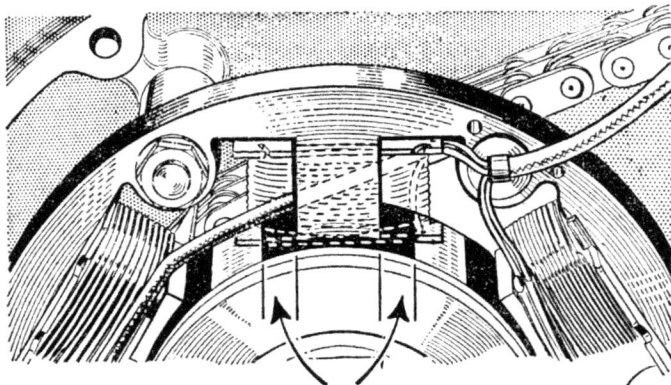

OVERLAP
MUST BE EQUAL ON BOTH
SIDES WHEN POINTS ARE
BREAKING

FIG. C32A.

### Sparking Plug

The machine is supplied with a Champion non-detachable type sparking plug to suit the characteristics of the engine. If the best performance with regard to both power and economy is to be obtained then it must remain clean and properly gapped.

The sparking plug should be removed periodically for examination. If the carburation is correct and the engine is in good condition the plug will remain clean for considerable periods. An over-rich mixture will however cause the formation of a sooty deposit on the plug points and eventually on the plug body (see upper view of Fig. C33A). Heavily leaded fuels may form a greyish deposit in a similar manner. If a heavy deposit is found, the plug should be cleaned, with the aid of the sand-blast type of plug cleaner found at most garages as, otherwise the performance of the machine may be affected. If a heavy deposit is allowed to build up inside the plug it may prevent the engine from firing altogether. A weak mixture will cause burning of the plug points and give the plug a whitish appearance (see Service Sheet No. 708).

Check that the gap between the sparking plug points is correct and if necessary reset to .020–.025 in. by bending the side wire.

.020–.025 in.

FIG. C33A. *The sparking plug.*

In no circumstances attempt to move the central electrode as this may damage the insulation. If the points are badly burnt away or cleaning fails to restore the plug to its full efficiency, then it should be replaced by a new one.

When replacing the plug make sure that the copper washer is in good condition. Use a tubular spanner to prevent damage to the plug and keep the ouside of the insulation free from oil and dirt by wiping with a clean rag.

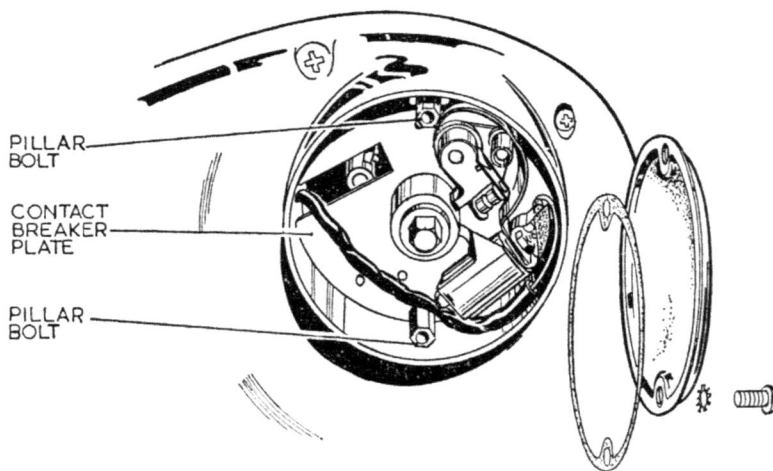

PILLAR BOLT

CONTACT BREAKER PLATE

PILLAR BOLT

FIG. C30B. *Contact Breaker and Auto Advance (Current Type)*

B.S.A. MOTOR CYCLES LTD., Service Department, Armoury Road, Birmingham 11

### USEFUL DATA

|  | C15 | C15T | C15S | C15 Sport Star | B40 |
|---|---|---|---|---|---|
| ENGINE NUMBER ... ... ... | | (on left side of crankcase below the cylinder) | | | |
| FRAME NUMBER ... ... ... | | (at the top of the steering head tube) | | | |
| **ENGINE:** | | | | | |
| Capacity (c.c.) ... ... ... | 249 | 249 | 249 | 249 | 343 |
| Cylinder bore (mm.) ... ... | 67 | 67 | 67 | 67 | 79 |
| Stroke (mm.) ... ... ... | 70 | 70 | 70 | 70 | 70 |
| Compression ratio ... ... | 8 : 1 | 8 : 1 | 10 : 1 | 8.75 : 1 | 7 : 1 |
|  | | *prior to eng. C15T-1251. | *prior to eng. C15S-2112. | | |
| Inlet opens B.T.D.C. ... ... | 26° | 41½° | 41½° | 51° | 26° |
| Inlet closes A.B.D.C. ... ... | 70° | 62½° | 62½° | 68° | 70° |
| Exhaust opens B.B.D.C. ... | 61½° | 62½° | 62½° | 78° | 61½° |
| Exhaust closes A.T.D.C. ... | 34½° | 41½° | 41½° | 37° | 34½° |
| Piston rings—compression, (in.) | .0625 wide | .0625 wide | .0625 wide | .0625 wide | .0625 wide |
| Piston rings—scraper, (in.) ... | .125 wide | .125 wide | .125 wide | .125 wide | .125 wide |
| Piston rings gaps—minimum (in.) | .009 | .009 | .009 | .009 | .009 |
| maximum (in.) | .013 | .013 | .013 | .013 | .014 |
| Sparking plug ... ... ... | Champion N5 | Champion N5 | Champion N3 | Champion N4 | Champion N5 |
| Plug points gap—minimum (in.) | .020 | .020 | .020 | .020 | .020 |
| maximum (in.) | .025 | .025 | .025 | .025 | .025 |
| **TRANSMISSION:** | | | | | |
| Gear ratios—top ... ... ... | 5.98 | 9.0 | 9.0 | 6.36 | 5.48 |
| third ... ... | 7.65 | 14.67 | 10.8 | 7.64 | 7.0 |
| second ... ... | 10.54 | 22.0 | 14.94 | 10.54 | 9.63 |
| first ... ... | 15.96 | 28.53 | 19.0 | 13.44 | 14.6 |
| Clutch friction plates ... ... | 4 | 4 | 4 | 4 | 4 |
| Chain sizes—front (in.) ... ... | ⅜ Duplex (70 pitches) | ⅜ Duplex (70 pitches) | ⅜ Duplex (70 pitches) | ⅜ Duplex (70 pitches) | ⅜ Duplex (70 pitches) |
| rear (in.) ... ... | ½ × .335 (112 pitches) | ½ × .335 (122 pitches) | ½ × .335 (122 pitches) | ½ × .335 (112 pitches) | ½ × .335 (116 pitches) |
| Teeth on—engine sprocket ... | 23T | 23T | 23T | 23T | 23T |
| gearbox sprocket ... | 17T | **15T | *15T | 16T | 19T |
| clutch sprocket ... | 52T | 52T | 52T | 52T | 52T |
| rear chainwheel ... | 45T | ††60T | †60T | 45T | 46T |
| **CAPACITIES:** | | | | | |
| Fuel tank (galls.) ... ... ... | 3 (13.6 litres) | 2 (9 litres) | 2 (9 litres) | 3 (13.6 litres) | 3 (13.6 litres) |
| Oil tank (pints) ... ... ... | 4 (2¼ litres) | 5 (2.8 litres) | 5 (2.8 litres) | 4 (2¼ litres) | 4 (2¼ litres) |
| Gearbox (pints) ... ... ... | †1/5 (220 c.c.) | 1/5 (220 c.c.) | 1/5 (220 c.c.) | 7/16 (250 c.c.) | 1/5 (220 c.c.) |
| Front forks (pints) ... ... | 1/6 (100 c.c.) | 1/3 (190 c.c.) | 1/3 (190 c.c.) | 1/6 (100 c.c.) | 1/3 (190 c.c.) |
| Primary chaincase (pints) ... | ¼ (140 c.c.) | ¼ (140 c.c.) | ¼ (140 c.c.) | ¼ (140 c.c.) | ¼ (140 c.c.) |

*After engine C15T-1251 and C15S-2112 valve timing is:—

|  |  |
|---|---|
| Inlet opens B.T.D.C. ... ... | 51° |
| Inlet closes A.B.D.C. ... ... | 68° |
| Exhaust opens B.B.D.C. ... | 78° |
| Exhaust closes A.T.D.C. ... | 37° |

†After engine C15-26792 and B40-2402 the gearbox capacity is increased to ½ pint (285 c.c.).

## USEFUL DATA—continued

| | C15 | C15T | C15S | C15 Sport Star | B40 |
|---|---|---|---|---|---|
| **WHEELS:** | | | | | |
| Rim size—front ... ... ... | WM2–17 | WM1–20 | WM1–20 | WM2–17 | WM2–18 |
| rear ... ... ... | WM2–17 | WM3–18 | WM3–18 | WM2–17 | WM2–18 |
| Tyre size—front ... ... ... | 3.25–17 | 3.00–20 | 3.00–20 | 3.25–17 | 3.25–18 |
| rear ... ... ... | 3.25–17 | 4.00–18 | 4.00–18 | 3.25–17 | 3.50–18 |
| Brakes, dia. × width—front (in.) | 6 × $\frac{7}{8}$ | 7 × $1\frac{1}{8}$ | 7 × $1\frac{1}{8}$ | 6 × $\frac{7}{8}$ | 7 × $1\frac{1}{8}$ |
| rear (in.) | 6 × $\frac{7}{8}$ | 6 × $\frac{7}{8}$ | 6 × $\frac{7}{8}$ | 6 × $\frac{7}{8}$ | 6 × $\frac{7}{8}$ |
| **CARBURATION (AMAL):** | | | | | |
| Bore (in.) ... ... ... ... | $\frac{7}{8}$ | $\frac{7}{8}$ | $1\frac{1}{16}$ | 1 | $1\frac{1}{16}$ |
| Main jet ... ... ... ... | 140 | 140 | 190 | 200 | 190 |
| Pilot jet ... ... ... ... | 25 | 25 | 25 | 25 | 20 |
| Throttle valve ... ... ... | 375/4 | 375/4 | 376/3½ | 376/4 | 376/3 |
| Needle position ... ... ... | 3 | 3 | 2 | 2 | 3 |
| Needle jet ... ... ... ... | .1055 | .1055 | .106 | .106 | .105 |
| **GENERAL DETAILS:** | | | | | |
| Front suspension movement (in.) | 5 | 5 | 5 | 5 | 5 |
| Rear suspension movement (in.) | $2\frac{3}{8}$ | $2\frac{3}{8}$ | $2\frac{3}{8}$ | $2\frac{3}{8}$ | $2\frac{3}{8}$ |
| Generator ouput ... ... ... | 60 watts | 60 watts | 60 watts | 60 watts | 60 watts |
| Contact breaker gap (in.) ... | .015 | .015 | .015 | .015 | .015 |
| Battery capacity ... ... ... | 13 amp/hr. at 20 hour rate. | — | — | 13 amp/hr. at 20 hour rate. | 13 amp/hr. at 20 hour rate. |
| Overall length ... ... ... | 78 | 81 | 81½ | 78 | 80 |
| Wheelbase (in.) ... ... ... | 51¼ | 51¾ | 51¾ | 51¼ | 52 |
| Ground clearance (in.) ... ... | 5 | 7¼ | 7 | 5 | 7 |
| Saddle height (in.) ... ... | 30 | 33 | 32 | 30 | 32 |
| Overall height (in.) ... ... | 37 | 42 | 41½ | 36 | 39½ |
| Handlebar width (in.) ... ... | 26 | 31⅛ | 31⅛ | 27 | 26 |
| Steering head angle ... ... | 65° | 63° | 63° | 65° | 65° |
| Steering lock angle ... ... | 50° | 60° | 60° | 50° | 40° |
| Weight (lbs.) ... ... ... | 275 | 265 | 265 | 275 | 295 |
| Tyre pressures—front (lbs.) ... | 16 | 19 | 19 | 17 | 17 |
| rear (lbs.) ... | 22 | 16 | 16 | 21 | 21 |

**Alternatives 17T, 18T, 19T and 20T.                    ††Alternatives 52T, 56T and 60T.

The recommended inflation pressures are based on a rider's weight of 140 lbs. If the rider's weight exceeds 140 lbs. increase the tyre pressures as follows:—

FRONT TYRE:   Add one lb. per square inch for every 28 lb. above 140 lb.
REAR TYRE:   Add one lb. per square inch for every 14 lb. increase above 140 lb.

If a pillion passenger or luggage is carried, the actual load bearing upon each tyre should be determined and the pressures increased in accordance with the Dunlop Load and Pressure Schedule.

B.S.A. MOTOR CYCLES LTD., Service Department, Armoury Road, Birmingham 11.
PRINTED IN ENGLAND — B.S.A. PRESS

## THE LUBRICATION SYSTEM

The engine lubrication system is of the dry sump type operated by a double gear pump, situated in the bottom of the crankcase on the right-hand side. The only external oilways are the supply and return pipes to the tank and the rocker feed and drainage pipes on the "B" Group. The oil drawn from the oil tank to the supply side of the pump first passes through a close mesh filter. This filter is not fitted to "M" Group machines as a felt filter is incorporated in the oil return pipe.

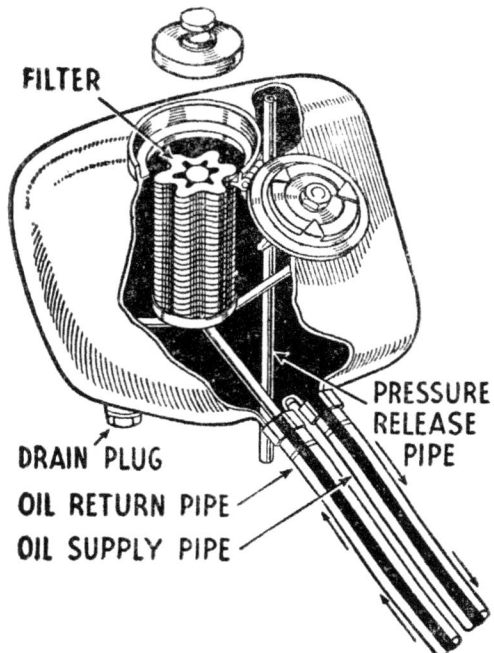

Fig. M3. *The Lubrication System* (*models M20 and M21*)

From the supply side of the pump the oil passes through a ball valve (A) and is then transferred to the hollow drive side mainshaft to supply the big-end roller bearing. On "B" and "M" models the transfer is made via a nozzle fitted in the timing cover which projects into the end of the drilled mainshaft and additional oilways in the timing cover provide positive lubrication to the cam pinion spindles. In the case of the "C" Group models, the oil passes through a hole in the main bearing bush, round an annular groove in the journal and thence via a radial drilling to the hollow centre of the shaft. (See Fig. M4). On C10L and C11G models a fine bleed hole from the main bearing meters a supply of oil to the camshaft and cam followers.

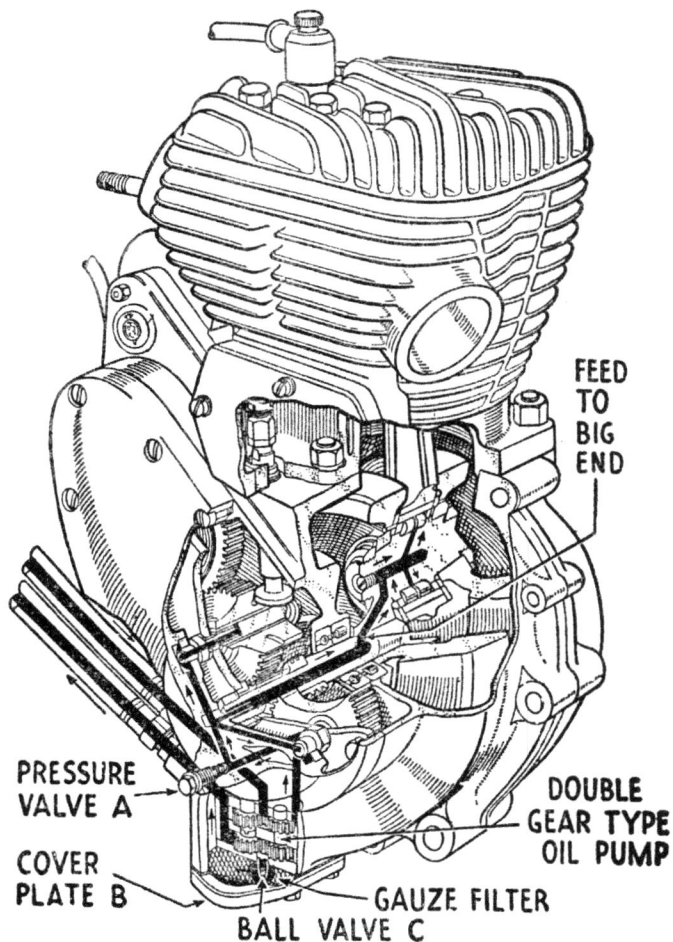

*The Oil Tank C15.*

## MODEL C15

**The** lubrication system is of the dry sump type and is operated by a double gear pump situated in the bottom of the crankcase on the right-hand side. The oil tank capacity is four pints and oil is drawn from the oil tank to the supply pump (top set of gears). It is then pumped past the non-return valve (A), and along the hollow mainshaft to the big-end.

After lubricating the engine the oil flows down through a filter to the bottom of the crankcase from which it is drawn by the return pump (lower set of gears) past the non-return oil valve (C), and delivered up the return pipe to the tank. At the junction of the return pipe to the tank a by-pass pipe leads a supply of oil to the rockers, push-rods end, etc.

*Lubrication System C*15.

The valve (A) prevents oil transfer from the tank to the crankcase while the machine is standing, and together with the sludge trap (F), does not require attention until such time as the engine is completely dismantled.

A by-pass valve (D) ensures a constant pressure in the system. Surplus quantities of oil are discharged into the crankcase.

If the ball valve (C) should be stuck in its seating there will be no return of oil to the tank. In this event remove the cover plate (B) below the pump, insert a piece of wire into the valve orifice and lift the ball off its seating to free it.

## THE CRANKCASE BREATHER VALVE

The crankcase air release valve is of similar construction on all models although its position in the crankcase is dependant on the model and the year of manufacture.

On all "C" Group models the breather is situated on the left-hand side of the crankcase behind the primary chaincase. 1946 and 1947 "B" and "M" machines have the breather positioned at the rear of the drive-side bearing boss. Later "B" and "M" Group models have the breather positioned in the lower edge of the timing chest cover.

In each case its purpose is to allow free release of air from the crankcase as the piston descends, and to prevent air being drawn back into the crankcase as the piston ascends. A crankcase breather valve which is faulty, or partially blocked, will result in oil leakage from the engine.

Before the breather valve can be withdrawn the air release pipe must be removed by unscrewing the union nut. The complete breather valve can then be unscrewed from the crankcase. To dismantle the breather, undo the large hexagon on the outer end of the valve, the valve retaining collar can then be unscrewed with the aid of a large screwdriver thus allowing the fibre disc valve to fall free. Before reassembling, wash the components thoroughly in petrol to free them from any oil residue that may cause the valve to stick.

Before replacing the breather valve on "C" Group models the movement of the disc valve should be checked to ensure that it does not exceed .010 in. If excessive clearance is found and the disc valve is undamaged the face of the retaining collar should be ground so as to reduce the depth of the recess in which the disc valve lies. Take care not to grind too much away so that the disc valve has no clearance.

If the breather valve is fitted into the timing case cover, ensure that it is positioned so that the hole drilled in the side of the pipe inside the cover is facing towards the cover and slightly towards the rear. Failure to observe this precaution may result in excessive oil loss. Correct positioning of the hole may be effected by varying the thickness of the fibre washer fitted between the air release valve and the timing case cover.

## MODELS C10L AND C11G

Instead of the pressure operated clack valve, a mechanically timed breather is employed. This takes the form of a hollow drive-side engine mainshaft with a radial drilling which, at the appropriate piston position, is brought in line with a drilled port in the crankcase thus allowing the gases to exhaust freely to the atmosphere. The engine sprocket distance sleeve, which fits over the portion of the mainshaft with the radial drilling, has six transfer ports so that it is immaterial which of the six spline-grooves locates the internal peg of the sleeve.

This type of breather is completely automatic and requires no adjustment or other maintenance whatsoever.

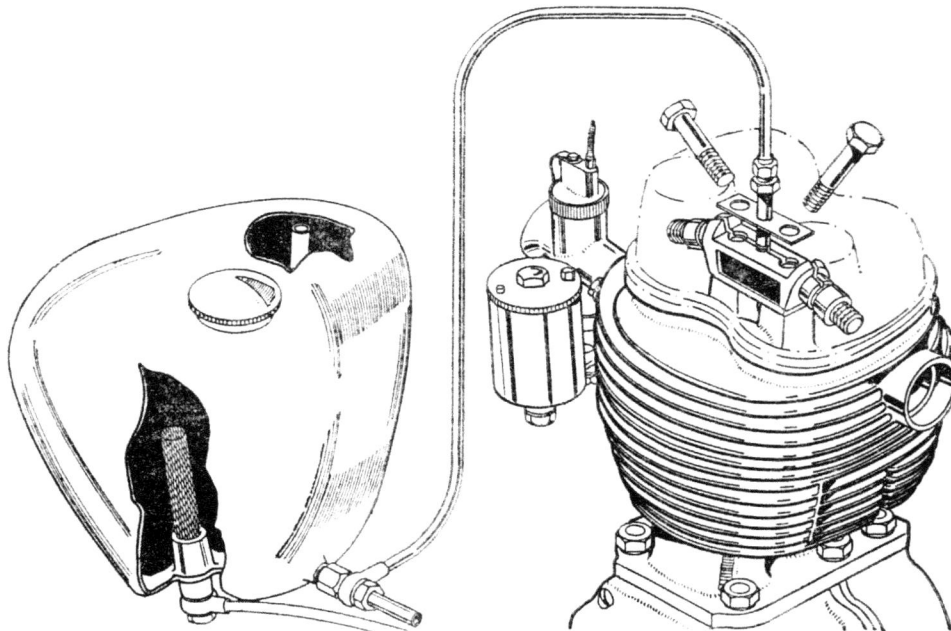

*Rocker Gear Lubrication C12 (1956).*

Parts required for conversion of C11 and C11G engines:—

| Part No. | Description |
|----------|-------------|
| 29–2086 | Rocker Oil Feed Pipe. |
| 29–2091 | Rocker Trunnion. |
| 29–2092 | Bolt. |
| 45–2454 | Locking Plate. |
| 65–8420 | Connection. |
| 65–8421 | Washer. |
| 65–8424 | Nut. |

## MODEL C12, 1956

The model C12 engine is identical with the C11G model. However, the lubrication system has been modified to provide positive lubrication to the valve rocker gear. The take off is from the oil tank return pipe, as on the "B" Group plunger models and the oil is fed through a rocker feed pipe to the rocker cover securing bolt which is drilled to allow the oil to pass to the trunnion. This trunnion incorporates oil grooves direct to each rocker fulcrum. After lubricating, the oil drains to the sump down the push rod tunnel, providing extra lubrication for the cams and cam followers in the process.

This modification can be adopted on the C11 and C11G engines at very low cost. The parts required are listed above, and they can be obtained through your dealer.

After lubricating the big-end and circulating throughout the engine in the form of oil mist, the oil drains down, through a filter to the bottom of the crankcase from which it is drawn by the return pump past ball valve (c) and delivered up the return pipe to the tank.

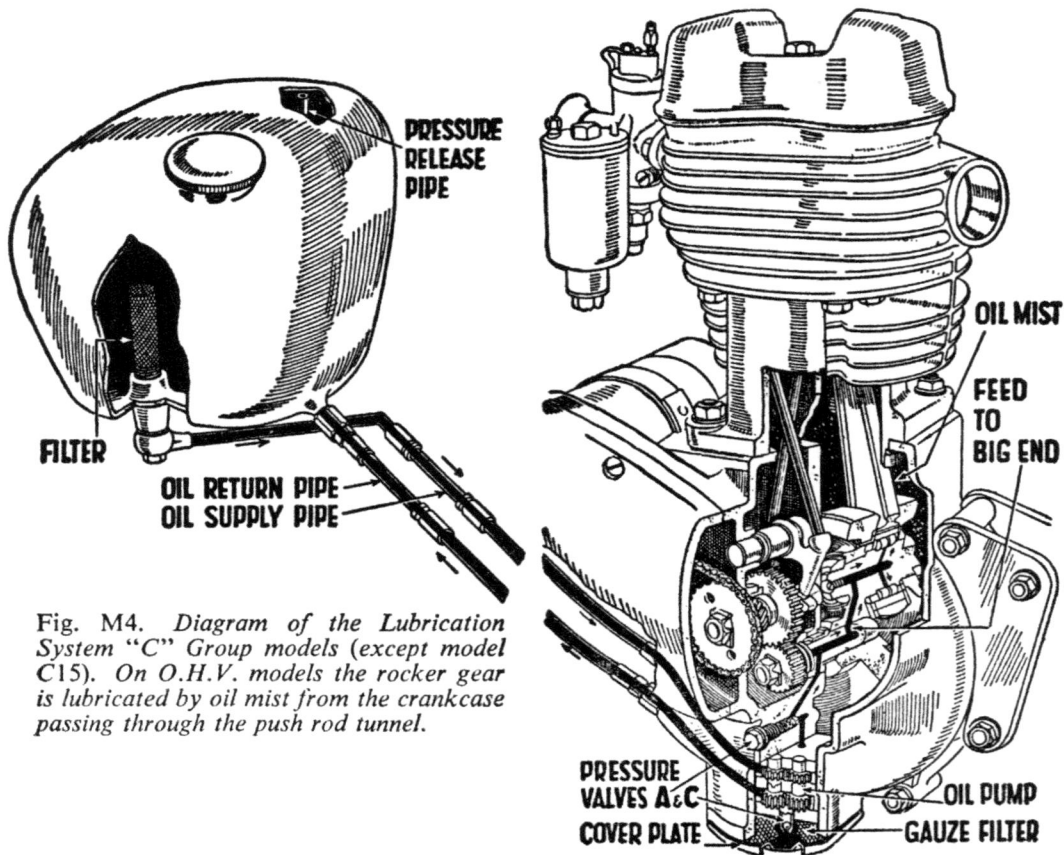

Fig. M4. *Diagram of the Lubrication System "C" Group models (except model C15). On O.H.V. models the rocker gear is lubricated by oil mist from the crankcase passing through the push rod tunnel.*

On "B" Group machines oil is fed through a union situated in the pipe between the return pump and the tank, to the rocker spindles, and after lubricating the rockers and enclosed valves, is returned to the crankcase through an external oil pipe attached to the base of the inlet valve spring housing (see Fig. M5). An internal oilway connects the two valve spring wells.

Incorrect seating of the ball valve (A) will allow oil to transfer from the tank to the engine, whilst the machine is stationary. In this event, unscrew the plug over the valve, and remove spring and ball. Clean the ball and its seating and replace. If the ball valve (C) should get stuck in its seating, there will be no return of oil to the tank. To correct, remove the cover plate below the pump and insert a piece of wire into the valve orifice, and lift the ball off its seating to free it. To check the flow of oil in the lubricating system, remove the tank filler cap whilst the engine is running. Oil should be seen issuing from the return pipe from the crankcase. The tank and crankcase should be drained periodically, and replenished with clean oil (see "Periodical Maintenance").

Any restriction in the pressure release pipe in the tank will cause an increase in pressure inside the oil tank, and will result in leakage of oil at the filler cap. This can be put right by inserting a length of flexible wire into the pipe at its lower end (just in front of the rear mudguard) and pushing the wire right up the pipe, thus clearing obstruction.

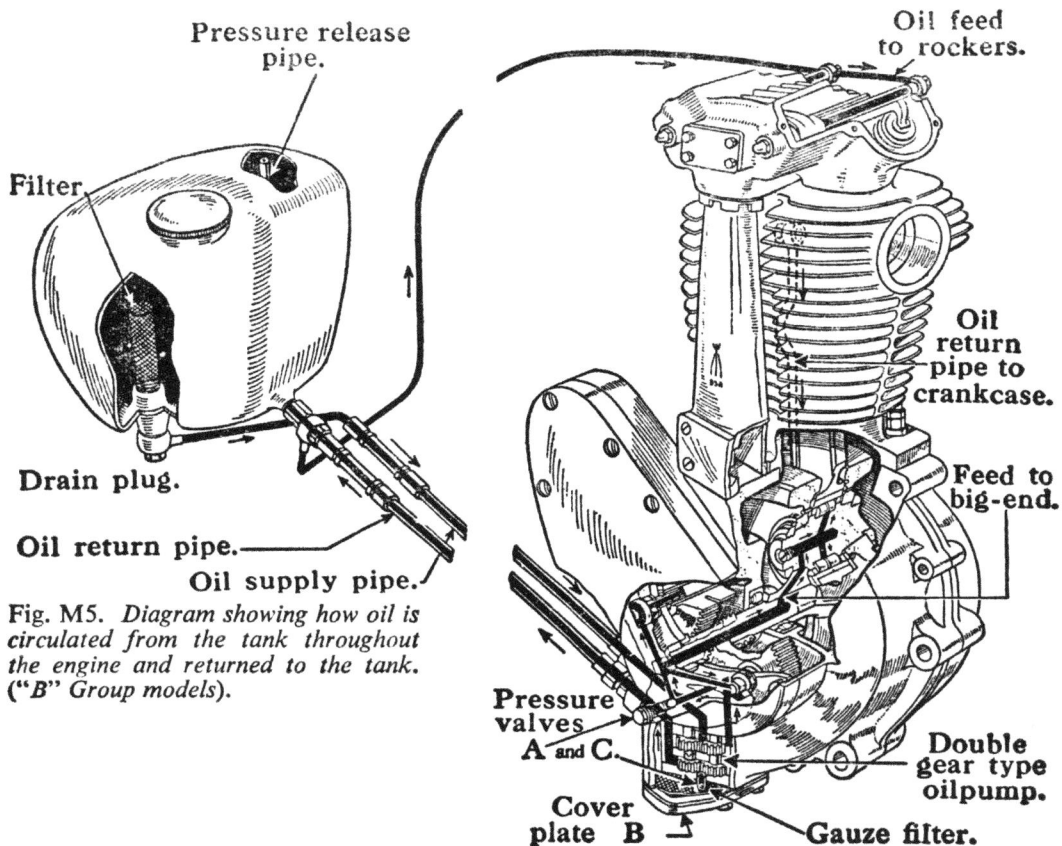

Pressure release pipe.

Oil feed to rockers.

Filter.

Oil return pipe to crankcase.

Drain plug.

Feed to big-end.

Oil return pipe.

Oil supply pipe.

Fig. M5. *Diagram showing how oil is circulated from the tank throughout the engine and returned to the tank. ("B" Group models).*

Pressure valves A and C.

Double gear type oilpump.

Cover plate B

Gauze filter.

To remove the "B" and "C" Group oil tank filter for cleaning, remove the oil pipe banjo union plug at the bottom of the tank. The filter will come out with the plug.

On models with the swinging arm type frame the oil tank is of slightly different construction but the system is the same. The oil tank filter is attached to the large hexagon nut in the outside of the tank and its removal does not entail interfering with the oil pipes.

To remove the "M" Group filter for cleaning, release the tank filler cap, release the filter cap thus exposed, and lift the filter out. In all cases the filter should be placed in a can big enough to cover it with petrol, and thoroughly washed. Before replacing make sure that it is quite dry of petrol.

The pump filter can be withdrawn after removing the cover plate (B) and should be thoroughly washed with petrol, dried and replaced.

On no account try to remove the oil pump unless it requires attention (see Service Sheet on complete "Dismantling of Engine").

### Crankcase Breather C15

The breather is mechanically timed as on the C10L and C11G models but takes the form of a hollow camshaft with a radial drilling which, at the appropriate piston position, is brought in line with a drilled port in the inner timing cover, this port has its outlet inside the outer timing cover. Pressure is then released through a small radial cut-away at the rear end of the outer cover joint face.

### Changing the Oil C15

This should preferably be done immediately after running, so that the oil is warm and will, therefore, flow more freely. Disconnect the oil pipe union nut (A), at the base of the tank and collect the old oil in a suitable receptacle.

### Filters

Remove the oil tank and crankcase filters for cleaning at regular intervals, this can be carried out in conjunction with the change of oil. After releasing the oil pipe at (A), unscrew the hexagon plug (B), which carries the filter in the tank, and wash thoroughly in petrol. Make sure that all the petrol has evaporated before replacing. Refill with the correct grade of oil.

The pump filter can be withdrawn after removing the crankcase cover plate and should be thoroughly washed with petrol, dried and replaced. The oil pump is extremely reliable and it is most unlikely that it will give trouble therefore it should not be disturbed unnecessarily. The pump is held in position by three bolts. The two other bolts hold the sections of the pump together.

**B.S.A. MOTOR CYCLES LTD.**, Service Department, Armoury Road, Birmingham 11.
B.S.A. Press

# BSA SERVICE SHEET No. 612

*Reprinted Sept. 1960*

## All Models

## BRAKE RELINING

### Brake Shoe Removal and Replacement

After the brake plate has been removed from the wheel, the brake cam lever A (Fig. M40) should be detached and the cam spindle B pushed in slightly to allow the shoes to clear the brake plate. Insert a screwdriver between the brake shoes at the fulcrum pin C and twist the screwdriver.

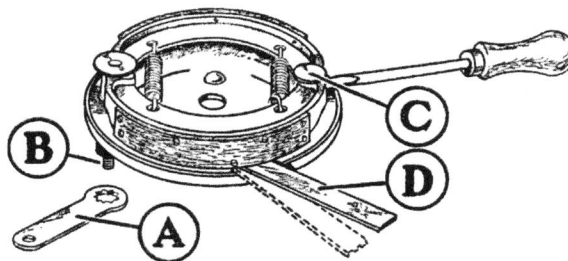

Fig. M40. Removing the Brake Shoes

Place a small lever D between one of the shoes and the cover plate and lever the shoe away from the cover plate until the spring pressure is released. Both shoes can then be lifted from the brake plate.

The shoes can be replaced by the reverse procedure. Hook the springs on to the shoes and place the ends of the shoes in position on the fulcrum pin and cam lever. Then push the shoes outwards until the springs pull them into their correct position.

NOTE: The brake shoe springs are quite strong and care should be taken that the fingers are not trapped by the brake shoes during these operations.

### Brake Shoe Relining

With the shoes removed the linings can best be removed by drilling away the heads of the rivets and punching the shanks out to the inside of the shoe with a suitable drift.

New linings are die pressed to suit the curvature of the shoes, but will require drilling and counter-boring for the rivets. Position the lining and hold it in place at one end by means of clamps. Using the holes in the shoes as guides, drill holes of the correct size for the rivets adjacent to the clamp. Turn the shoe over, and counterbore the holes just drilled sufficiently deep so that the rivet heads will stand below the lining surface; this is important, since the rivets will otherwise score the brake drum.

**B.S.A. Service Sheet No. 612 (continued)**

Insert the rivets into the holes and rivet them over on the inside of the shoe. This is easily accomplished by holding in a vice a short length of rod, whose diameter is equal to that of the rivet head, and using it as an anvil upon which to rest the rivet head while hammering the shank over. (See Fig. M41.) This will also make sure that the rivets do not stand proud of the lining.

Move the clamps to the next pair of holes, taking care that the lining is kept in firm contact with the shoe the whole time, and repeat the above procedure. When the lining is finally riveted down, bevel off the ends of the linings and file off any local high spots.

Precautions to be observed when fitting the relined shoes to the hubs are given in the Service Sheet on Hubs and Brakes.

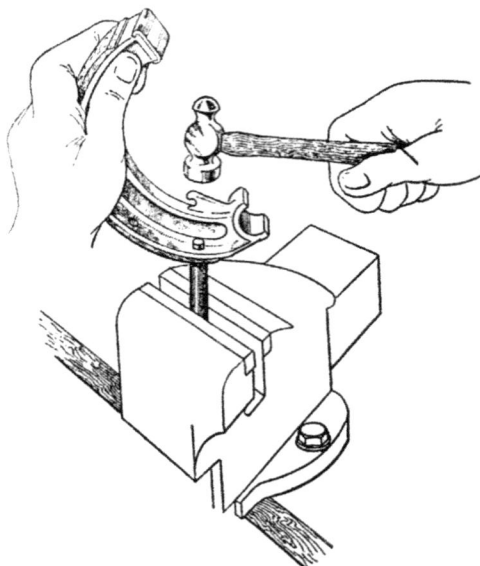

Fig. M41.  Riveting the Linings

Works reconditioned brake shoes can be obtained through the medium of your Dealer from the B.S.A. Exchange Replacement Service.

B.S.A. MOTOR CYCLES LTD.
Service Dept., Waverley Works, Birmingham 10
Printed in England.

U/B5305

# BSA SERVICE SHEET No. 701

## ALL MODELS — USEFUL DATA

| MODEL | C10 | C11 | C12 | C15 Std. | B31 | B32 | B33 | B34 | M20 |
|---|---|---|---|---|---|---|---|---|---|
| Engine bore (mm.) | 63 | 63 | 63 | 67 | 71 | 71 | 85 | 85 | 82 |
| Engine stroke (mm.) | 80 | 80 | 80 | 70 | 88 | 88 | 88 | 88 | 94 |
| Engine capacity (c.c.) | 249 | 249 | 249 | 249 | 348 | 348 | 499 | 499 | 496 |
| Petrol tank capacity (galls.) | 2½ | 2½ | 2¾ | 2½ | 3 | 3 | 3 | 3 | 3 |
| Oil tank capacity (pints) | 4 | 4 | 4 | 4 | 4 | 4 | 4 | 4 | 5 |
| Gearbox capacity (pint) | *½ | *½ | ½ | ½ | 1 | 1 | 1 | 1 | 1 |
| Tappet clearance cold: | | | | | | | | | |
| inlet (in.) | .004 | .003 | .010 | .008 | .003 | .003 | .003 | .003 | .010 |
| exhaust (in.) | .006 | .003 | .012 | .010 | .003 | .003 | .003 | .003 | .012 |
| Tyres—front | 3.00×19 | 3.00×20† | 3.00×19 | 3.25×17 | 3.25×19 | 2.75×21 | 3.25×19 | 2.75×21 | 3.25×19 |
| Tyres—rear | 3.00×19 | 3.00×20† | 3.00×19 | 3.25×17 | 3.25×19 | 4.00×19 | 3.25×19 | 4.00×19 | 3.25×19 |
| Piston ring gap: | | | | | | | | | |
| plain (in.) | .010 | .010 | .010 | .010 | .010 | .010 | .010 | .010 | .010 |
| oil control (in.) | .010 | .010 | .010 | .010 | .010 | .010 | .010 | .010 | .010 |
| Piston ring side clearance (in.) | .002–.004 | .002–.004 | .002–.004 | .002–.004 | .002–.004 | .002–.004 | .002–.004 | .002–.004 | .002–.004 |
| Piston clearance: | | | | | | | | | |
| bottom of skirt | .0045—.0065 | .0035—.0055 | .0035—.0055 | .0025—.004 | .0040—.0055 | .0040—.0055 | .0045—.0065 | .0045—.0065 | .0040—.0060 |
| Gear ratios: | | | | | | | | | |
| Top | 6.6 | 6.6 | 6.26 | 5.98 | 5.6 | 7.1 | 5.0 | 5.6 | 5.3 |
| third | — | — | 7.64 | 7.65 | 7.3 | 9.2 | 6.5 | 7.4 | 7.0 |
| second | 9.8 | 9.8 | 11.1 | 10.54 | 11.1 | 14.2 | 10.0 | 11.5 | 10.9 |
| first | 14.5 | 14.5 | 16.15 | 15.96 | 15.9 | 20.2 | 14.2 | 16.8 | 15.8 |
| Ignition setting (in. before T.D.C.): | | | | | | | | | |
| fully advanced | — | — | — | 11/32 | 7/16 | 7/16 | 7/16 | 7/16 | 7/16 |
| fully retarded | 1/32 | 1/32 | T.D.C. | — | — | — | — | — | — |
| Carburetter: | | | | | | | | | |
| jet | 90 | 80 | 140 | — | 150 | 150 | 200 | 200 | 170 |
| with air cleaner | 90 | 80 | 100 | 140 | 150 | 150 | 170 | 170 | — |
| Sparking plug: | | | | | | | | | |
| C.I. cylinder head | L.10 | L.10S | L.10S | — | L.10S | L.10S | L.10S | L.10S | — |
| Al. alloy cylinder head | N.8 | — | — | N.5 | — | NA.8 | — | NA.8 | N.8 |
| Compression ratio | 5.1 : 1 | 6.5 : 1 | 6.5 : 1 | 7.25 : 1 | 6.5 : 1 | 6.5 : 1 | 6.8 : 1 | 6.8 : 1 | 4.9 : 1 |
| Valve timing—inlet (deg.): | | | | | | | | | |
| opens before T.D.C. | 25 | 25 | 34 | 26 | 25 | 25 | 25 | 25 | 25 |
| closes after B.D.C. | 70 | 70 | 78 | 70 | 65 | 65 | 65 | 65 | 65 |
| Valve timing—exhaust (deg.): | | | | | | | | | |
| opens before B.D.C. | 70 | 70 | 74 | 61½ | 65 | 65 | 65 | 65 | 65 |
| closes after T.D.C. | 25 | 25 | 38 | 34½ | 25 | 25 | 25 | 25 | 25 |
| Distributor points gap (in.) | .012 | .012 | .015 | .012 | — | — | — | — | — |
| Magneto points gap (in.) | — | — | — | — | .012 | .012 | .012 | .012 | .012 |
| Plug points gap (in.) | .015–.018 | .015–.018 | .018–.020 | .020–.025 | .015–.018 | .015–.018 | .015–.018 | .015–.018 | .015–.018 |
| Tyre pressures: | | | | | | | | | |
| front (lb. per sq. in.) | 20 | 20 | 18 | 16 | 16 | — | 16 | — | 17 |
| rear (lb. per sq. in.) | 28 | 28 | 26 | 22 | 20 | — | 17 | — | 22 |

For Swinging Arm and other models not listed see appropriate series.

*Four-speed gearbox, 1 pint.          †3.00 × 19 on later models.

| MODEL | M21 | M33 | A7 (up to Eng. No. ZA7-11192 | A7 ST 2 carbu-retters) | A7 (and after Eng. No. AA7-101) | A7 S/T & S/S (on & Eng. No. AA7S-101) | A10 | R/R & S/R |
|---|---|---|---|---|---|---|---|---|
| Engine bore (mm.) ... ... ... | 82 | 85 | 62 | 62 | 66 | 66 | 70 | 70 |
| Engine stroke (mm.) ... ... ... | 112 | 88 | 82 | 82 | 72.6 | 72.6 | 84 | 84 |
| Engine capacity (c.c.) ... ... | 591 | 499 | 495 | 495 | 497 | 497 | 646 | 646 |
| Petrol tank capacity (galls.) ... ... | 3 | 3 | 3 | 3½ | 3½ | 3½ | 4¼ | 2 or 4 |
| Oil tank capacity (pints) ... ... | 5 | 5 | 4 | 4 | 4 | 4 | 4 | 5½ |
| Gearbox capacity (pint) ... ... | 1 | 1 | 1 | 1 | 1 | 1 | 1 | 14 fl. oz. |
| Tappet clearance—cold: | | | | | | | | |
| inlet (in.) ... ... ... ... | .010 | .003 | .015 | .015 | .010 | .008 | .010 | .008 |
| exhaust (in.) ... ... ... ... | .012 | .003 | .015 | .015 | .016 | .012 | .016 | .008 |
| Tyres—front ... ... ... | 3.50×19 | 3.25×19 | 3.25×19 | 3.25×19 | 3.25×19 | 3.25×19 | 3.25×19 | — |
| Tyres—rear ... ... ... | 3.50×19 | 3.50×19 | 3.50×19 | 3.50×19 | 3.50×19 | 3.50×19 | 3.50×19 | — |
| Piston ring gap: | | | | | | | | |
| plain (in.) ... ... ... ... | .010 | .010 | .013 | .013 | .013 | .013 | .013 | — |
| oil control (in.) ... ... ... | .010 | .010 | .011 | .011 | .011 | .011 | .011 | — |
| Piston ring side clearance ... ... | .002–.004 | .002–.004 | .002–.004 | .002–.004 | .002–.004 | .002–.004 | .002–.004 | .002–.004 |
| Piston clearance: | | | | | | | | |
| bottom of skirt (in.) ... ... ... | .0040—.0060 | .0045—.0065 | .0030—.0050 | .0030—.0050 | .0030—.0050 | .0030—.0050 | .0030—.0050 | .0030—.0050 |
| Gear ratios: | | | | | | s/T    s/s | | |
| Top ... ... ... ... ... | 5.9 | 4.8 | 5.1 | 5.1 | 5.1 | 5.0    5.28 | 4.42 | 4.53 |
| third ... ... ... ... ... | 7.8 | 6.3 | 6.2 | 6.2 | 6.2 | 6.05    6.38 | 5.36 | 5.48 |
| second ... ... ... ... ... | 12.2 | 9.9 | 9.0 | 9.0 | 9.0 | 8.8    9.28 | 7.77 | 7.96 |
| first ... ... ... ... ... | 17.8 | 14.3 | 13.2 | 13.2 | 13.2 | 12.9    13.62 | 11.41 | 11.68 |
| Ignition setting (in. before T.D.C. fully advanced) ... ... ... | 7/16 | 7/16 | 3/8 | 3/8 | 5/16 | 3/8 | 11/32 | 3/8 |
| Carburetter: | | | | | | | | |
| jet ... ... ... ... | 170 | 200 | — | 110 | — | — | — | 250 |
| with air cleaner ... ... ... ... | — | 170 | 140 | — | 140 | 160 | 170 | 240 |
| Sparking plug: | | | | | | | | |
| C.I. cylinder head ... ... ... | L.10 | L.10S | L.10S | L.10S | L.10S | L.10S | L.10S | NA.10 |
| Al. alloy cylinder head ... ... | N.8 | — | — | — | — | — | — | — |
| Compression ratio ... ... ... | 5 : 1 | 6.8 : 1 | 6.6 : 1 | 7 : 1 | 6.6 : 1 | 7.25 : 1 | 6.5 : 1 | R/R 8 : 1 S/R 8.26:1 |
| Valve timing—inlet (deg.): | | | | | | | | |
| opens before T.D.C. ... ... ... | 25 | 25 | 24 | 24 | 30 | 42 | 30 | 42 |
| closes after B.D.C. ... ... ... | 65 | 65 | 65 | 65 | 70 | 62 | 70 | 62 |
| *Valve timing—exhaust (deg.): | | | | | | | | |
| opens before B.D.C. ... ... ... | 65 | 65 | 60 | 60 | 65 | 67 | 65 | 67 |
| closes after T.D.C. ... ... ... | 25 | 25 | 21½ | 21½ | 25 | 37 | 25 | 37 |
| Distributor points gap ... ... ... | — | — | — | — | — | — | — | — |
| Magneto points gap (in.) ... ... | .012 | .012 | .012 | .012 | .012 | .012 | .012 | .012 |
| Plug points gap (in.) ... ... ... | .015–.018 | .015–.018 | .015–.018 | .015–.018 | .015–.018 | .015–.018 | .015–.018 | .018–.020 |
| Tyre pressures: | | | | | | | | |
| front (lb. per square inch) ... ... | 16 | 17 | 17 | 17 | 17 | 17 | 17 | 17 |
| rear (lb. per square inch) ... ... | 18 | 18 | 18 | 18 | 18 | 18 | 18 | 19 |

*NOTE.—Standard A7's after engine number CA7-5232 and Standard A10's after engine number DA10-1647 have the same camshaft as the S/S and R/R machines and valve timing is therefore the same.

**B.S.A. MOTOR CYCLES LTD.,** Service Department, Armoury Road, Birmingham 11.

PRINTED IN ENGLAND—B.S.A. PRESS

# *BSA* SERVICE SHEET No. 703

*Revised Dec. 1958.*

## All Models

## WORKSHOP DATA (BEARINGS) 1956

| B.S.A. Part No. | Hoffman No. | Skefko No. | Ransome & Marles No. | British Timkin No. | Fischer No. |
|---|---|---|---|---|---|
| 24–722 | RM.9L | CFM7/C2 | MRJA.$\frac{7}{8}$ | — | RFM.9 |
| 24–724 | R.325L | 402454.B | MRJA.25 | — | MFM.25 |
| 24–732 | 325 | 6305 | MJ.25 | | 6305 |
| 24–4065 | 135 | 6207 | LJ.35 | — | 6207 |
| 24–4217 | L.S.8 | RLS.6 | LJ$\frac{3}{4}$ | | LS.8 |
| 24–6860 | | 2K.1178X 2K.1130N1 | | 1178X 1130.N1 | |
| 27–261 | MS.9 | RM.S7 | MJ.$\frac{7}{8}$ | — | MS.9 |
| 27–4027 | LS.11 | RL.S9 | LJ.1$\frac{1}{8}$ | | — |
| 29–3857 | 130 | 6206 | LJ.30 | | 6206 |
| 29–6211 | MS.7 | RM.S5 | MJ.$\frac{5}{8}$ | — | MS.7 |
| 42–5819 | 120 | — | | — | |
| 65–1388 | RMS.11 | CRM.9 | MRJ.1$\frac{1}{8}$ | — | RMS.11 |
| 65–2045 | 125 | 6205 | LJ.25 | — | 6205 |
| 65–5883 | LS.9 | RLS.7 | LJ.$\frac{7}{8}$ | | LS.9 |
| 67–670 | R.130L | NFL.30 | LRJA.30 | — | NFL.30 |
| 89–3022 | LS.10 | RLS.8 | LJ.1 | | LS.10 |
| 89–3023 | LS.8 | RLS.6 | LJ.$\frac{3}{4}$ | | LS.8 |
| 90–10 | 117 | 6203 | LJ.17 | — | 6203 |
| 90–11 | LS.7 | RLS.5 | LJ.$\frac{5}{8}$ | | LS.7 |
| 90–12 | S.9 | EE.8J | KLNJ.$\frac{7}{8}$ | — | EE.8 |
| 90–5525 | 112 | 6201 | LJ.12 | | 6201 |
| 90–5559 | — | | | A.2126 | — |
| 90–6063 | 115 | 6202 | LJ.15 | — | 6202 |

# LOCATION OF BEARINGS

| Model | Crankcase Roller Bearing Driveside | Crankcase Ball Bearing Driveside | Crankcase Roller Bearing Gearside | Crankcase Ball Bearing Gearside | Crankcase Ball Bearing (Small) | Crankcase Ball Bearing (Large) | Gearbox Pinion Sleeve Ball Bearing | Gearbox Mainshaft Ball Bearing | Front Hub Ball Bearing | Rear Hub Ball Bearing | Rear Hub Brake Drum and C/Wheel Ball Bearing |
|---|---|---|---|---|---|---|---|---|---|---|---|
| Dandy | — | — | — | | 90 6063 | 24 4217 | 90–6063 (Output shaft) | 90–6063 (Input shaft) | — | | |
| D1, D3 & D5 | | — | — | — | 90–10 | 24–4217 | 90 12 | 90 11 | 90 5525 | 90 6063 | |
| D1, D3 (Comp.) | | — | — | | | | | | 90 5559 | | |
| C10L | — | 24–732 | | | | | 29 3857 | 90–11 | — | 90–6063 | |
| C12 | — | 24–732 | | | | | 29–3857 | 90–11 | 65–5383 | 90 11 O/S  29–6211 N/S | |
| C15 | | 24–782 | | | | | 29 3857 | | 90–10 | 90 10 O/S  42 5819 N/S | |
| B31 S/A | 24 724 | 65–2045 | 24–722 | | | | 24–4065 | 24–4217 | 89–3022 | 89 3022 | 89–3022 |
| B31 S/A (1958) | — | — | — | | | | | | 42 5819 | 42 5819 | 89–3022 |
| B32 Comp. Rigid | 24–724 | 65–2045 | 24 722 | | | | 24–4065 | 24 4217 | 65–5883 | 65–5883 | 65 5883 |
| B32/34 Gold Star | 65 1338 | 65 2045 | 24–722 | | | | 24–4065 | 24 4217 | 65–5883 | 65 5883 | 65 5883 |
| B33 S/A | 24–724 | 65–2045 | 24–722 | | | | 24–4065 | 24 4217 | 89 3022 | 89 3022 | 89–3022 |
| B33 S/A (1958) | — | — | | | | | | — | 42–5819 | 42 5819 | 89–3022 |
| B34 Comp. Rigid | 24–724 | 65 2045 | 24 722 | — | | | 24–4065 | 24–4217 | 65–5883 | 65–5883 | 65 5883 |
| M21 Rigid | 24 724 | 65 2045 | 24 722 | 27–261 | | | 24 4065 | 24–4217 | 65–5883 | 24 6860 (Tapered Roller) | |
| M21 Plunger | 24–724 | 65 2045 | 24–722 | 27–261 | | | 24 4065 | 24–4217 | 65–5883 | 65 5883 | 89 3022 |
| M33 | 24 724 | 65–2045 | 24–722 | | | | 24–4065 | 24–4217 | 65–5883 | 65–5883 | 89–3022 |
| A7 and Shooting Star | 67 670 | — | — | | | | 24 4065 | 24–4217 | 89–3022 | 89 3022 | 89–3022 |
| A7 & S/S (1958) | — | | | | — | | | — | 42–5819 | 42–5819 | 89–3022 |
| A10 S/A | 67 670 | — | — | | — | | 24–4065 | 24–4217 | 89–3022 | 89–3022 | 89 3022 |
| A10 S/A (1958) | — | | — | | — | | | — | 42–5819 | 42 5819 | 89 3022 |
| A10 Plunger | 67 670 | — | — | | | | 24–4065 | 24–4217 | 65–5883 | 65 5883 | 89–3022 |
| A10 Road Rocket | 67 670 | — | — | | | | 24 4065 | 24 4217 | 65–5883 | 89 3022 | 89–3022 |
| A10 Super Rocket | 67–670 | — | — | | | | 24–4065 | 24–4217 | 42–5819 | 42–5819 | 89–3022 |

*Printed in England*     B.S.A. MOTOR CYCLES LTD., Service Dept., Birmingham 11.

# ***BSA*** SERVICE SHEET No. 704

## ALL MODELS
## PISTON CLEARANCES

To avoid the possibility of seizure or piston tap, pistons must be fitted with adequate but not excessive clearance.

The following are the recommended total clearances between the bottom of the piston and the cylinder wall.

| MODEL | | | Tolerances |
|---|---|---|---|
| Dandy 70 ... ... ... | 7.25 : 1 ... ... ... ... | | .003—.004″ |
| D1 ... ... ... ... | ... ... ... ... ... ... | | .0027—.0045″ |
| D3, C15 ... ... ... | ... ... ... ... ... ... | | .0025—.004″ |
| D5, D7 ... ... ... | ... ... ... ... ... ... | | .003—.005″ |
| C10, C10L ... ... ... | ... ... ... ... ... ... | | .0045—.0065″ |
| C11, C11G, C12 ... ... | ... ... ... ... ... ... | | .0035—.0055″ |
| C15 (Star Group) ... | 6.4 : 1 to 10 : 1 ... ... ... | | .0017—.0033″ |
| B31 ... ... ... ... | ... ... ... ... ... | | .004—.0055″ |
| B31 (Split skirt) ... | ... ... ... ... ... | | .0005—.0016″ |
| B32A ... ... ... | ... ... ... ... ... | | .002—.004″ |
| BB32 Gold Star | 8 : 1 ... ... ... ... | | .003—.0045″ |
| | 6.5 : 1 ... ... ... ... | | .004—.0055″ |
| | 7.5 : 1 ... ... ... ... | | .002—.004″ |
| | 9 : 1 ... ... ... ... | | .003—.0045″ |
| CB32 Gold Star | 6.5 : 1 ... ... ... ... | | .002—.004″ |
| | 8 : 1 ... ... ... ... | | .003—.0045″ |
| | 8.5 : 1 ... ... ... ... | | .003—.0045″ |
| | 9 : 1 ... ... ... ... | | .003—.0045″ |
| | 12.25 : 1 ... ... ... | | .004—.0055″ |
| | 13 : 1 ... ... ... | | .004—.0055″ |
| DB32 Gold Star | 7.25 : 1 ... ... ... | | .0025—.004″ |
| | 8 : 1 ... ... ... ... | | .003—.0045″ |
| | 9 : 1 ... ... ... ... | | .003—.0045″ |
| B40 (Star Group) ... | 7.0 : 1 to 8.7 : 1 ... ... | | .0015—.003″ |
| B33 ... ... ... ... | ... ... ... ... ... | | .0045—.0065″ |
| B33 (Split skirt) ... | ... ... ... ... ... | | .0006—.00275″ |
| B34A ... ... ... | ... ... ... ... ... | | .0045—.0065″ |
| BB34 Gold Star | 7.5 : 1 Standard ... ... | | .0045—.0065″ |
| | 8 : 1 ... ... ... ... | | .0025—.0045″ |
| | 9 : 1 ... ... ... ... | | .0025—.0045″ |
| | 6.8 : 1 ... ... ... ... | | .0045—.0065″ |
| | 11.1 ... ... ... ... | | .0025—.0045″ |
| CB34 Gold Star | 7.25 : 1 ... ... ... | | .003—.0045″ |
| | 8 : 1 ... ... ... ... | | .003—.0045″ |
| | 9 : 1 ... ... ... ... | | .003—.0045″ |
| DB34 Gold Star ⎫ | 8 : 1 ... ... ... ... | | .003—.0045″ |
| DBD34 Gold Star ⎰ | 8.75 : 1 ... ... ... | | .003—.0045″ |

| MODEL | | | | | | | | | | Tolerances |
|---|---|---|---|---|---|---|---|---|---|---|
| M20 ... | ... | ... | ... | ... | ... | ... | ... | ... | ... | .004—.006″ |
| M21 ... | ... | ... | ... | ... | ... | ... | ... | ... | ... | .004—.006″ |
| M33 ... | ... | ... | ... | ... | ... | ... | ... | ... | ... | .0045—.0065″ |
| M33 | (Split skirt) | ... | ... | ... | ... | ... | ... | ... | | .0006—.00275″ |
| A7 ... | ... | ... | ... | 6.7 : 1 ... | ... | ... | ... | ... | | .002—.004″ |
| | (Split skirt) | ... | 6.7 : 1 ... | | ... | ... | ... | ... | | .0011—.0031″ |
| | | | 7.25 : 1 | | ... | ... | ... | ... | | .002—.004″ |
| | (Split skirt) | ... | ... | ... | ... | ... | ... | ... | | .0011—.0031″ |
| A7 | (Star Twin) | ... | ... | ... | ... | ... | ... | ... | | .002—.004″ |
| A7 | (Split skirt) | ... | (Star Twin and Shooting Star) | | | | | ... | | .001—.0031″ |
| A7 | (Shooting Star) | | 8 : 1 (after Engine No. CA7SS-4501) | | | | | | | .0035—.005″ |
| A50 | (Star Twin) | ... | 8.0 : 1 to 9.0 : 1 | | | ... | ... | ... | | .0011—.0025″ |
| A10 | (Golden Flash) | | 6.5 : 1 ... | | ... | ... | ... | ... | | .003—.0045″ |
| | (Split skirt) | ... | 6.5 : 1 ... | | ... | ... | ... | ... | | .0025—.0045″ |
| | (Split skirt) | ... | 7.25 : 1 | | ... | ... | ... | ... | | .0025—.0045″ |
| A10 | (Super Flash and Road Rocket) | | 8 : 1 | ... | ... | ... | ... | ... | | .003—.0045″ |
| A10 | (Golden Flash) | | 7.5 : 1 (after Engine No. DA10-651) | | | | | | | .0035—.005″ |
| A10 | (Super Rocket) | | 8.5:1 (after Engine No. CA10R-6001) | | | | | | | .004—.0055″ |
| A10 | (Rocket Gold Star) | | 8.75 : 1 | | ... | ... | ... | ... | | .001—.0025″ |
| A65 | (Star Twin) | ... | 7.5 : 1 to 9.0 : 1 | | | ... | ... | ... | | .0012—.0027″ |

**B.S.A. MOTOR CYCLES LTD.,** Service Department, Armoury Road, **Birm**ingham 11

B.S.A. PRESS

# BSA SERVICE SHEET No. 705

## All Models

*October*, 1948
*Reprinted April*, 1960

### PERIODICAL ATTENTIONS.

**HUBS.**              **Every 1,000 miles.**

Inject grease through the nipples located in the centres of the hubs.    Do not overdo this, otherwise grease will penetrate to the brake linings and cause ineffective brakes. Three or four strokes of the gun should be ample.    Where no grease nipple is provided the bearings should be removed and packed with grease when the machine is in need of complete overhaul.

**BRAKE CAM SPINDLES.**

Grease sparingly.    Two or three strokes of the gun only, or if no grease nipple is provided, apply a few drops of engine oil between the brake arm and the spindle.

**SPEEDOMETER DRIVE.**

Grease well.    Three or four strokes of the gun regularly.

**ENGINE OIL.**              **Every 2,000 miles (except 2-stroke models).**

The oil tank and sump should be drained (preferably when the engine is warm after a longish run), and the tank refilled with fresh oil.

In case of new or re-conditioned engines, the oil should be drained and renewed after the first 250 miles, and again after 1,000 miles.

**REAR CHAIN.**

Remove the rear chain, clean thoroughly in paraffin, and soak in engine oil or molten grease and graphite.

**CONTACT BREAKER (except A and C Group Models).**

A very small quantity of thin oil should be injected into the lubrication wick, and the face cam smeared with oil.    The wick is accessible after removing the spring contact arm (held by the round-headed screw at the opposite end to the contact point) and is located in the hollow end of the round-headed screw which is revealed when the spring arm is removed.

When replacing the arm, it is important that the small curved backing spring is refitted correctly, i.e., with the bent portion facing outwards.

**DYNAMO ARMATURE BUSH (A and C Group Models fitted with lubricator).**

A few drops of oil injected through the lubricator are sufficient.

### Every 5,000 miles.

Drain the gearbox and refill with new oil up to the level of the filler plug.

Drain the telescopic forks and refill each leg with correct amount of new oil.

In the case of new or re-conditioned gearboxes, change the oil after the first 1,000 miles.

### New Machines.

**CYLINDER HEAD BOLTS (except B and M O.H.V. engines).**

Examine the cylinder head joint daily, and if leakage becomes apparent, tighten the bolts, working diagonally so as to pull the head down evenly.    Do not over-tighten otherwise there is a possibility of distortion or bolt stretch.

**CYLINDER BASE NUTS (except B and M O.H.V. engines).**

There are five of these—one at each of the four corners outside, and one inside the tappet chest on the single cylinder models.    A Group Models have eight cylinder base nuts and Model C11 six nuts.    Tighten after the first 100 miles.

**CYLINDER BARREL AND HEAD FIXING (B and M O.H.V. engines).**

The barrel and head are both secured to the crankcase by four long bolts coupled to bushes screwed into the latter.    Apply a spanner to the upper hexagon for tightening. These bolts have right-hand threads, and, being inverted, are tightened by turning the spanner to the right.

B.S.A. MOTOR CYCLES LTD.,
Service Dept., Waverley Works, Birmingham, 10
*(PRINTED IN ENGLAND)*

# BSA SERVICE SHEET No. 708

### ALL MODELS

## CARBURATION.   Monobloc and Seperate Float Chamber Type

### How the Carburetter Works

The function of the carburetter is to atomise the petrol and proportion it correctly with the air drawn in through the intake on the induction stroke.  The action of the float and needle in the float chamber maintains the level of fuel at the needle jet, and when the engine is stopped and no further fuel is being used the needle valve cuts off the supply.

The twist-grip controls, by means of a cable, the position of the throttle slide and the throttle needle and so governs the volume of mixture supplied to the engine.

The mixture is correct at all throttle openings, if the carburetter is correctly tuned.

The opening of the throttle brings first into action the mixture supply from the pilot jet, then as it progressively opens, via the pilot by-pass the mixture is augmented from the needle jet.  Up to three-quarter throttle this action is controlled by the tapered needle in the needle jet, and from three-quarters onwards the mixture is controlled by the main jet.

The pilot jet (J), which in the older type of carburetter is embodied in the jet block, has been replaced in the Monobloc carburetter by a detachable jet (9) Fig. X5, assembled in the carburetter body and sealed by a cover nut.

The main jet does not spray directly into the mixing chamber, but discharges through the needle jet into the primary air chamber and goes from there as a rich petrol/air mixture through the primary air choke into the main air choke.

Although the maintenance and tuning instruction contained in this Service Sheet apply equally well to the Monobloc and separate float chamber types of carburetter, the new instrument has been designed with a view to giving improved performance, and certain constructional changes have been made.

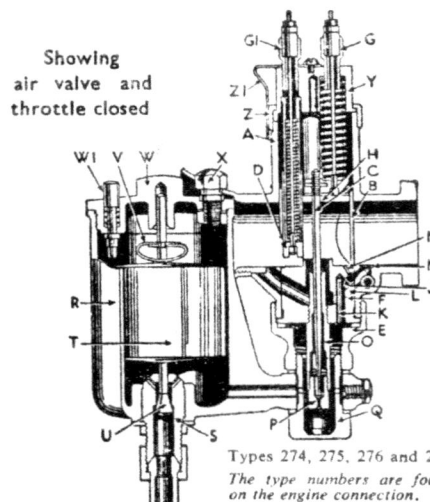

Showing
air valve and
throttle closed

Types 274, 275, 276 and 289
*The type numbers are found
on the engine connection.*

| | | | |
|---|---|---|---|
| A. | Mixing Chamber. | P. | Main Jet. |
| B. | Throttle Valve. | Q. | Float Chamber Holding Bolt. |
| C. | Jet Needle and Clip above. | R. | Float Chamber. |
| D. | Air Valve. | S. | Needle Valve Seating. |
| E. | Mixing Chamber Union Nut. | T. | Float. |
| F. | Jet Block. | U. | Float Needle Valve. |
| G/GI. | Cable Adjusters. | V. | Float Needle Clip. |
| H. | Jet Block Barrel. | W. | Float Chamber Cover. |
| J. | Pilot Jet. | WI. | Tickler. |
| K. | Passage to Pilot. | X. | Float Chamber Lock Screw. |
| L. | Pilot Air Passage. | Y. | Mixing Chamber Top Cap. |
| M. | Pilot Mixture Outlet. | Z. | Mixing Chamber Lock Ring. |
| N. | Pilot by-pass. | ZI. | Mixing Chamber Security |
| O. | Needle Jet. | | Spring. |

Fig. X4.   *A sectioned illustration of Needle Jet
Carburetter.*

The float chamber is a drum-shaped reservoir, die cast in one piece with the mixing chamber. The material used being zinc-alloy. The float is designed to pivot instead of rising and falling, as in the separate float chamber type, and as it does so, it impinges on a nylon needle controlling the inflow of fuel.

Variations of up to 20° in the angle of the carburetter when fitted, do not affect the working of the float, therefore it lends itself to use for down draught carburation and is not so greatly effected by the degree of lean when cornering. Access to the float (Fig. X6) is gained by removing a plate held in place by three screws.

Compensation for over-rich mixture which results from snap throttle openings, is provided by bleed holes in the needle jet (Fig. X5). A compensatory air bleed is provided, this is the larger of the two holes at the mouth of the air intake, which leads to the space around the needle jet (Fig. X5).

The pilot intake is the smaller of the two holes, and operates in conjunction with the detachable pilot jet (Fig. X5). This pilot mixture is adjusted as before, by an adjusting screw (Fig. 8a).

### Hints and Tips—Starting from Cold
Flood the carburetter by depressing the tickler and close the air control, set the ignition say, half-retarded. Then open the throttle about ⅛ in., then kick-start. If the throttle is too far open, starting will be difficult.

### Starting—Engine Hot
Do not flood the carburetter, but it may be found necessary with some engines to close the air lever, set the ignition to half-retarded, the throttle to ⅛ in. open and kick-start. If the carburetter has been flooded and won't start because the mixture is too rich—open the throttle wide and give the engine several turns to clear the richness, then start again with the throttle ⅛ in. open, and air valve wide open. Generally speaking it is not advisable to flood at all when an engine is hot.

### Starting—General
By experiment, find out if and when it is necessary to flood, also note the best position for the air lever and the throttle for the easiest starting. Excessive flooding, particularly when the engine is hot, will make starting more difficult. It is necessary only to raise the level of petrol in the float chamber, by depressing the tickler.

### Starting—Single Lever Carburetters
Open the throttle very slightly from the idling position and flood the carburetter more or less according to the engine being cold or hot respectively.

## SECTIONAL ILLUSTRATIONS OF CARBURETTERS. Types 375, 376 and 389

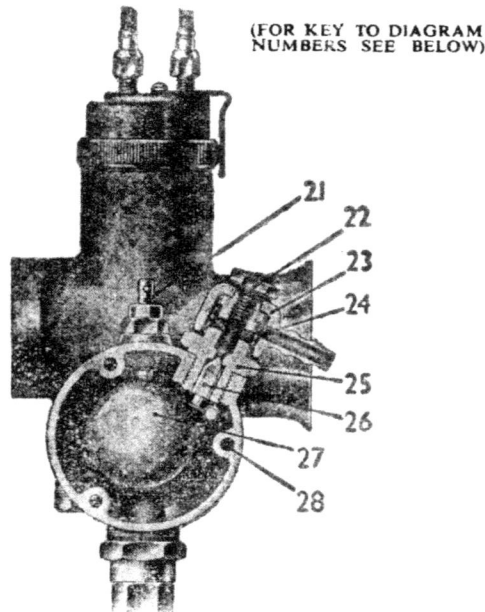

(FOR KEY TO DIAGRAM NUMBERS SEE BELOW)

(MONOBLOC)

Fig. X6.  *Section through Float Chamber.*

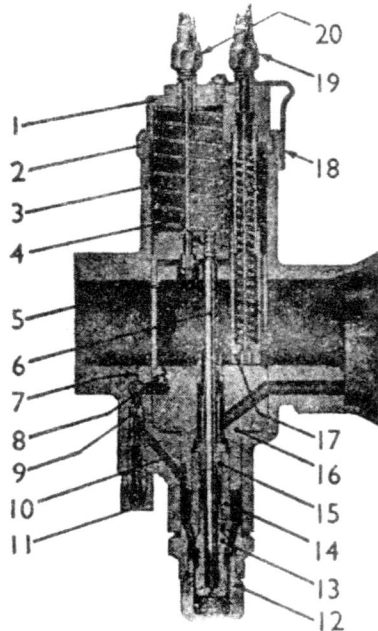

Diagrammatic section of Carburetter showing only the lower half of the throttle chamber with the throttle a little open—and the internal primary air passages to the main jet and pilot system.

FOR KEY TO DIAGRAM NUMBERS SEE BELOW

Fig. X5.

| | |
|---|---|
| 1. Mixing Chamber Top. | 18. Mixing Chamber Cap Spring. |
| 2. Mixing Chamber Cap. | 19. Cable Adjuster (air). |
| 3. Carburetter Body. | 20. Cable Adjuster (throttle). |
| 4. Jet Needle Clip. | 21. Tickler. |
| 5. Throttle Valve. | 22. Banjo Bolt. |
| 6. Jet Needle. | 23. Banjo. |
| 7. Pilot outlet. | 24. Filter Gauze. |
| 8. Pilot by-pass. | 25. Needle Seating. |
| 9. Pilot Jet. | 26. Needle. |
| 10. Petrol Feed to Pilot Jet. | 27. Float. |
| 11. Pilot Jet Cover Nut. | 28. Side Cover Screws. |
| 12. Main Jet Cover. | 31. Air to Pilot Jet. |
| 13. Main Jet. | 32. Feed Holes in Pilot Jet. |
| 14. Jet Holder. | 33. Bleed Holes in Needle Jet. |
| 15. Needle Jet. | 34. Primary Air Choke. |
| 16. Jet Block. | 35. Primary Air Passage. |
| 17. Air Valve | 36. Throttle Valve Cut-away |

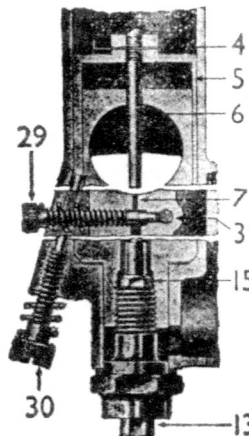

Fig. 7.  *Secttion through Mixing Chamber, showing Air Valve and Thaottle closed.*

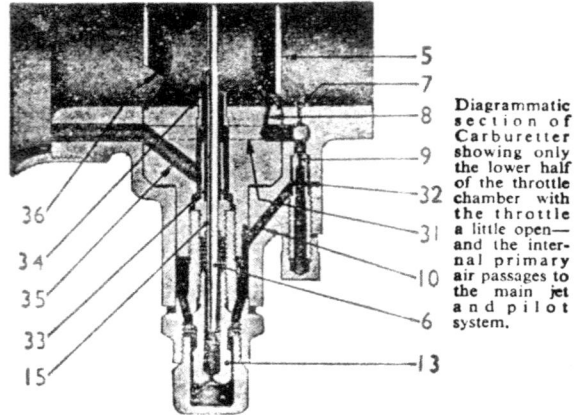

### 29. PILOT AIR ADJUSTING SCREW

This screw regulates the strength of the mixture for "idling" and for the initial opening of the throttle. The screw controls the depression on the pilot jet by metering the amount of air that mixes with the petrol.

### 30. THROTTLE ADJUSTING SCREW

Set this screw to hold the throttle open sufficiently to keep the engine running when the twist-grip is shut off.

## Cable Controls

See that there is a minimum of backlash when the controls are set back and that any movement of the handlebar does not cause the throttle to open; this is done by the adjusters on the top of the carburetter. See that the throttle shuts down freely.

## Petrol Feed

Verification. Detach petrol pipe union at the float chamber end; turn on petrol tap momentarily and see that fuel gushes out. Avoid petrol pipes with vertical loops as they cause air-locks. Flooding may be due to a worn or bent needle or a leaky float ,but nearly all flooding with new machines is due to impurities (grit, fluff, etc.) in the tank—so clean out the float chamber periodically till the trouble ceases. If the trouble persists the tank might be drained, swilled out, etc. Note that if the carburetter, either vertical or horizontal, is flooding with the engine stopped, the overflow from the main jet will not run into the engine but out of the carburetter through a hole at the base of the mixing chamber.

## Fixing Carburetter and Air Leaks

Erratic slow running is often caused by air leaks, so verify there are none at the point of attachment to the cylinder or inlet pipe—check by means of oil placed around the joint, if there are leaks the oil will be sucked in, and eliminate by new washers and the equal tightening up of the flange nuts. Also in old machines look out for air leaks caused by a worn throttle or worn inlet valve guides.

## Explosions in Exhaust

May be caused by too weak a pilot mixture when the throttle is closed or nearly closed—also, it may be caused by too rich a pilot mixture and an air leak in the exhaust system; the reason in either case is that the mixture has not fired in the cylinder and has fired in the hot silencer. If the explosion occurs when the throttle is fairly wide open the trouble will be ignition—not carburation.

## Excessive Petrol Consumption

On a new machine may be due to flooding, caused by impurities from the petrol tank lodging on the float needle seat and so preventing its valve from closing. If the machine has had several years use, flooding may be caused by a worn float needle valve. Also excessive petrol consumption will be apparent if the throttle needle jet (o) Fig. X4. or (15) Fig. X5, has worn; it may be remedied or improved by lowering the needle in the throttle, but if it cannot be, then the only remedy is to get a new needle jet.

## Air Filters

These may affect the jet setting, so if one is fitted afterwards to the carburetter the main jet may have to be smaller If a carburetter is set with an air filter and the engine is run without it, take care not to overheat the engine due to too weak a mixture; testing with the air control will indicate if a larger main jet and higher needle position are required.

## Faults

The trouble may not be carburation; if the trouble cannot be remedied by making mixtures richer or weaker with the air control, and you know the petrol feed is good and the carburetter is not flooding, the trouble is elsewhere.

## Fault Finding

There are only *two* possible faults in carburation, either *richness* of mixture or *weakness* of mixture, so in case of trouble decide which is the cause, by:—

1. Examining the petrol feed ...
   - Verify jets and passages are clear.
   - Verify ample flow.
   - Verify there is no flooding.

2. Looking for air leaks ...
   - At the connection to the engine.
   - Or due to leaky inlet valve stems.

3. Defective or worn parts ...
   - As a slack throttle-worn needle jet.
   - The mixing chamber union nut not tightened up, or loose jets.

4. *Testing with the air control* to see if by richening the mixture the results are better or worse.

## Indications of

| Richness: | Weakness: |
|---|---|
| Black smoke in exhaust. | Spitting in carburetter. |
| Petrol spraying out of carburetter. | Erratic slow running. |
| Four strokes, eight-stroking | Overheating. |
| Two strokes, four-stroking. | Acceleration poor. |
| Heavy, lumpy running. | Engine goes better if:— |
| Heavy petrol consumption. | Throttle not wide open, or air control is partially closed. |
| ? If the jet block (F) is not tightened up by washer and nut (E) richness will be caused through leakage of petrol. | ? Has air cleaner been removed. |
| ? Air cleaner choked up. | ? Jets partially choked up |
| ? Needle jet worn large. | Removing the silencer or running with a racing silencer requires a richer setting and large main jet. |
| Sparking plug sooty. | |

## Note

Verify correctness of fuel feed, stop air leaks, check over ignition and valve operation and timing. *Decide by test whether richness or weakness is the trouble and at what throttle position.* See throttle opening diagrams, Fig. X6.

## Procedure

If at a particular throttle opening you partially close the air control, and the engine goes better, weakness is indicated; or on the other hand the running is worse, richness is indicated. *Then you proceed to adjust the appropriate part as indicated for that position.*

### Fault at Throttle Positions indicated on Fig. X9

| To Cure Richness: | | To Cure Weakness: |
|---|---|---|
| Fit smaller main jet. | 1st | Fit larger main jet. |
| Screw out pilot air screw. | 2nd | Screw pilot air screw in. |
| Fit a throttle with larger cut-away. | 3rd | Fit a throttle with smaller cut-away. |
| Lower needle one or two grooves. | 4th | Raise needle one or two grooves. |

### Notes

It is not correct to cure a rich mixture at half-throttle by fitting a smaller main jet because the main jet may be correct for power at full throttle: the proper thing to do is to lower the needle.

Information on throttle slides and needle position is given in paragraphs (*f*) and (*e*) respectively in the next section entitled "Tuning".

### Changing from Standard Petrols to Special Fuels.

Such as alcohol mixtures will, with the same setting in the carburetter, certainly cause weakness of mixture and possible damage from overheating.

## TUNING

(*a*) Figs. X8 and 8a are two diagrammatic sections of the carburetter to show:

1. The throttle stop screw.
2. The pilot air screw.

### (*b*) Throttle Stop Screw

Set this screw to prop the throttle open sufficiently to keep the engine running when the twist-grip is shut off.

### (*c*) Pilot Air Screw

This screw regulates the strength of the mixture for "idling" and for the initial opening of the throttle. The screw controls the suction on the pilot petrol jet by metering the amount of air that mixes with the petrol.

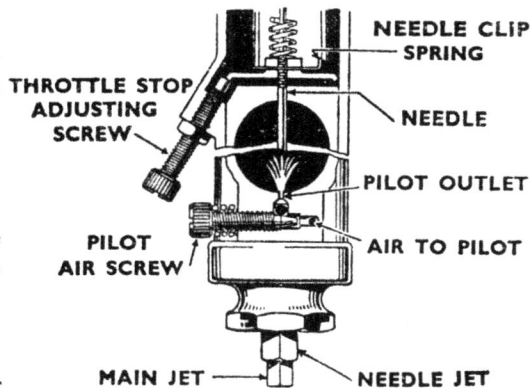

Fig. X8

NOTE:—The air for the pilot jet may be admitted internally or externally according to one or other of the designs, but there is no difference in tuning.

### (*d*) Main Jet

The main jet controls the petrol supply when the throttle is more than three-quarters open, but at smaller throttle openings although the supply of fuel goes through the main jet, the amount is diminished by the metering effect of the needle in the needle jet.

Each jet is calibrated and numbered so that its exact discharge is known and two jets of the same number are alike.

**Never reamer a Jet out, get another of the right size**

The bigger the number the bigger the jet. Spare jets *are sealed*.

To get at the main jet, undo the float chamber holding bolt (Q) Fig. X4, or main jet cover number 12 (Fig. X7). The jet is screwed into the needle jet so if the jet is tight, hold the needle jet also carefully with a spanner whilst unscrewing the main jet.

### (e) Needle and Needle Jet

The needle is attached to the throttle and being tapered either allows more or less petrol to pass through the needle jets as the throttle is opened or closed throughout the range, except when idling or nearly full throttle. The needle jet is of a defined size and is only altered from standard when using alcohol fuels.

The taper needle position in relation to the throttle opening can be set according to the mixture required by fixing it to the throttle with the needle clip spring in a certain groove (see illustration above), thus either raising or lowering it. Raising the needle richens the mixture and lowering it weakens the mixture at throttle openings from quarter to three-quarter open (see illustration, Fig. X9).

### (f) Throttle Valve Cut-away

The atmospheric side of the throttle is cut away to influence the depression on the main fuel supply and thus gives a means of tuning between the pilot and needle jet range of throttle opening. The amount of cut-away is recorded by a number marked on the throttle, viz.: 6/3 means throttle type 6 with number 3 cut-away; larger cut-aways, say 4 and 5, give weaker mixtures, and 2 and 1 richer mixtures.

### (g) Air Valve

Is used only for starting and running when cold, and for experimenting with, otherwise run with it wide open.

### (h) Tickler

A small plunger located in the float chamber lid. When pressed down on the float, the neddle valve is pushed off its seat and so "flooding" is achieved. Flooding temporarily enriches the mixture until the level of the petrol subsides to normal.

## Phases of Amal Needle Jet Carburettor Throttle Openings

| Up to $\frac{1}{8}$ open | from $\frac{1}{8}$ to $\frac{1}{4}$ open | $\frac{1}{4}$ to $\frac{3}{4}$ open | $\frac{3}{4}$ to full open |
|---|---|---|---|
| **PILOT JET** | **THROTTLE CUT-AWAY** | **NEEDLE POSITION** | **MAIN JET SIZE** |

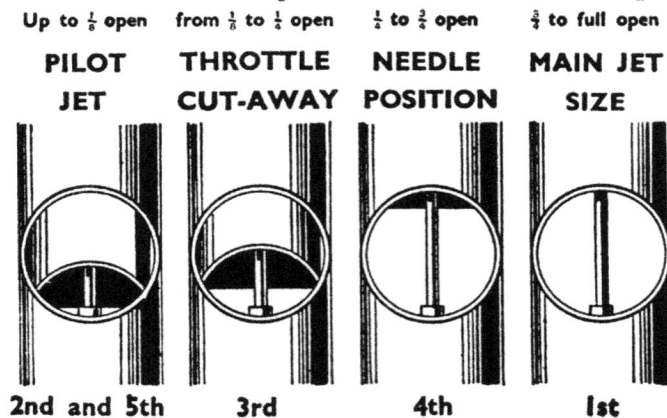

| 2nd and 5th | 3rd | 4th | 1st |
|---|---|---|---|

**SEQUENCE OF TUNING**
Fig. X9

## Sequence of Tuning

Tune up. In the following order only, by so doing you will not upset good results obtained.

NOTE.—The carburetter is automatic throughout the throttle range—the air control should always be wide open except when used for starting or until the engine has warmed up. We assume normal petrols are used.

Read remarks on "Fault Finding" and "Tuning" for each tuning device and get the motor going perfectly on a quiet road with a slight up gradient so that on test the engine is pulling.

## 1st Main Jet with Throttle in position

Test the engine for full throttle; if when at full throttle, the power seems better with the throttle less than wide open or with the air valve closed slightly the main jet is too small. If the engine runs "heavily" the main jet is too large. If testing for speed work note the jet size is rich enough to keep engine cool, and to verify this, examine the sparking plug by taking a fast run, declutching and stopping engine quickly. If the plug body at the end has a bright black appearance, the mixture is correct; if sooty, the mixture is rich; or if a dry grey colour, the mixture is too weak and a larger jet is necessary.

## 2nd Pilot Jet with Throttle in positions 2 and 5

With engine idling too fast with the twist-grip shut off and the throttle shut down on to the throttle stop screw, and ignition set for best slow running: (1) Loosen stop screw nut and screw down until engine runs slower and begins to falter, then screw the pilot air screw in or out to make engine run regularly and faster. (2) Now gently lower the throttle stop screw until the engine runs slower and just begins to falter, then lock the nut lightly and begin again to adjust the pilot air screw to get best slow running; if this second adjustment makes engine run too fast, go over the job again a third time. Finally, lock up tight the throttle stop screw nut without disturbing the screw's position.

## 3rd Throttle Cut-away with Throttle in position

If, as you take off from the idling position, there is objectionable spitting from the carburetter, slightly richen the pilot mixture by screwing the air screw in about half a turn, but if this is not effective, screw it back again and fit a throttle with a smaller cut-away. If the engine jerks under load at this throttle position and there is no spitting, either the throttle needle is much too high or a larger throttle cut-away is required to cure richness.

## 4th Needle with Throttle in position 4

The needle controls a wide range of throttle opening and also the acceleration. Try the needle in as low a position as possible, viz., with the clip in a groove as near the end as possible; if acceleration is poor and with air valve partially closed the results are better, raise the needle by two grooves; if very much better try lowering needle by one groove and leave it where it is best.

NOTE:—If mixture is still too rich with clip in groove number 1 nearest the end—the needle jet probably wants replacement because of wear. The needle itself never wears out.

**5th** Finally go over the idling again for final touches.

B.S.A. MOTOR CYCLES LTD., Service Department, Armoury Road, Birmingham 11.
Printed in England                                                                                    B.S.A. Press.

# *BSA* SERVICE SHEET No. 708B

## ALL MODELS

## CARBURATION AT HIGH ALTITUDES

The carburetter settings of all B.S.A. motor cycles are designed to give the best all round performance at altitudes of a few thousand feet.

At greater altitudes the air becomes rarefied with the result that the mixture is incorrect.

To overcome this difficulty it is necessary to reduce the size of the main jet, the reduction depending on the altitude at which the machine is mainly used.

The table below shows the percentage of reduction at given altitudes, but it must be emphasised that while the alteration to jet size will correct the mixture, it will not replace the lost power. This can only be corrected by "blowing" or super-charging.

It may also be advisable to re-tune the carburetter for smaller throttle openings this should be done in accordance with Service Sheet 708.

| Altitude. | | | | | | | Percentage of reduction in jet size. |
|---|---|---|---|---|---|---|---|
| 3,000 feet | ... | ... | ... | ... | ... | ... | 5% |
| 6,000 feet | ... | ... | ... | ... | ... | ... | 9% |
| 9,000 feet | ... | ... | ... | ... | ... | ... | 13% |
| 12,000 feet | ... | ... | ... | ... | ... | ... | 17% |

B.S.A. MOTOR CYCLES LTD., Service Dept., Armoury Road, Birmingham 11.

B.S.A. Press.

# *BSA* SERVICE SHEET No. 709

## ALL MODELS
## FAULT FINDING

No adjustments should be made, or any part tampered with, until the cause of the trouble is known. Otherwise adjustments which are correct may be deranged.

**Engine Stops Suddenly:**
    Petrol shortage in tank, or choked petrol supply pipe or tap.
    Choked main jet, or water in float chamber.
    Oiled up or fouled sparking plug.
    Water on high-tension pick-up or on sparking plug.

**Engine Fails to Start, or is difficult to start:**
    Lack of fuel, or insufficient flooding if cold.
    Excessive flooding, allowing neat petrol to enter the cylinder.
    Oil sparking plug, or stuck-up valve or valve stem sticky.
    Weak valve spring, or valve not seating properly.
    Throttle opening too large, or pilot jet choked.
    Contact points dirty, or gap incorrect.
    Flat battery, if coil ignition, or faulty electrical connections in ignition circuit.

**Loss of Power:**
    Valve, or valves, not seating properly.
    Weak valve spring or springs, or sticking valve.
    No tappet clearance, or excessive clearance.
    Lack of oil in tank.
    Brakes adjusted too closely.
    Badly fitting or broken piston rings.
    Punctured carburettor float.
    Incorrect ignition timing.

**Engine Overheats:**
    Lack of proper lubrication.
    Weak valve springs, or pitted valve seats.
    Worn piston rings, or late ignition setting.
    Carburettor setting too weak, or partly choked petrol pipe.

**Engine Misses Fire:**
    Weak valve spring.
    Defective or oiled sparking plug, or oil on contact points.
    Incorrectly adjusted contact points or tappets.
    Faulty condenser.
    Defective sparking plug or high-tension cable.
    Loose sparking plug terminal.
    Carburettor flooding, due to stuck or defective float.
    Partly choked main jet.
    Choked vent hole in petrol tank filler cap.

**Excessive Oil Consumption:**
    Stoppage, or partial stoppage, in pipe returning oil from engine to tank.
    Clogged, or partially clogged, filter in sump, or oil tank.
    Badly worn or stuck-up piston rings, causing high pressure in engine crankcase.
    High crankcase pressure, caused by release valve (breather) action.
    Air leak in dry sump oiling system.
    Non-return valve in system not seating.
    Ball valve in oil pump stuck on its seat.

B.S.A. MOTOR CYCLES LTD., Service Department, Armoury Road, Birmingham 11
**B.S.A. PRESS**

# *BSA* SERVICE SHEET No. 710

## ALL MODELS
## CHAIN ALTERATIONS AND REPAIRS

A chain rarely breaks if it is kept properly lubricated and adjusted. Usually it is worn out long before it reaches breaking point. The rear chain is the most heavily stressed and is therefore the one most likely to give trouble. Spare parts should be carried to enable the rider to carry out a repair on the road with the aid of a chain rivet extractor (see Fig. X7). The front chain will probably be worn out before it requires shortening.

**How to use the Chain Rivet Extractor**

First press down lever (A) Fig. X7 to open the two jaws (B). Insert the link to be removed so that the jaws grip the roller and support the uppermost inner side plate. The punch (C) is then screwed on to the rivet head until the rivet is forced through the outer plate.

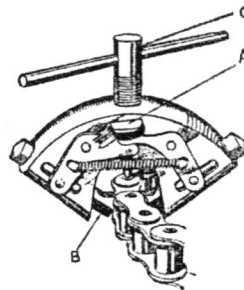

Fig. X7.

**To shorten a worn Rear Chain**

After a big mileage, the rear chain may have stretched so that no further adjustment is possible by the usual method. In this case it is possible to shorten the chain by one link or pitch, so increasing its useful life. First remove the single connecting spring link (A) securing the two ends of the chain, Fig. X8. If the chain terminates in two ordinary links as in Fig. X8 (in which case the chain will be an even number of pitches) extract the third and fourth rivets (B) from the end and replace the detached three pitches by a single connecting link (C). The connection is made with an additional spring link (D). If one end of the chain has a double cranked link, Fig. X9—in which case the chain will have an odd

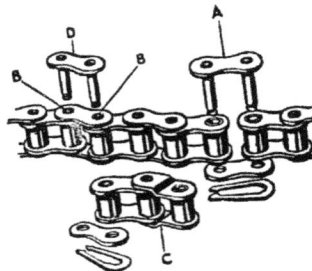

Fig. X8.

number of pitches—extract the second and third rivets (A), releasing the cranked link unit complete, which can be retained for further use. Replace with one inner link (B) and again connect up with an additional single connecting link (C).

**To repair a damaged Chain**
If a roller or link has been damaged (x) Fig. X9, remove rivets (D), take out the damaged link and replace with one inner link, secured by two single connecting links.

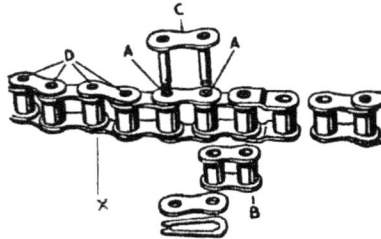

Fig. X9.

It is important that the spring clip fastener should always be put on so that the *closed* end faces the direction of travel of the chain—i.e. when clip is on top run of chain, closed end is toward front of machine—when clip is on bottom run, closed end is towards rear of machine.

It should be noted that once a rivet has been extracted it must not be used again, so that it is important to check that the correct rivet is being removed before actually removing it. In the case of double cranked links, the complete unit comprises an inner link and the cranked outer link—three rollers in all—and these must never be separated.

**Fitting Rear Chain**
To fit a new rear chain, turn wheel until the spring link of the old chain is located on rear sprocket. Disconnect, and allow the lower run to drop down. Join the top run of the old chain to the new chain by means of the connecting link, and then by pulling on the bottom run of the old chain the new one will be carried round the gearbox sprocket. Then the old chain can be disconnected and the ends of the new one joined together.

When the rear chain breaks and falls from its sprockets, the new or repaired chain can be replaced without taking off the chainguards. One end of the chain must be fed (from the rear) under the front end of the rear top chainguard on to the gearbox sprocket A long bladed screwdriver or a piece of stiff wire may assist this operation When the chain has located on the sprocket teeth, engage a gear and gently turn gearbox over with the kickstarter This will feed chain round gearbox sprocket When sufficient length of chain is hanging below sprocket, disengage gear and chain can then be pulled round until both runs can be fed inside rear chainguard and engaged on rear wheel sprocket.

**B.S.A. MOTOR CYCLES LTD.**, Service Department, Armoury Road, Birmingham 11.

# BSA

# SERVICE SHEET No. 710x

MARCH, 1969

# FRAME REPAIRS

## ALL MODELS

Frame repairs must not be attempted unless adequate workshop facilities are available.

The information given in this sheet is intended for the use of Dealers who are unable to take advantage of the B.S.A. repair service and who have frame repair facilities.

Spotting points to enable frame trueing to be carried out can be determined by making use of the dimensions given.

B.S.A. Motor Cycles Ltd., Armoury Road Birmingham II.

PRINTED IN ENGLAND

IT IS DIFFICULT TO UNDERSTAND WHY B.S.A. ISSUED THE FOLLOWING FRAME DRAWINGS IN VARYING SCALES AND AT SUCH SMALL SIZES - MAKING SOME OF THE DIMENSIONS ALMOST IMPOSSIBLE TO READ. HOWEVER, THEY ARE INCLUDED FOR THE SAKE OF COMPLETENESS

## A7-10
## RIGID FRAME

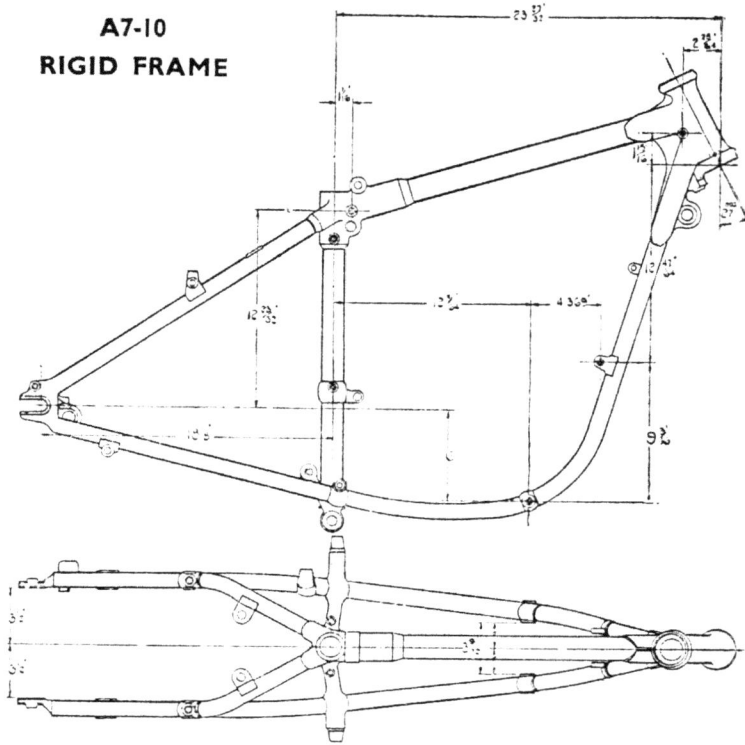

## A7-10
## SPRING FRAME

# 1953 SUPER FLASH
## SPRING FRAME

# M20, M21 and M33
## RIGID FRAME
### 1945 - 1948

**M20, M21 and M33**
**RIGID FRAME**
**1949 onwards**

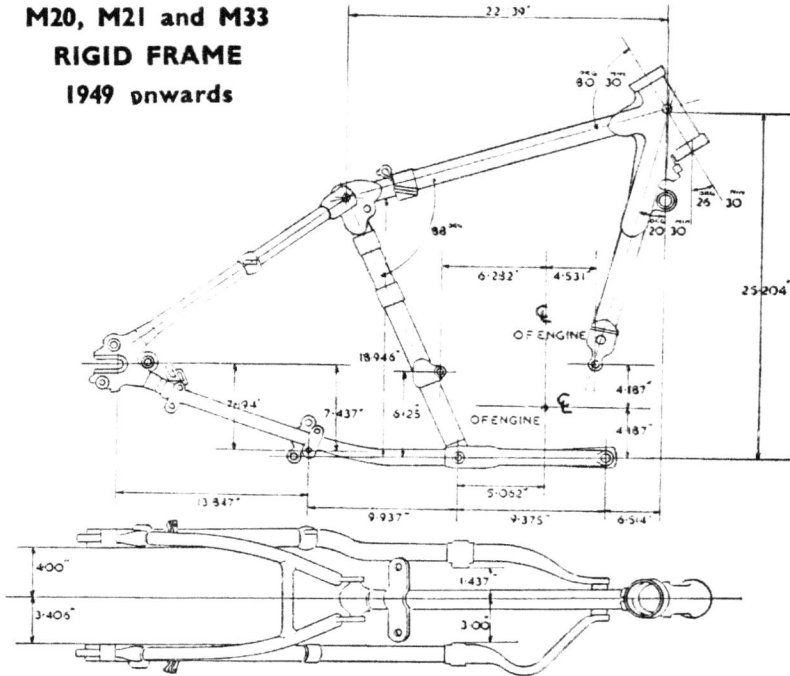

**M20, M21 and M33**
**SPRING FRAME**

## B31 - 32 - 33 - 34
### RIGID FRAME

## B31 - 32 - 33 - 34
### SPRING FRAME

# D1 and D3
## RIGID FRAME

# D1 and D3
## SPRING FRAME

**C10L**
**SPRING FRAME**

1954 C10L
(SPRING FRAME)

**C10, C11, C11G**
**RIGID FRAME**

# C10, C11, C11G
## SPRING FRAME
## 3 SPEED GEARBOX

# C10, C11, C11G
## SPRING FRAME
## 4 SPEED GEARBOX

# 1953 GOLD STAR SWINGING ARM

1953 GOLD STAR SWINGING ARM

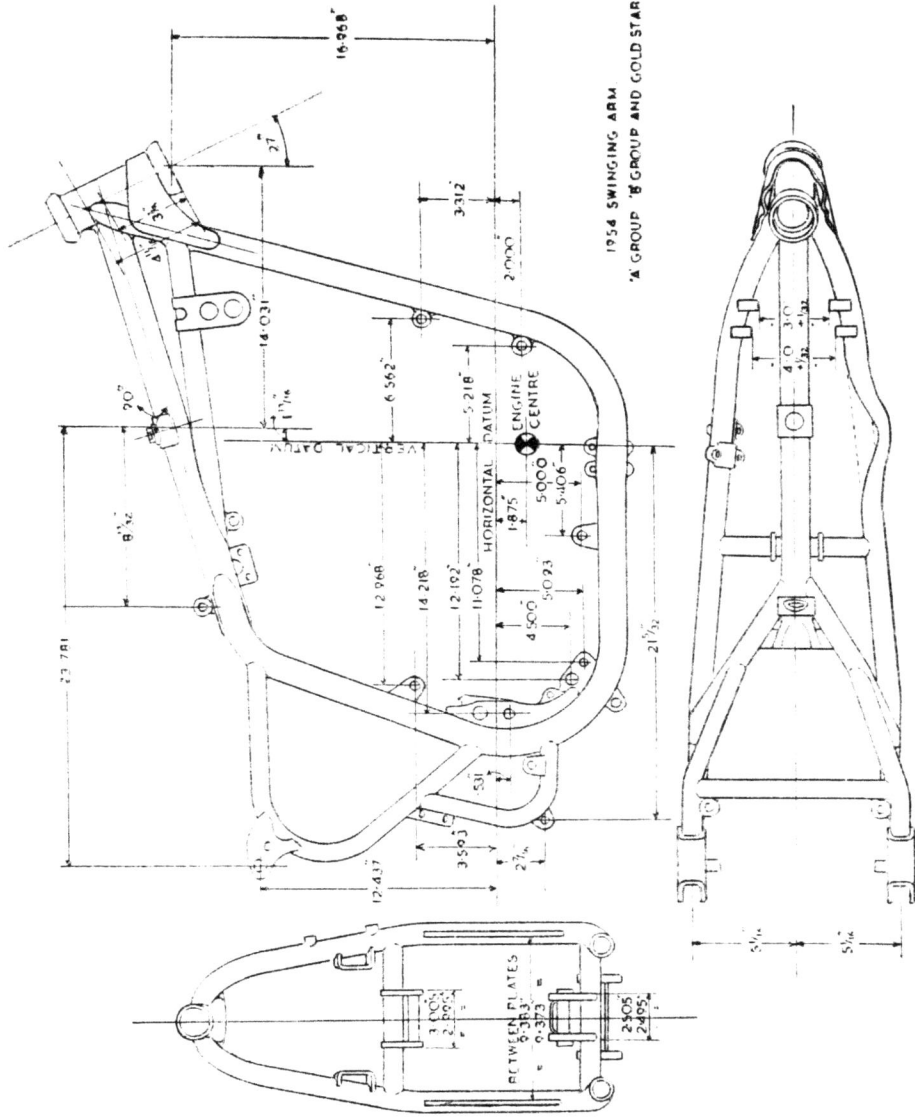

A GROUP, B GROUP and GOLD STAR    1954 SWINGING ARM

1954 SWINGING ARM
'A' GROUP 'B' GROUP and GOLD STAR

95

## B32 and B34
## 1954 RIGID FRAME

## D3 SWINGING ARM

96

## C12 SWINGING ARM

## D5 SWINGING ARM

# D7 SWINGING ARM

**C15 STAR AND C15 SPORTS STAR**

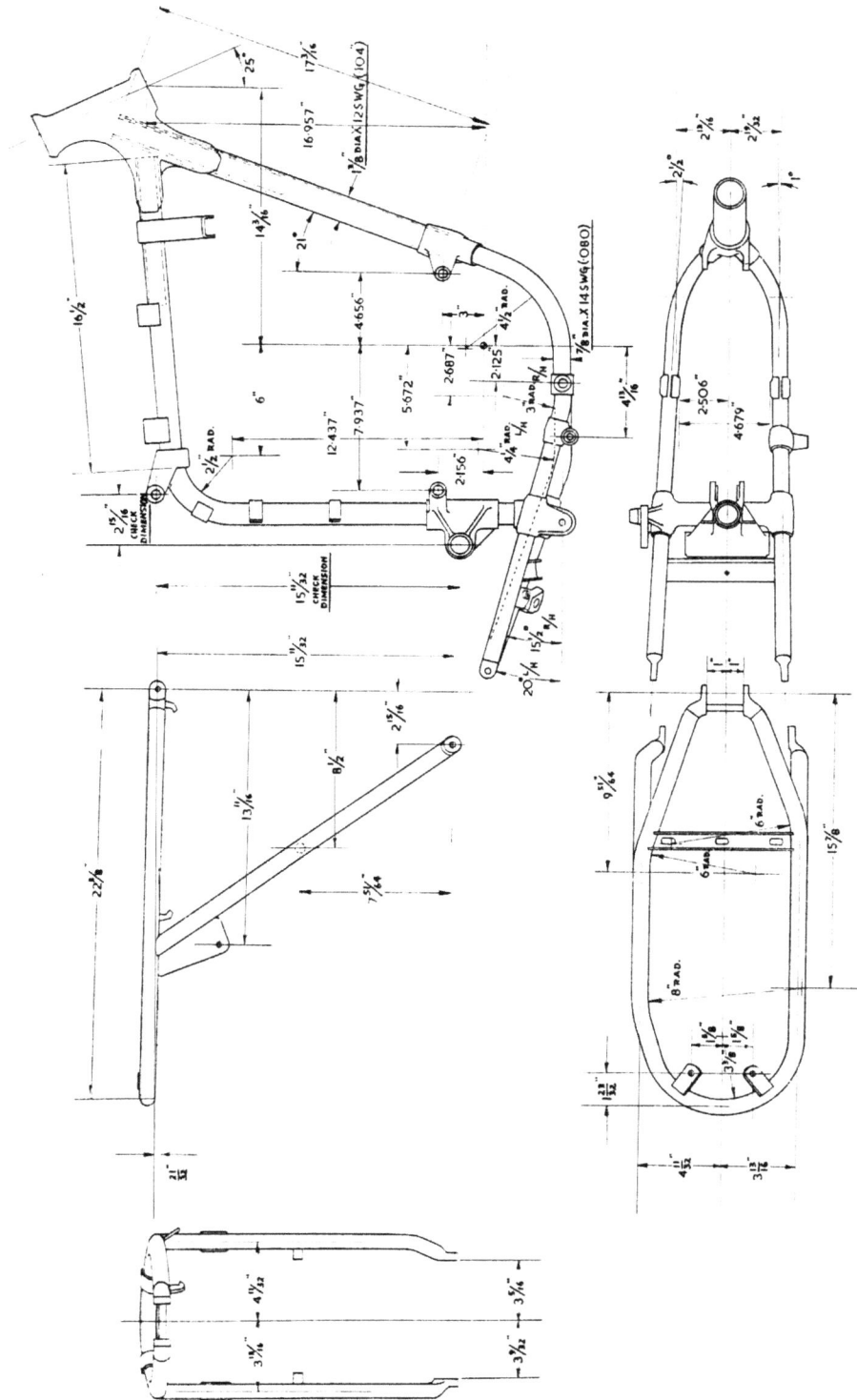

# C15 TRIALS AND C15 SCRAMBLES

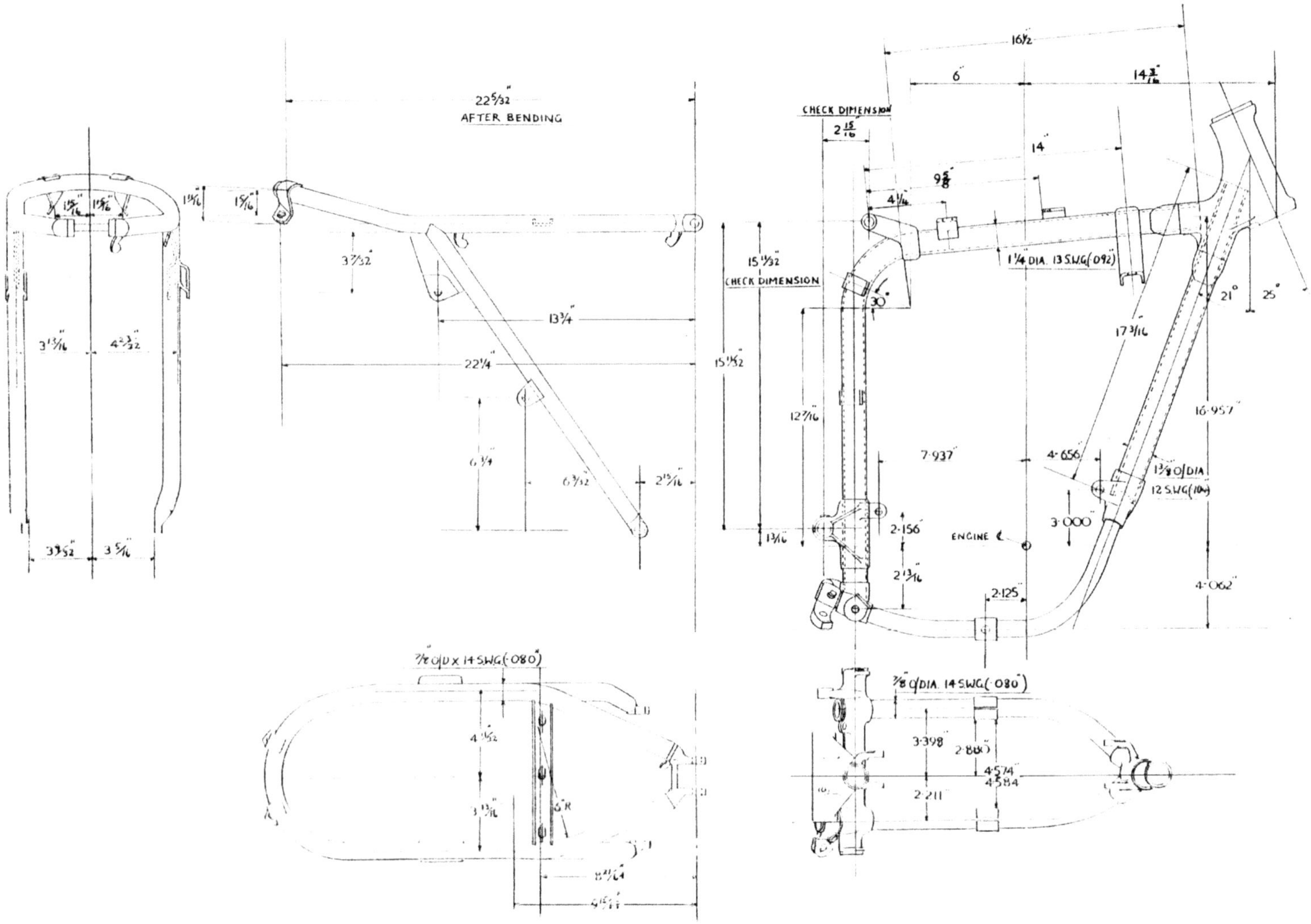

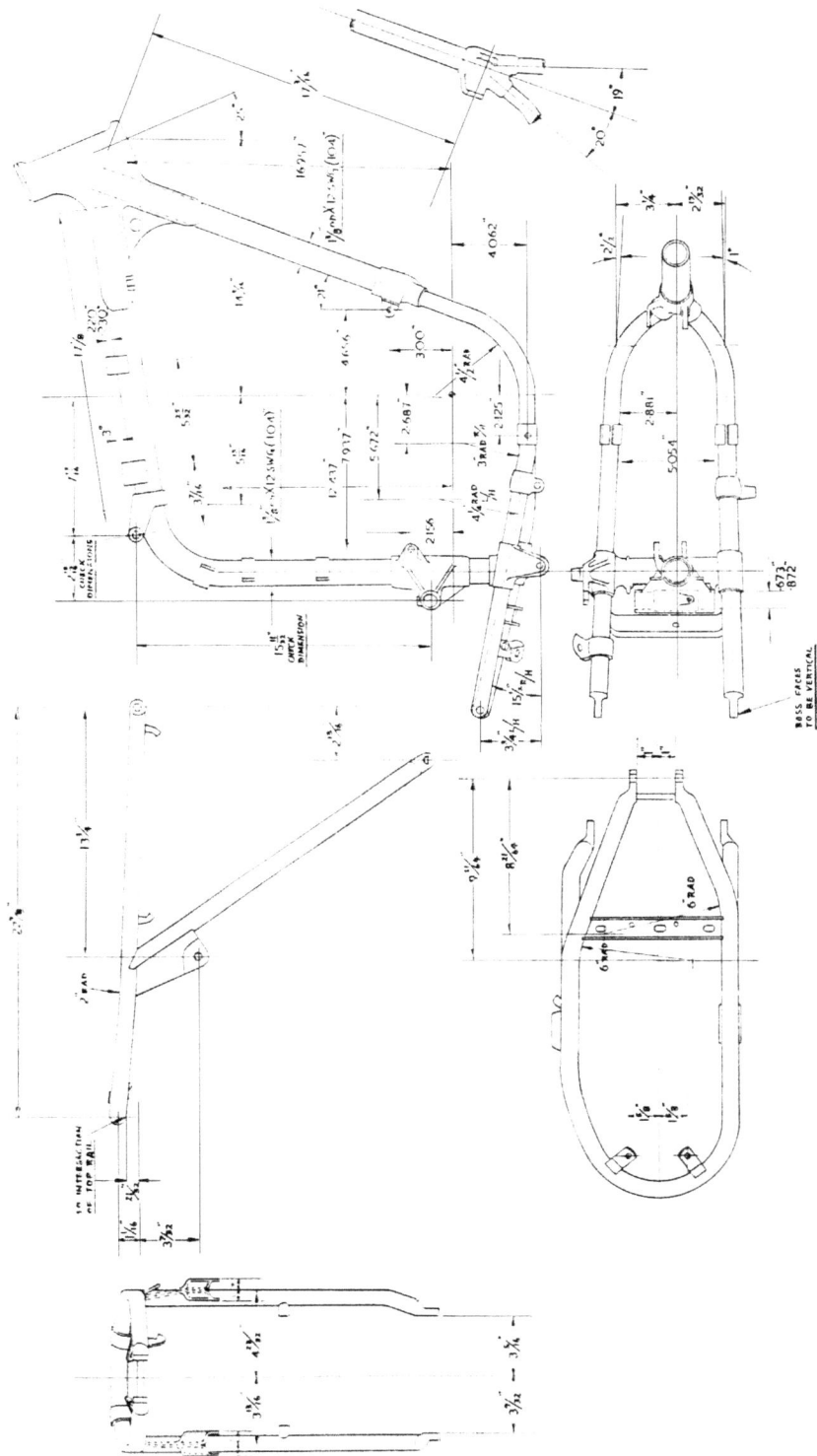

# B40 STAR

# 500 c.c. STAR AND 650 c.c. STAR MODELS A50 AND A65

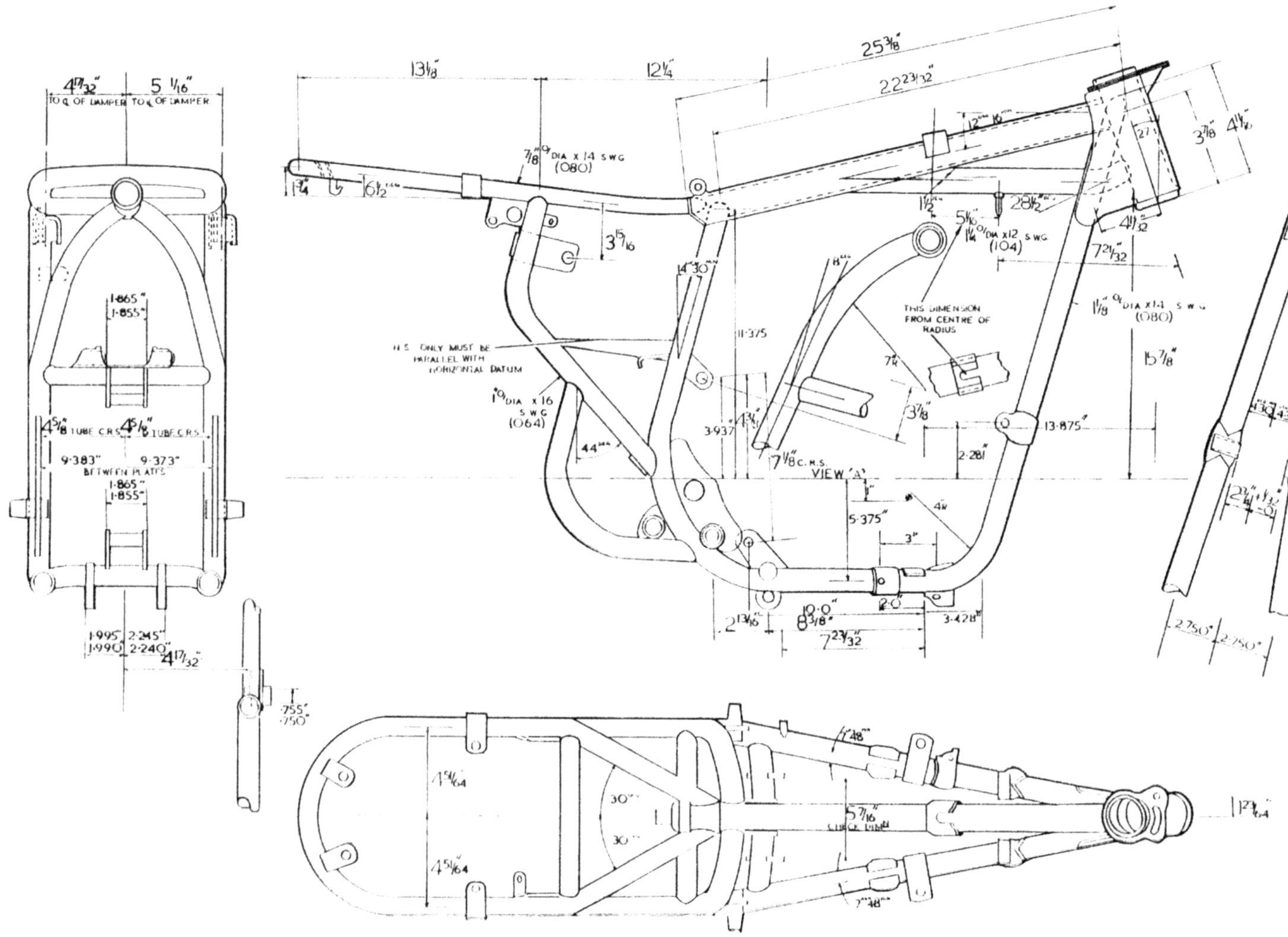

# SERVICE TOOLS

## for all

## MOTOR CYCLES

## 1946 to 1958 Inclusive

---

## Use in conjunction with
## Service Sheet No. 711A

**For Details of Models and Prices.**

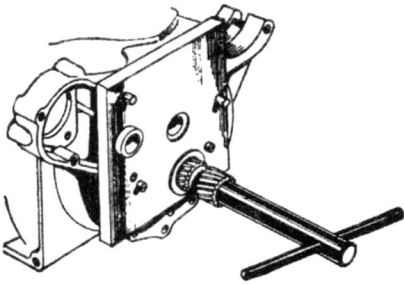

61-3281   Reaming Jig (mainshaft and cam-
          shaft gear bushes)
61-3275   Reaming Jig (mainshaft and cam-
          shaft gear bushes)

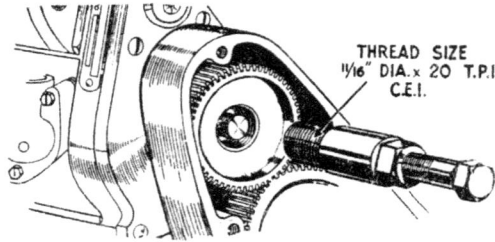

THREAD SIZE
$1\frac{1}{16}$" DIA. x 20 T.P.I.
C.E.I.

61-1903   Magdyno Driving Pinion Extractor
          Tool complete.

For Models fitted with Magdyno Lighting Equipment.

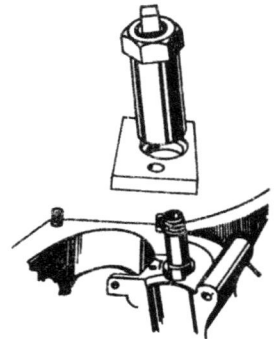

61-3069   Inlet Tappet
          Guide Extractor

61-3284   Mainshaft Bush Reamer
61-3285   Pilot for Jigs 61-3275
61-3286   Pilot for Jigs 61-3281
61-3287   Shell Reamer Holder
61-3288   Tommy Bar for 61-3287

61-3167   Reamer for use with 61-3162
          61-3281 and 61-3275

INSIDE DIA. $3\frac{1}{32}$" MIN.
LENGTH INSIDE
$2\frac{5}{8}$" MIN.

$\frac{5}{16}$" DIA.
x 26 T.P.I.
C.E.I.

NOTE RELATION
OF FLATS AND TAPPET.

61-691   Cam Pinion Post Extractor

67-9114   Push Rod Assembly Tool

61-1733
61-1732
61-3198
61-3548

61-3187

61-3256   Extractor Set Complete

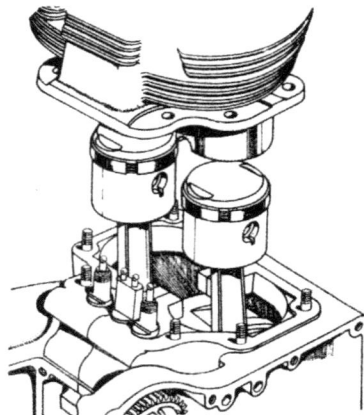

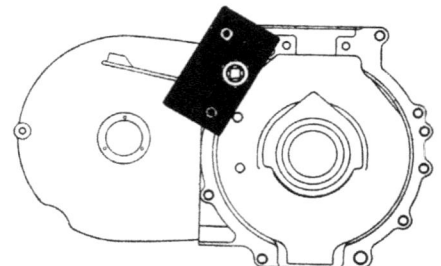

61-3061   Piston Ring Slipper
61-3334   Piston Ring Slipper,
61-3262   Piston Ring Slipper,
          (2 per set)

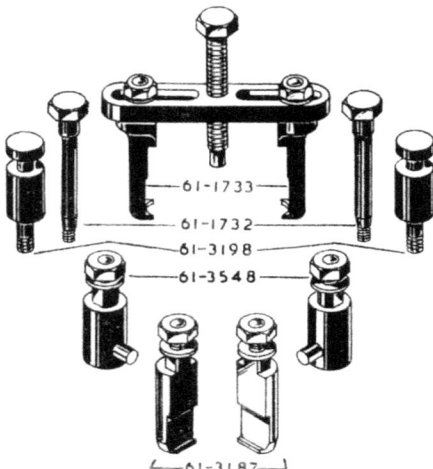

61-3159   Camshaft Bush Extractor

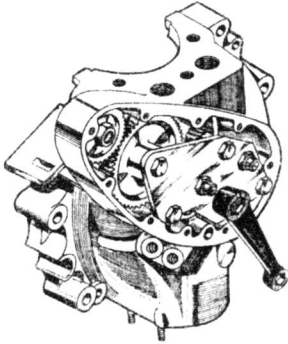

15-832   Mainshaft Nut Spanner

61-1817   Crankpin Nut Spanner

Tool comprises Holder, Locknut and
three Sockets

Sockets
for 61-1817
61-1754
61-1755
61-3228

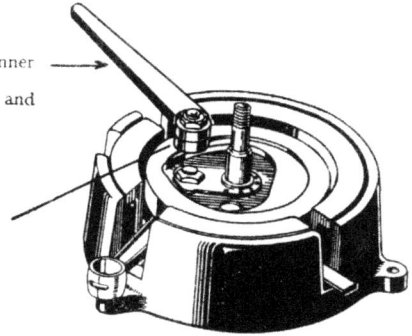

61-1751   Flywheel Bolster
61-1750      ,,      ,,   Gauge Rod
61-1747      ,,      ,,   Ring
61-1749      ,,      ,,      ,,

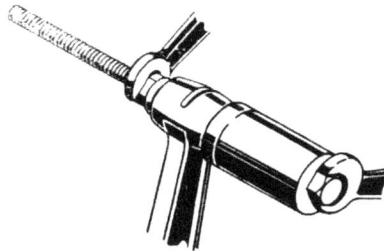

65-9243   C Spanner and Fork Top Nut Spanner

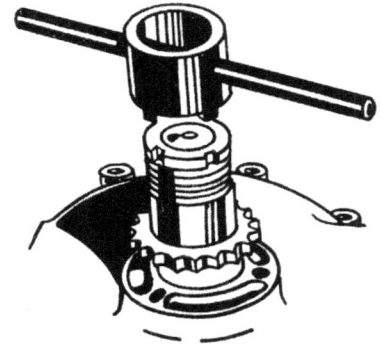

61-658   Gudgeon Pin Bush Extractor comprising Spindle with various size bushes.

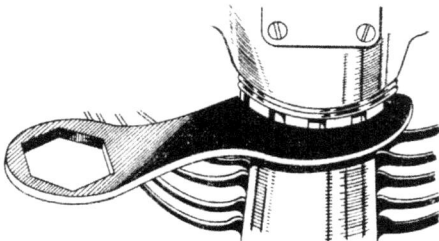

61-3220   Cush Drive Nut Tube Spanner

**61-3305   Valve Seating Tool complete**

Comprising Tommy Bar 61-3291
Holder 61-3290

Cutters

| | | |
|---|---|---|
| 61-3298 | .. | $1\frac{5}{16}'' \times 45° \times 20°$ |
| 61-3299 | .. | $1\frac{1}{2}'' \times 45° \times 20°$ |
| 61-3300 | .. | $1\frac{5}{8}'' \times 45° \times 20°$ |
| 61-3301 | .. | $1\frac{3}{4}'' \times 45° \times 20°$ |
| 61-3302 | .. | $1\frac{7}{8}'' \times 45° \times 20°$ |

Pilots

| | | |
|---|---|---|
| 61-3293 | .. | $\frac{5}{16}''$ |
| 61-3294 | .. | .350″ |
| 61-3295 | .. | $\frac{3}{8}''$ |

61-3263  61-3264  61-3265  61-3267  61-3268
Valve Guide fitting and extracting punches

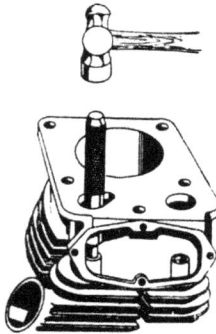

65-9240   Valve Grinding Tool

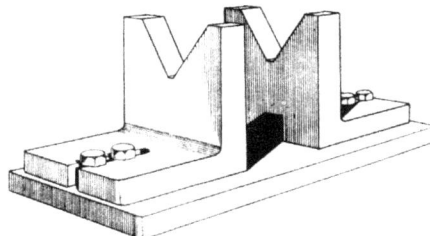

61-692   Vee Block and Base Plate

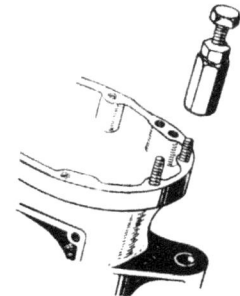

| | | |
|---|---|---|
| 61-699 | $\frac{1}{4}''$ | C.E.I. Stud Boxes |
| 61-317 | $\frac{5}{16}''$ | ,,   ,,   ,, |
| 61-545 | $\frac{3}{8}''$ | ,,   ,,   ,, |

61-3049   Cylinder Head Spanner

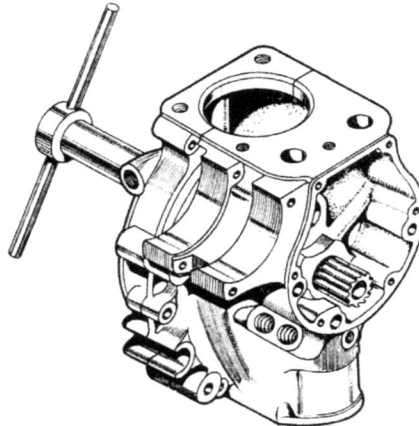

61-1932   Reamer and Holder complete (mainshaft bush)
61-1922   Reamer for 61-1932

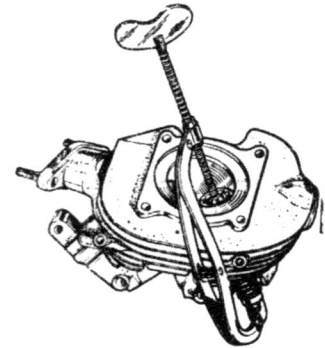

61-3340   Valve Spring Compressor with Adaptor
Models M33
"B" Group, "A" Group, and Sunbeam

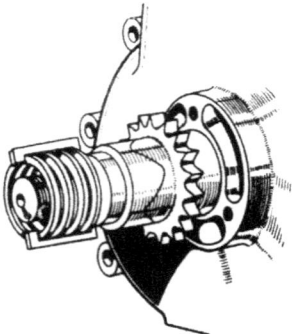

61-1822   Cush Drive Spring Assembly Tool
For holding Spring compressed whilst fitting Lockring.
(2 per set)

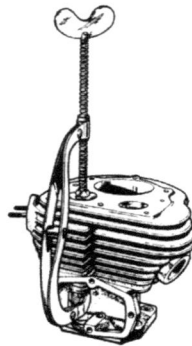

61-3340   Valve Spring Compressor
Models C10, C11, M20, M21
(Use without adaptor)

Service Tool 61-3206
See Service Sheet 711A for details.
Press is not included

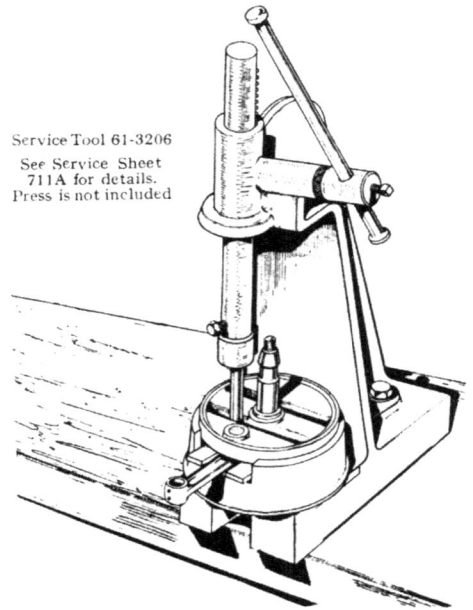

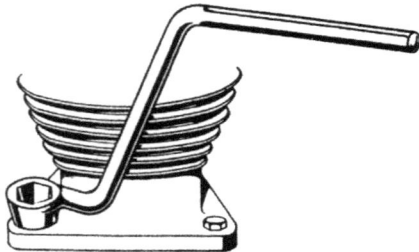

61-3052   Cylinder Base Nut Spanner

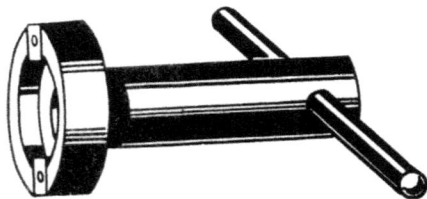

61-3257   Gearbox Sprocket Locknut Spanner,
61-3258   Gearbox Sprocket Locknut Spanner,

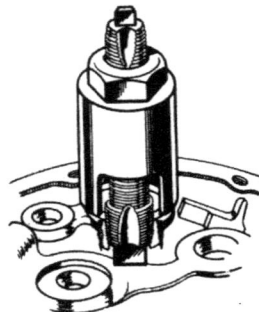

61-3185   Bush Extractor

61 3246   Gudgeon Pin Bush Reamer (.4687")
61-3367   Gudgeon Pin Bush Reamer (.625")
61 3556   Gudgeon Pin Bush Reamer (.6875")
61-3366   Gudgeon Pin Bush Reamer (.750")
61-3580   Gudgeon Pin Bush Reamer (.4375")
61-3581   Gudgeon Pin Bush Reamer (.5625")

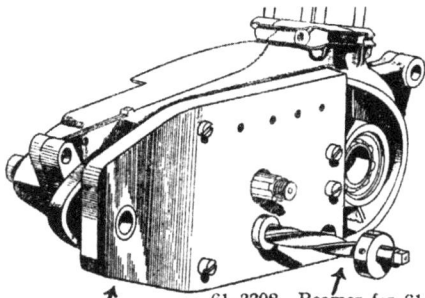

Service Tool 61-3199.

61-3308　Reamer for 61-3199
Line Reaming the Gearbox Bushes

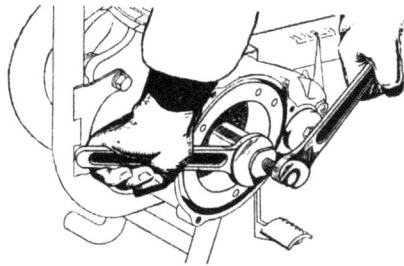

61-3188　Generator Flywheel Removal Tool
　　　　　(Wico Pacy)
90-297　　Generator Flywheel Removal Tool
　　　　　(Lucas)

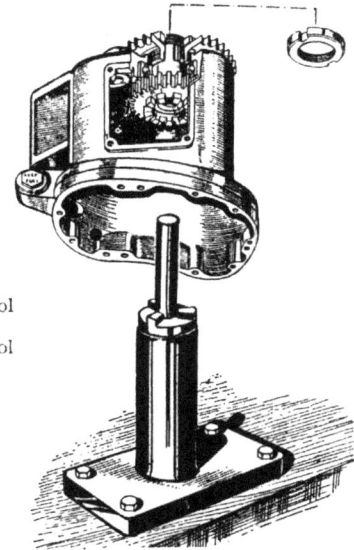

61-3064　Pinion Sleeve Extractor

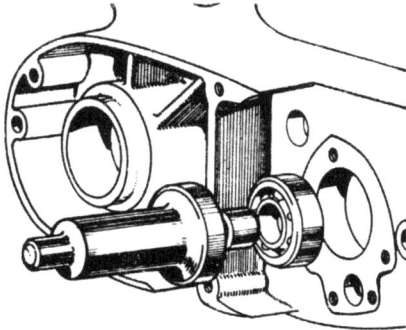

61-3214　Ballrace Pilot (gearbox pinion bearing)
61-3215　Ballrace Pilot (gearbox mainshaft bearing)

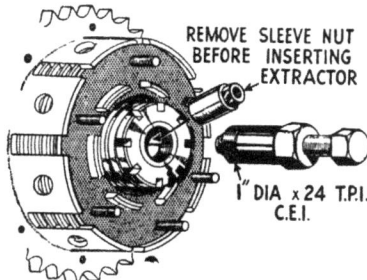

REMOVE SLEEVE NUT
BEFORE INSERTING
EXTRACTOR

1" DIA x 24 T.P.I.
C.E.I.

61-1912　Clutch Extractor Tool

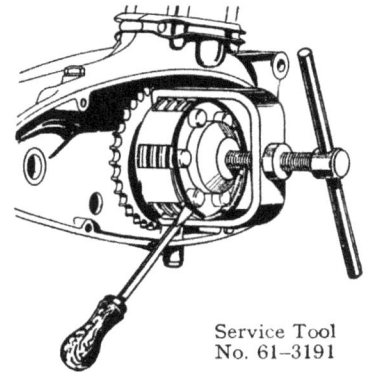

Service Tool
No. 61-3191

Removing the Clutch Plate Circlip

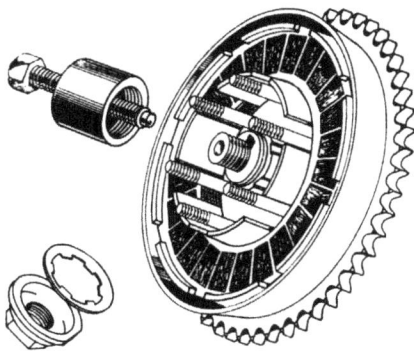

61-3362　Clutch Extractor Tool

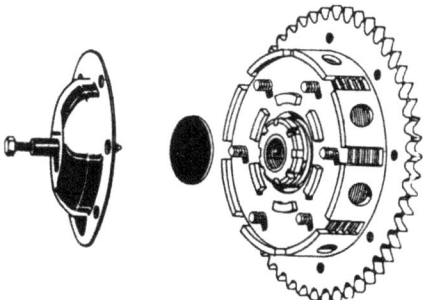

61-3055　Clutch Testing Tool

61-3212　Ballrace Pilot for large engine bearing
61-3213　Ballrace Pilot for small engine bearing

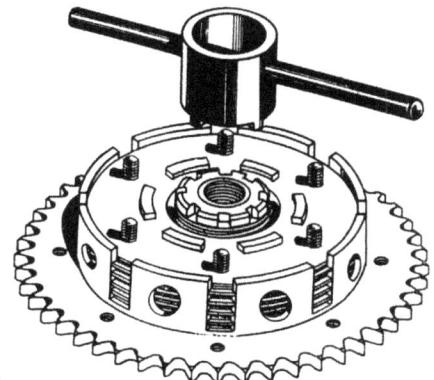

61-1915　Clutch Spring Nut Tube Spanner.

61-3006  Oil Seal Extractor

61-3007  Oil Seal Assembly Tool

61-3003  Spanner for Fork Plug Assembly

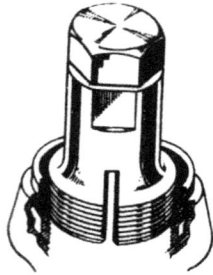

61-3060  Ballrace Extractor (steering head)
for all $\frac{3}{16}$″ balls

61-3063  Ballrace Extractor (steering head)
for all $\frac{1}{4}$″ balls

61-3002  Assembly Tool for Adjuster Sleeve
61-3008  Assembly Tool for Adjuster Sleeve

61-3350  Fork Shaft Dismantling and Assembly Tool

61-3005  Assembly Tool for Oil Seal Holder

61-3001  Spanner for Fork Top Nut Assembly

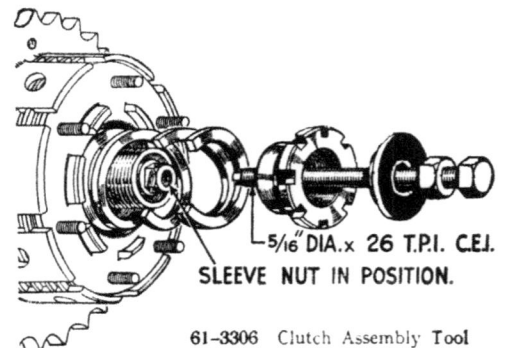

61-3222  Rear Suspension Strip and Assembly Tool

5/16″ DIA. x 26 T.P.I. C.E.I. SLEEVE NUT IN POSITION.

61-3306  Clutch Assembly Tool

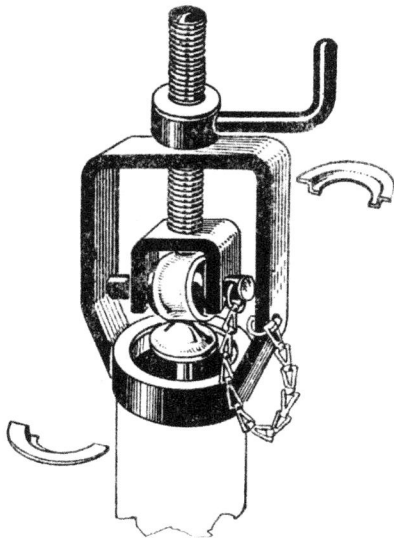

61-3503
Rear Suspension
Dismantling Tool

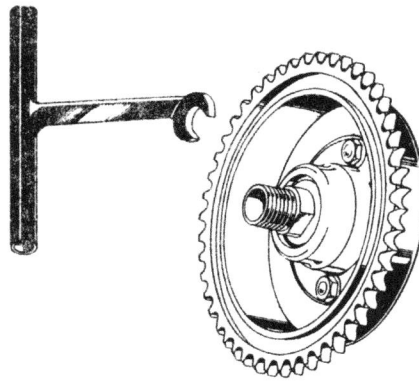

61-3217   Spanner for rear chain sprocket

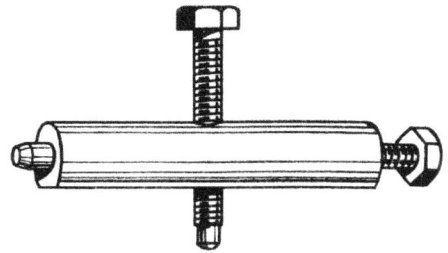

61-3540   Flywheel Removal Tool

61-3542   Wheel Bearing Nut Peg Spanner

61-3536   Flywheel Assembly Tool

61-705   Spoke Nipple Key, (10 and 12 gauge)

61-773   Spoke Nipple Key (8 and 10 gauge)

61-3552   Starter Ratchet Circlip
Assembly Tool

61-3554   Gearbox Sprocket Locking Tool

61-3513
Rear Suspension
Dismantling Tool

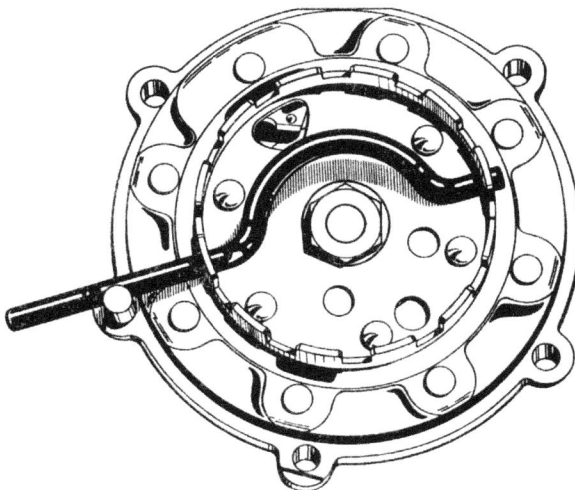

61-3551   Flywheel Locking Tool

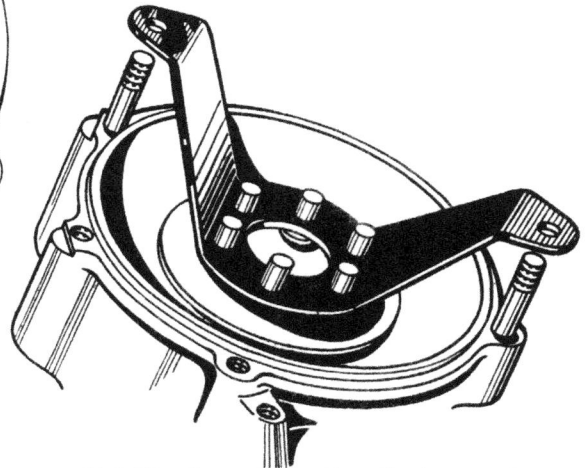

61-3553   Clutch Back Plate Locking Tool

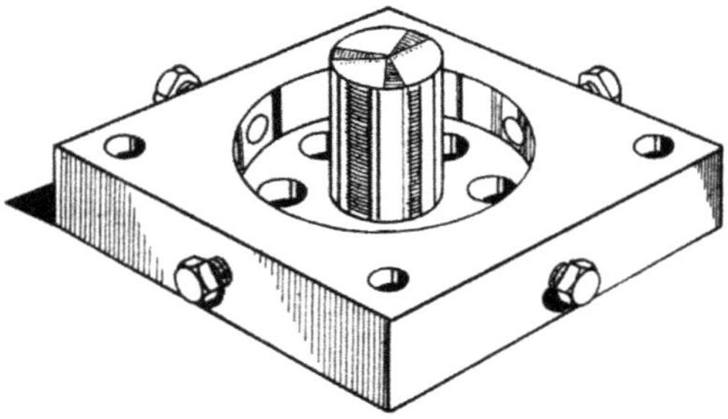

61–3499 Bench Die Holder

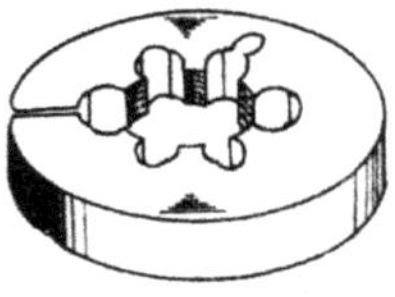

61–3483 Die

Tap

Die Nut

| Part No. | Description | For |
|---|---|---|
| 61–3574 | Tap and Die Set in wooden case comprising tools listed below except 61–3483 ... ... ... ... ... ... ... | General Workshop use |
| 61–3575 | Tap and Die Set in wooden case comprising all tools listed below | General Workshop use |

## TAPS.

| Part No. | Taps. | | For |
|---|---|---|---|
| 61–3461 | ⅜″ x 19 TPI B.S.P. ... ... ... ... | (R/H) | Petrol Tap Hole. |
| 61–3462 | ⅜″ x 20 TPI B.S.F. ... ... ... ... | (L/H) | Sunbeam Dynamo. |
| 61–3463 | 7/16″ x 20 TPI C.E.I. ... ... ... ... | (R/H) | General. |
| 61–3464 | ½″ x 20 TPI C.E.I. ... ... ... ... | (R/H) | General. |
| 61–3502 | 9/16″ x 20 TPI C.E.I. ... ... ... ... | (R/H) | General. |
| 61–3465 | 9/16″ x 20 TPI C.E.I. ... ... ... ... | (L/H) | Front Fork Spindle Hole. |
| 61–3466 | ⅝″ x 20 TPI C.E.I. ... ... ... ... | (R/H) | General. |
| 61–3467 | ¾″ x 20 TPI C.E.I. ... ... ... ... | (R/H) | General. |
| 65–3468 | ¾″ x 20 TPI B.S.W. ... ... ... ... | (R/H) | General. |
| 61–3469 | ¾″ x 12 TPI B.S.F. ... ... ... ... | (L/H) | Sunbeam Rear Spindle Hole. |
| 61–3470 | ⅞″ x 20 TPI B.S.W. ... ... ... ... | (R/H) | Rear Suspension Shaft. |
| 61–3471 | 1-1/16″ x 20 TPI C.E.I. ... ... ... ... | (R/H) | Fork Shaft Top. |
| 61–3472 | 1⅛″ x 28 TPI B.S.W. ... ... ... ... | (R/H) | Fork Shaft Bottom. |
| 61–3473 | 1½″ x 20 TPI B.S.W. ... ... ... ... | (R/H) | Filler Caps. |
| 61–3531 | 14 mm. x 1.25 mm. ... ... .. ... | (R/H) | 14-mm. Spark Plug Hole |
| 61–3533 | 1.250″ x 20 TPI B.S.W. ... ... ... ... | (R/H) | Bantam Fork Tube (90–5021) |

## DIES.

| Part No. | Dies. | | For |
|---|---|---|---|
| 61–3474 | 7/16″ x 20 TPI C.E.I. ... ... ... ... | (R/H) | General. |
| 61–3475 | ½″ x 20 TPI C.E.I. ... ... ... ... | (R/H) | General. |
| 61–3476 | 9/16″ x 20 TPI C.E.I. ... ... ... ... | (R/H) | Gearbox Mainshaft. |
| 61–3477 | 9/16″ x 20 TPI C.E.I. ... ... ... ... | (L/H) | "A" Group Mainshaft. |
| 61–3478 | ⅝″ x 20 TPI C.E.I. ... ... ... ... | (R/H) | General. |
| 61–3479 | ¾″ x 20 TPI C.E.I. ... ... ... ... | (R/H) | General. |
| 61–3480 | ¾″ x 12 TPI B.S.F. ... ... ... ... | (L/H) | Sunbeam Rear Spindle. |
| 61–3481 | 1″ x 24 TPI C.E.I. ... ... ... ... | (R/H) | Fork Stem. |
| 61–3482 | 1.120″ x 24 TPI C.E.I. ... ... ... | (R/H) | Fork Stem. |
| 61–3483 | 1⅞″ x 28 TPI WHIT. ... ... ... | (R/H) | Fork Sliding Tube Top. |
| 61–3499 | Bench Die Holder (for use with 61–3483) ... | | |

**B.S.A. MOTOR CYCLES LTD.**
**Service Dept., Birmingham 11**
*Printed in England*

# PRICE LIST

## for

# SERVICE TOOLS

# 1946 to 1958 Inclusive

## Use in conjunction with Service Sheet No. 711

| Part No. | Description | Used on Model | £ | s. | d. |
|---|---|---|---|---|---|
| 15–832 | Rear Hub Nut Spanner ... ... ... ... | A, B, C and M ... ... ... | | 4 | 5 |
| 61–317 | Stud Box 5/16" c.e.i. ... ... ... ... | General ... ... ... ... | | 3 | 0 |
| 61–545 | Stud Box 3/8" c.e.i. ... ... ... ... | General ... ... ... ... | | 3 | 0 |
| 61–658 | Gudgeon Pin Bush Extractor ... ... ... | All Models ... ... ... | | 10 | 6 |
| 61–691 | Cam Pinion Post Extractor ... ... ... | B and M ... ... ... | | 4 | 6 |
| 61–692 | Flywheel "V" Blocks (used with 61–1821) ... | B, C and M ... ... ... | 2 | 5 | 4 |
| 61–696 | Socket Nut (used with 61–1817) ... ... ... | B, C and M ... ... ... | | 1 | 5 |
| 61–698 | Crankpin Nut Spanner only (used with 61–1817) ... | B, C and M ... ... ... | 1 | 1 | 0 |
| 61–699 | Stud Box 1/4" c.e.i. ... ... ... ... | General ... ... ... ... | | 3 | 0 |
| 61–705 | Nipple Key (10 and 12 gauge) ... ... ... | General ... ... ... ... | | 3 | 10 |
| 61–773 | Nipple Key (8 and 10 gauge) ... ... ... | General ... ... ... ... | | 3 | 10 |
| 61–1747 | Flywheel Bolster Ring ... ... ... ... | C Group ... ... ... ... | 4 | 1 | 3 |
| 61–1749 | Flywheel Bolster Ring ... ... ... ... | B and M 500 c.c. ... ... | 4 | 1 | 3 |
| 61–1750 | Flywheel Bolster Gauge Rod (2 per set) ... ... | B, C and M ... ... ... | | 7 | 7 |
| 61–1751 | Flywheel Bolster ... ... ... ... ... | B, C and M ... ... ... | 3 | 11 | 9 |
| 61–1754 | Crankpin Nut Socket (used with 61–1817) ... | C Group ... ... ... ... | | 8 | 0 |
| 61–1755 | Crankpin Nut Socket (used with 61–1817) ... | B and M ... ... ... | | 8 | 0 |
| 61–1817 | Crankpin Nut Spanner complete ... ... ... | B, C and M ... ... ... | 2 | 7 | 6 |
| | *Comprising:—* | | | | |
| | 61–696 Socket Nut ... ... ... ... | | | 1 | 5 |
| | 61–698 Spanner ... ... ... ... | | 1 | 1 | 0 |
| | 61–1754 Socket ... ... ... ... ... | C Group ... ... ... | | 8 | 0 |
| | 61–1755 Socket ... ... ... ... ... | B and M ... ... ... | | 8 | 0 |
| | 61–3228 Socket ... ... ... ... ... | Gold Star ... ... ... | | 9 | 1 |

| Part No. | Description | Used on Model | Per Unit Retail Price |
|---|---|---|---|
| | | | £ s. d. |
| 61–1821 | "V" Block Base Plate (used with 61–692) ... ... | B, C and M ... ... ... | 1 10 3 |
| 61–1822 | Cush Drive Spring Assembly Tool (2 per set) ... | A, B, C and M ... ... ... | 4 6 |
| 61–1903 | Magdyno Drive Pinion Extractor ... ... ... | B and M ... ... ... | 3 0 |
| 61–1912 | Clutch Extractor ... ... ... ... | M to 1948 ... ... ... | 6 0 |
| 61–1915 | Clutch Spring Nut Tube Spanner ... ... ... | M to 1948 ... ... ... | 4 6 |
| 61–1922 | Reamer (used with 61–1932) (mainshaft bush) ... | C Group ... ... ... ... | 3 5 0 |
| 61–1932 | Reamer and Holder complete (used with 61–1922) | C Group ... ... ... ... | 4 4 9 |
| 61–3001 | Fork Top Nut Spanner (front fork) ... ... | A, B, C and M ... ... ... | 13 6 |
| 61–3002 | Adjuster Sleeve Assembly Tool (steering head) ... | B, C and M ... ... ... | 12 1 |
| 61–3003 | Fork Plug Spanner (front fork) ... ... | A, B, C and M ... ... ... | 13 6 |
| 61–3005 | Oil Seal Holder Assembly Tool (front fork) ... | A, B, C and M ... ... ... | 1 1 2 |
| 61–3006 | Oil Seal Extractor (front fork) ... ... | A, B, C and M ... ... ... | 15 1 |
| 61–3007 | Oil Seal Assembly Tool (front fork) ... ... | A, B, C and M ... ... ... | 6 0 |
| 61–3008 | Adjuster Sleeve Assembly Tool (steering head) ... | A7/10, S7/8 ... ... ... | 12 1 |
| 61–3049 | Cylinder Head Spanner ... ... ... | M20/21 ... ... ... | 10 6 |
| 61–3052 | Cylinder Base Nut Spanner ... ... ... | M20/21 ... ... ... | 1 1 2 |
| 61–3055 | Clutch Testing Tool ... ... ... ... | M to 1948 ... ... ... | 15 1 |
| 61–3060 | Steering Head Ballrace Extractor ... ... | For 3/16" Balls ... ... | 8 3 |
| 61–3061 | Piston Ring Slipper (2 per set) ... ... | A7 to 1950 ... ... ... | 7 6 |
| 61–3063 | Steering Head Ballrace Extractor ... ... | For 1/4" Balls ... ... | 8 3 |
| 61–3064 | Pinion Sleeve Extractor ... ... ... | B, C and M ... ... ... | 2 11 5 |
| 61–3069 | Inlet Tappet Guide Extractor ... ... ... | A7 to 1950 ... ... ... | 7 7 |
| 61–3159 | Camshaft Bush Extractor ... ... ... | A7, A10 ... ... ... | 12 8 |
| 61–3167 | Camshaft Bush Reamer (used with 61–3275/81) ... | A Group ... ... ... | 3 0 6 |
| 61–3185 | Gearbox Bush Extractor ... ... ... | M Group ... ... | 15 9 |
| 61–3188 | Flywheel Magneto Removal Tool (Wico Pacy) ... | D1, D3 and D5 ... ... ... | 6 8 |
| 61–3191 | Clutch Plate Circlip Removal Tool ... ... ... | D1, D3 and D5 ... ... ... | 1 10 3 |
| 61–3199 | Gearbox Bush Line Reaming Plate (used with 61–3205) | D1, D3 and D5 ... ... ... | 2 1 6 |
| 61–3205 | Layshaft Bush Reamer only (used with 61–3199) ... | D1, D3 and D5 ... ... ... | 2 1 11 |
| 61–3206 | Flywheel Dismantling and Assembly Tool ... ... | D1, D3 and D5 ... ... ... | 3 15 6 |

*Comprising :—*
    61–3207    Jig Body
    61–3208(2)  Dismantling Bar
    61–3209    Dismantling Punch
    61–3210    Assembly Bridge
(*Note :—* Press as illustrated is not included).

| Part No. | Description | Used on Model | Per Unit Retail Price |
|---|---|---|---|
| 61–3212 | Ballrace Pilot for large engine bearing ... ... | D1, D3 and D5 ... ... ... | 7 7 |
| 61–3213 | Ballrace Pilot for small engine bearing ... ... | D1, D3 and D5 ... ... ... | 6 8 |
| 61–3214 | Ballrace Pilot for gearbox pinion bearing ... ... | D1, D3 and D5 ... ... ... | 7 7 |
| 61–3215 | Ballrace Pilot for gearbox mainshaft bearing ... | D1, D3 and D5 ... ... ... | 6 8 |
| 61–3217 | Spanner for rear wheel sprocket ... ... ... | A7, A10 ... ... ... | 11 3 |
| 61–3220 | Tube Spanner for cush drive nut ... ... | A, B, C and M ... ... ... | 3 6 |
| 61–3222 | Rear Suspension Strip and Assembly Tool ... | A, B and M ... ... ... | 13 6 |
| 61–3228 | Crankpin Nut Socket (used with 61–1817) ... | B32/4 G/S ... ... ... | 9 1 |
| 61–3246 | Reamer Gudgeon Pin Bush ... ... ... | D1, D3 ... ... ... | 14 6 |
| 61–3256 | Extractor Set complete ... ... ... ... | All Models ... ... ... | 1 12 7 |

*Comprising :—*
    61–351(1)    Plate
    61–776(1)    Bolt
    61–1732(2)  Extractor Leg (A Group cam pinion)
    61–1733(2)  Extractor Leg (engine pinion B,
                  C and M).
    61–3187(2)  Extractor Leg (crankshaft pinion
                  A7/10).
    61–3198(2)  Extractor Leg (engine sprocket etc.,
                  D, C and A).
    61–3548(2)  Extractor Leg (Dandy flywheel) ...

# *BSA* SERVICE TOOLS

| Part No. | Description | Used on Model | Retail Price Per Unit |
|---|---|---|---|
| | | | £ s. d. |
| 61-3257 | Gearbox Sprocket Locknut Spanner ... ... | A, B and M ... ... ... | 15 1 |
| 61-3258 | Gearbox Sprocket Locknut Spanner ... ... ... | C ... ... ... ... | 15 1 |
| 61-3262 | Piston Ring Slipper (2 per set) ... ... | A10 ... ... ... ... | 6 0 |
| 61-3263 | Valve Guide Punch (used on B33/34, exhaust and G/Stars with .374 dia. valve stems). ... ... | | 3 0 |
| 61-3264 | Valve Guide Punch (comprising 61-3265/66 and 61-3307) ... ... ... ... ... | C10 In. and Ex. ... ... | 12 8 |
| 61-3265 | Valve Guide Punch (B31/32 inlet, A7/10, C11, C12 inlet and exhaust and G/Stars with .310" dia. valve stems) ... ... ... ... ... | | 6 0 |
| 61-3267 | Valve Guide Punch (comprising 61-3268/9/70) ... | M20, M21 In. and Ex. ... | 8 3 |
| 61-3268 | Valve Guide Punch (B31/32 exhaust, B33/34 inlet and G/Stars with .348" dia. valve stems) ... ... | | 6 0 |
| 61-3275 | Mainshaft and Camshaft Bush Reaming Jig ... | A7 to 1950 ... ... | 2 12 11 |
| 61-3281 | Mainshaft and Camshaft Bush Reaming Jig ... | A10, AA7 onwards ... | 2 12 11 |
| 61-3284 | Reamer (mainshaft used with 61-3275/81) ... | A7, A10 ... ... ... ... | 4 6 2 |
| 61-3285 | Pilot for 61-3275 ... ... ... ... | A7 to 1950 ... ... | 15 1 |
| 61-3286 | Pilot for 61-3281 ... ... ... ... | A10, AA7 onwards ... | 15 1 |
| 61-3287 | Reamer Holder (used with 61-3284) ... ... | A7, A10 ... ... ... ... | 9 1 |
| 61-3290 | Valve Seat Cutter Holder ... ... ... | A, B, C and M ... ... | 5 3 |
| 61-3293 | Valve Seat Cutter Pilot ($\frac{5}{16}$") ... ... ... | A, B and C ... ... | 6 8 |
| 61-3294 | Valve Seat Cutter Pilot (.350") ... ... | B and M ... ... ... | 6 8 |
| 61-3295 | Valve Seat Cutter Pilot (.375") ... ... | B, and M33 ... ... | 6 8 |
| 61-3298 | Valve Seat Cutter (1$\frac{7}{16}$" dia x 45° x 20°) ... | A7 and C ... ... ... | 2 6 2 |
| 61-3299 | Valve Seat Cutter (1$\frac{1}{2}$" dia. x 45° x 20°) ... | A10 and C ... ... | 2 6 2 |
| 61-3300 | Valve Seat Cutter (1$\frac{5}{8}$" dia. x 45° x 20°) ... | B ... ... ... ... | 2 6 2 |
| 61-3301 | Valve Seat Cutter (1$\frac{3}{4}$" dia. x 45° x 20°) ... | B and M ... ... ... | 2 6 2 |
| 61-3302 | Valve Seat Cutter (1$\frac{7}{8}$" dia. x 45° x 20°) ... | B and M ... ... ... | 2 6 2 |
| 61-3305 | Valve Seating Tool complete ... ... ... ... | A, B, C and M ... ... | 12 16 2 |
| 61-3306 | Clutch Assembly Tool ... ... ... ... | M to 1948 ... ... | 3 0 |
| 61-3308 | Reamer for 61-3199 (comprising 61-3205 and 61-3309) | D1, and D3 ... ... | 2 8 1 |
| 61-3311 | Crankshaft Balance Weight (18 ozs., 12 drms.) ... | A7 1951 onwards ... | 15 1 |
| 61-3312 | Crankshaft Balance Weight (16 ozs., 14 drms.) ... | A7 to 1951 ... ... | 15 1 |
| 61-3334 | Piston Ring Slipper (2 per set) ... ... ... | A7 1951 onwards ... | 6 0 |
| 61-3340 | Valve Spring Compressor complete ... ... ... | A, B, C and M ... ... | 1 1 2 |
| 61-3350 | Front Fork Dismantling and Assembly Tool ... | A, B, C, M and S7/8 ... | 15 1 |
| 61-3362 | Clutch Extractor Tool ... ... ... | A, B, C and M 1949 onwards ... | 6 8 |
| 61-3366 | Gudgeon Pin Bush Reamer (.750") ... ... | B, M and A10 ... ... | 1 1 10 |
| 61-3367 | Gudgeon Pin Bush Reamer (.625") ... ... | C only ... ... | 1 2 8 |
| 61-3487 | Valve Guide Assembly Punch ... ... ... | S7 and S8 ... ... | 15 1 |
| 61-3497 | Crankshaft Balance Weight (19 ozs. 8 drms.) ... | A10R/R and S/R ... | 13 9 |
| 61-3499 | Bench Die Holder (used with 61-3483) ... ... | A, B, C and M ... ... | 2 18 6 |
| 61-3503 | Rear Suspension Dismantling Tool ... ... | A and B S/A ... ... | 1 17 10 |
| 61-3513 | Rear Suspension Dismantling Tool ... ... | C12 and D3 S/A ... | 1 14 4 |
| 61-3536 | Flywheel Assembly Tool ... ... ... | Dandy ... ... ... | 5 6 |
| 61-3540 | Flywheel Removal Tool ... ... ... ... | Dandy ... ... ... | 6 3 |
| 61-3542 | Wheel Bearing Nut Peg Spanner ... ... | A and B, S/A ... ... | 10 4 |
| 61-3548 | Flywheel Removal Tool (2) (used with 61-3256) ... | Dandy ... ... ... | 4 7 |
| 61-3551 | Flywheel Locking Tool ... ... ... | Dandy ... ... ... | 1 2 |
| 61-3552 | Starter Ratchet Circlip Assembly Tool ... ... | Dandy ... ... ... | 5 3 |
| 61-3553 | Clutch Back Plate Locking Tool ... ... | Dandy ... ... ... | 9 2 |
| 61-3554 | Gearbox Sprocket Locking Tool ... ... | Dandy ... ... ... | 5 5 |
| 61-3556 | Gudgeon Pin Bush Reamer ($\frac{11}{16}$") ... ... | A7 ... ... ... | 1 17 10 |
| 61-3558 | Locking Ring Spanner ... ... ... | 8" Brake ... ... | 11 10 |
| 61-3580 | Gudgeon Pin Bush Reamer ($\frac{7}{16}$") ... ... | Dandy ... ... ... | 1 0 0 |
| 61-3581 | Gudgeon Pin Bush Reamer ($\frac{9}{16}$") ... ... | D5 ... ... ... | 1 6 10 |
| 65-9240 | Valve Grinding Tool ... ... ... ... | A, B, C and M ... ... | 1 10 |
| 65-9243 | Combined "C" and Fork Top Nut spanner ... ... | A, B, C and M ... ... | 1 10 |
| 67-9114 | Push Rod Assembly Tool ... ... ... ... | A7/10 1951 onwards ... | 1 5 |
| 90-297 | Lucas Rotor Removal Tool ... ... ... ... | D1 ... ... ... | 1 3 |

# ✈BSA SERVICE TOOLS

| Part No. | Description | Used on Models | Retail Price |
|---|---|---|---|
| | | | £  s.  d. |
| 61–3574 | Tap and Die Set in wood case comprising taps and dies listed below except 61–3483 ... ... ... | General ... ... ... ... | 23 15 0 |
| 61–3575 | Tap and Die Set in wood case comprising taps and dies listed below ... ... ... ... ... | General ... ... ... ... | 32 7 0 |

## TAPS

| Part No. | Taps | | | | | | | Description | Retail Price |
|---|---|---|---|---|---|---|---|---|---|
| | | | | | | | | | £  s.  d. |
| 61–3461 | ⅜″ | x 19 | T.P.I. | B.S.P. | R/H | ... | ... ... | Petrol Tap Hole ... ... | 7 7 |
| 61–3462 | ⅜″ | x 20 | T.P.I. | B.S.F. | L/H | ... | ... ... | Sunbeam Dynamo ... ... | 7 7 |
| 61–3463 | ⁷⁄₁₆″ | x 20 | T.P.I. | C.E.I. | R/H | ... | ... ... | General ... ... ... ... | 13 1 |
| 61–3464 | ½″ | x 20 | T.P.I. | C.E.I. | R/H | ... | ... ... | General ... ... ... ... | 14 6 |
| 61–3502 | ⁹⁄₁₆″ | x 20 | T.P.I. | C.E.I. | R/H | ... | ... ... | General ... ... ... ... | 18 7 |
| 61–3465 | ⁹⁄₁₆″ | x 20 | T.P.I. | C.E.I. | L/H | ... | ... ... | Front Fork Spindle Hole ... | 1 0 0 |
| 61–3466 | ⅝″ | x 20 | T.P.I. | C.E.I. | R/H | ... | ... ... | General ... ... ... ... | 17 3 |
| 61–3467 | ¾″ | x 20 | T.P.I. | C.E.I. | R/H | ... | ... ... | General ... ... ... ... | 18 7 |
| 61–3468 | ¾″ | x 20 | T.P.I. | B.S.W. | R/H | ... | ... ... | General ... ... ... ... | 18 7 |
| 61–3469 | ¾″ | x 12 | T.P.I. | B.S.F. | L/H | ... | ... ... | Sunbeam Rear Spindle Hole ... | 1 0 0 |
| 61–3470 | ⅞″ | x 20 | T.P.I. | B.S.W. | R/H | ... | ... ... | Rear Suspension Shaft ... | 1 7 6 |
| 61–3471 | 1 ¹⁄₁₆″ | x 20 | T.P.I. | C.E.I. | R/H | ... | ... ... | Fork Shaft Top ... ... | 1 5 6 |
| 61–3472 | 1 ⅛″ | x 28 | T.P.I. | B.S.W. | R/H | ... | ... ... | Fork Shaft ... ... ... | 1 14 4 |
| 61–3473 | 1 ½″ | x 20 | T.P.I. | B.S.W. | R/H | ... | ... ... | Filler Cap ... ... ... | 2 14 7 |
| 61–3531 | 14 mm. x 1.25 mm. | | | | R/H | ... | ... ... | Spark Plug ... ... ... | 1 0 7 |
| 61–3533 | 1.250″ x 20 T.P.I. | | | B.S.W. | R/H | ... | ... ... | D1 Fork Tube ... ... ... | 1 11 0 |

## DIES

| Part No. | Dies | | | | | | | Description | Retail Price |
|---|---|---|---|---|---|---|---|---|---|
| | | | | | | | | | £  s.  d. |
| 61–3474 | ⁷⁄₁₆″ | x 20 | T.P.I. | C.E.I. | R/H | ... | ... ... | General ... ... ... ... | 11 0 |
| 61–3475 | ½″ | x 20 | T.P.I. | C.E.I. | R/H | ... | ... ... | General ... ... ... ... | 12 4 |
| 61–3476 | ⁹⁄₁₆″ | x 20 | T.P.I. | C.E.I. | R/H | ... | ... ... | Gearbox Mainshaft ... ... | 13 9 |
| 61–3477 | ⁹⁄₁₆″ | x 20 | T.P.I. | C.E.I. | L/H | ... | ... ... | A Group Mainshaft ... ... | 17 3 |
| 61–3478 | ⅝″ | x 20 | T.P.I. | C.E.I. | R/H | ... | ... ... | General ... ... ... ... | 13 9 |
| 61–3479 | ¾″ | x 20 | T.P.I. | C.E.I. | R/H | ... | ... ... | General ... ... ... ... | 18 7 |
| 61–3480 | ¾″ | x 12 | T.P.I. | B.S.F. | L/H | ... | ... ... | Sunbeam Rear Spindle ... | 1 2 0 |
| 61–3481 | 1″ | x 24 | T.P.I. | C.E.I. | R/H | ... | ... ... | Fork Stem ... ... ... | 1 4 1 |
| 61–3482 | 1.120″ x 24 T.P.I. | | | C.E.I. | R/H | ... | ... ... | Fork Stem ... ... ... | 1 13 9 |
| 61–3483 | 1 ⅞″ | x 28 | T.P.I. | Whit. | R/H | ... | ... ... | Fork Sliding Tube Top ... | 9 9 1 |
| | (Used with holder 61–3499) | | | | | | | | |

~~B.S.A. Cycles Ltd., Service Department, Birmingham 11~~
B.S.A. Motor Cycles Ltd., Service Department, Birmingham 11

*Printed in England.  Sept. 1958*

# SERVICE TOOLS

## for

## MOTOR CYCLES

Removing the Clutch Centre with Extractor No. 61–3583 (Model C15).

Removing the Crankshaft Pinion with Extractor No. 61–3681 using Legs No. 61–3588 (fitted with Legs 61–3585 for removing the Worm Wheel) (Model C15).

Parting the Flywheels using Bolster 61–3589, Stripping Bars 61–3590 and Punch 61–3601 (Model C15).

Assembling the Crankpin into the Gear Side Flywheel using Locating Gauge No. 61–3597 and Punch No. 61–3601 (Model C15).

Assembling the Drive Side Flywheel on to the Gear Side, using Bolster No. 61–3589, Bridge Piece No. 61–3591 and Punch No. 61–3601 (Model C15).

Flywheel Truing Sleeve No. 61–3592 used with Drive Side bearing on "V" blocks No. 61–692 (Model C15).

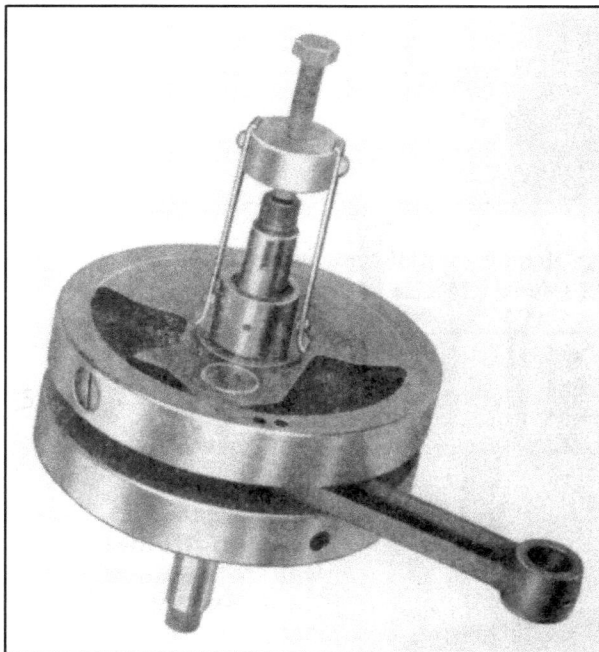

Removing the Gear Side Sleeve with Tool No. 61–3593 (Model C15).

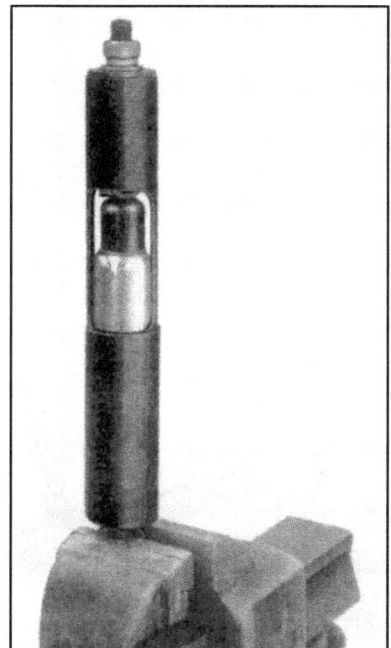

Dismantling the Rear Damper with Tool No. 61–3642 (for Models C15 and D7).

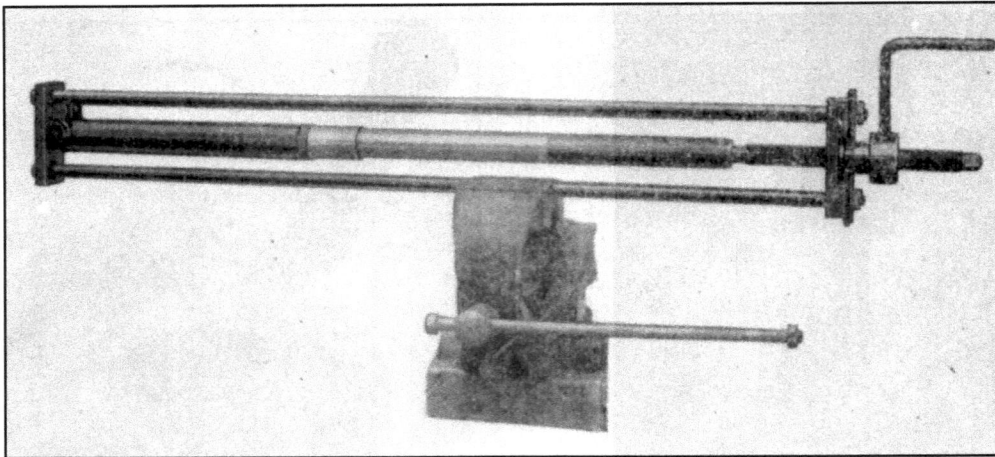

Withdrawing the Fork Main Member and Bushes from the Sliding Member using Tool No. 61–3587.

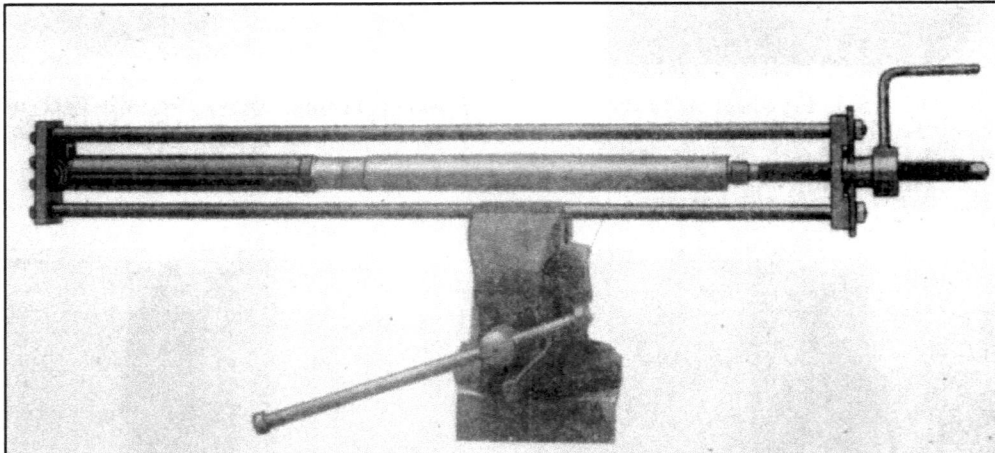

Reassembling the Fork Main Member, Sliding Member and Bushes using Tools No. 61–3587 and 61–3602 (Model C15).

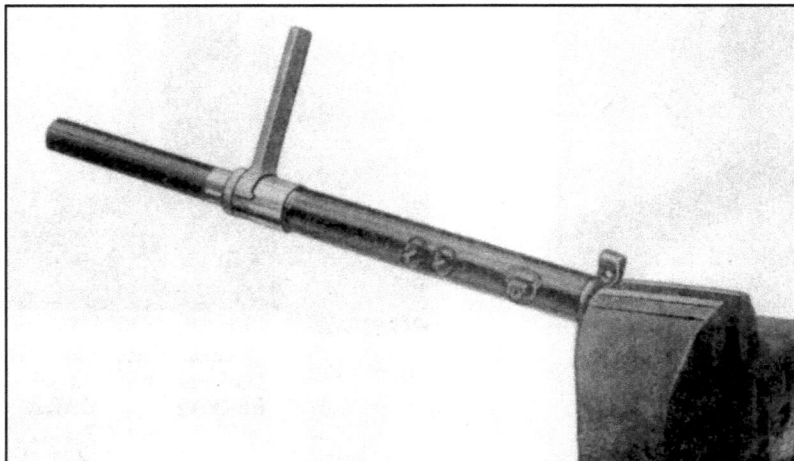

Removing the Fork Oil Seal Holder with "C" Spanner No. 61–3586 (Model C15).

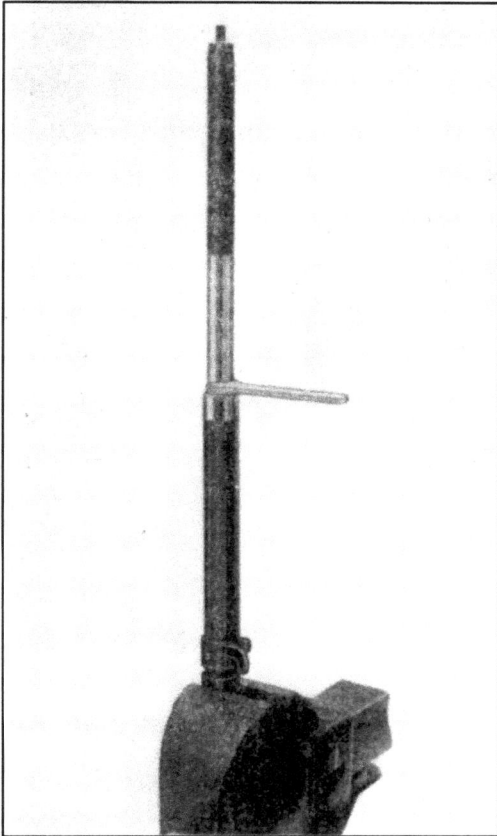

Taking off the Fork Leg Oil Seal Holder
with Tool No. 3633 (Model D7).

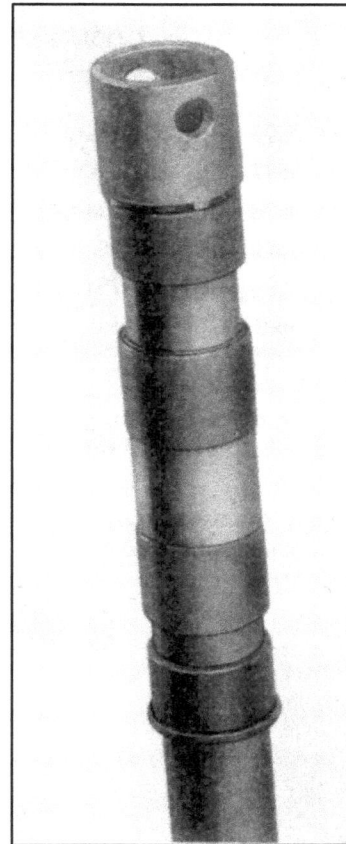

(Model C15).
Removing the Fork Leg
Bottom Nut with Dog Span-
ner No. 61–3606 (Tommy
Bar not supplied).

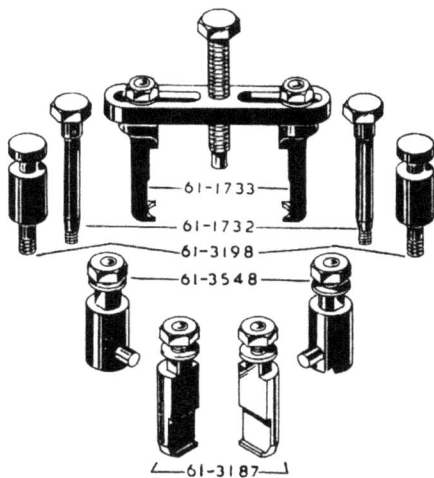

Pinion Extractor showing some of the
special Legs.

## PINION EXTRACTOR SETS

| | | | |
|---|---|---|---|
| A Group ... ... ... | | | Part No. 61–3676 |
| B and M Groups ... ... | | | Part No. 61–3677 |
| C Group (excepting C15) | | | Part No. 61–3678 |
| C15 ... ... ... ... | | | Part No. 61–3681 |
| D Group ... ... ... | | | Part No. 61–3679 |
| Dandy ... ... ... | | | Part No. 61–3680 |
| Complete Set ... ... | | | Part No. 61–3256 |

Details of comprising parts and applications are
given overleaf.

## COMPRISING PARTS OF EXTRACTOR SETS

61–3676 = 61–351 Plate, 61–776 Bolt, 61–1732 Leg (2), 61–3187 Leg (2), 61–3198 Leg (2).

61–3677 = 61–351 Plate, 61–776 Bolt, 61–1733 Leg (2).

61–3678 = 61–351 Plate, 61–776 Bolt, 61–1732 Leg (2), 61–1733 Leg (2), 61–3198 Leg (2).

61–3679 = 61–351 Plate, 61–776 Bolt, 61–3198 Leg (2).

61–3680 = 61–351 Plate, 61–776 Bolt, 61–3548 Leg (2).

61–3681 = 61–351 Plate, 61–776 Bolt, 61–3585 Leg (2), 61–3588 Leg (2).

These extractors are extremely useful for the removal of timing, worm or other gears, the legs being specially designed for the particular models.

They can also be used for other jobs of a like nature where a puller is required. All the legs are interchangeable and can be purchased separately if required.

## 61-358 GUDGEON PIN BUSH EXTRACTOR

is now cancelled and replaced by 61–3672.

This tool is now available for the individual models as detailed below:—

| Tool No. | Model | Comprising |
|---|---|---|
| 61–3651 | — | Holder, Rod and Nut only. |
| 61–3652 | A7, A10 ... ... | 61–3651, and Bushes 61–3319/20. |
| 61–3653 | B Group ... ... | 61–3651, and Bushes 61–3654/5. |
| 61–3656 | C10, C11, C12 ... | 61–3651, and Bushes 61–3657/8. |
| 61–3659 | C15, A7 (Steel Rod) | 61–3651, and Bushes 61–3660/1. |
| 61–3662 | D1, D3 ... ... | 61–3651, and Bushes 61–3663/4. |
| 61–3665 | D5, D7 ... ... | 61–3651, and Bushes 61–3666/7. |
| 61–3668 | M20, M21 ... ... | 61–3651, and Bushes 61–654/5. |
| 61–3669 | Dandy ... ... | 61–3651, and Bushes 61–3670/71. |

Using a piston
Ring Slipper
makes replace-
ment easier.

## Piston Ring Slippers (Terry).

Now available for the following models:—

| | | |
|---|---|---|
| 61–5004 | 55–60 mm. Bore | Models D1, D3. |
| 61–5051 | 60–65 mm. Bore | Models C10L, C11, C12, D5, D7. |
| 61–3682 | 65–70 mm. Bore | Models A Group, C15. |

## Additional Tools not illustrated

61–5035 valve grinding tool (Suction type). This tool is similar to 65–9240 shown on Service Sheet No. 711 but is suitable for valves with $\frac{3}{4}$ in. to 1 in. diameter heads.

61–3673 clutch nut screwdriver, designed specially for the moded C15.

# BSA SERVICE SHEET No. 712X

## ALL GROUPS
## FLYWHEEL BALANCING (STATIC)

*Revised and Reprinted October 1956.*
*Revised May 1958.*

Flywheel balancing should not be undertaken except by an expert mechanic, who is fully equipped with the tools described in this Service Sheet.

Unless very great care is exercised, excessive engine vibration may result from any change of balance, and unless extreme care is practised in flywheel drilling, flywheels may be seriously weakened.

All flywheel assemblies are accurately balanced before leaving the Works and there should be no need to re-balance when fitting new big end assemblies unless the difference in weight between the old and new assembly is more than 1 to 1¾ozs.

When a fabricated crankshaft is employed as on the "C", "B" and "M" Group models, the method of flywheel truing is described in Service Sheet No. 607 in the case of "M" group machines and No. 305 in the case of "B" group and No. 407 - 414 - 424 - 424A for "C" group machines.

The equipment required for balancing is a drilling machine and knife edge rollers (see Fig. X10) which must be set up perfectly horizontal and sufficiently high to allow the flywheels to revolve with the Con Rod hanging.

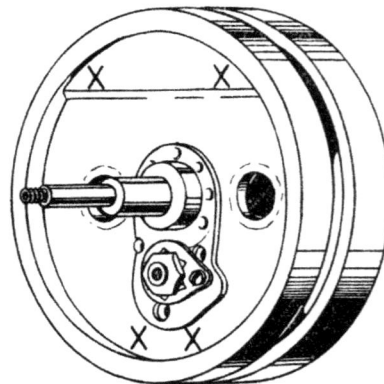

**X, DENOTES SUGGESTED DRILLING POINTS.**

Fig. X10.   Knife Edge Rollers.      Fig. X11.   "B" and "M" Group Flywheels.

For balancing purposes a small weight equivalent to part of the reciprocating weight must be attached to the small end of the Con Rod.   A table of these weights is given below.

Place the assembly on the knife edges and allow to revolve till it stops, mark the lowest spot with chalk and check again two or three times.

To find the amount of the out-of-balance apply plasticine to the rim of the wheels diametrically opposite the heaviest point until the wheels remain stationary when placed in any position.

The wheels must now be drilled at the heaviest spot to remove metal equal to the weight of plasticine.   Care must be taken to drill each wheel equally (see Fig. X11).

## BALANCING "A" GROUP FLYWHEELS.

A group flywheels are treated similarly to the single cylinder models except that the Con Rods are not fitted, a balance weight being attached to each crank pin. These are available as Service Tools, 61–3310 for A7, 61–3312 for A7 after Engine No. AA7–101, 61–3311 for A10 and 61–3497 for A10 Road Rocket. New bolts and nuts must be used to secure the flywheel and the ends of the bolts peined over after locking.

Drilling is carried out on the periphery of the flywheel instead of the webs and care must be taken to keep the holes central and not too deep, the maximum depth should not be more than 3/16″ (see Fig. X12). It is preferable to start with a smaller diameter hole which can be opened out if necessary, rather than a large diameter to then find that too much metal has been removed.

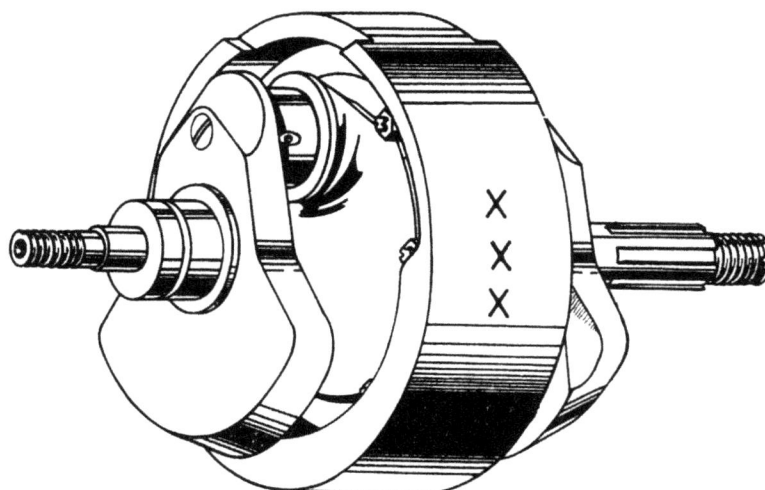

## X, DENOTES SUGGESTED DRILLING POINTS.

Fig. X12. "A" Group Crankshaft.

| Model | | | Weight attached | | | | Model | | Weight attached | | |
|---|---|---|---|---|---|---|---|---|---|---|---|
| A7 | ... | ... | ... | 2 @ | 19 ozs. | 10 drams | B32 Competition | ... | 5 ozs. | 4 drams |
| A7 after AA7–101 | | ... | 2 @ | 16 ozs. | 12 drams | B34 Competition | ... | 9 ozs. | 9 drams |
| A10 | ... | ... | ... | 2 @ | 18 ozs. | 10 drams | B32 Gold Star | ... | 6 ozs. | 5 drams |
| A10 Road Rocket | | ... | 2 @ | 19 ozs. | 8 drams | B34 Gold Star | ... | 11 ozs. | 4 drams |
| C Group | ... | ... | | 3 ozs. | 5 drams | M20 ... | ... | ... | 7 ozs. | |
| B31 | ... | ... | ... | | 4 ozs. | 6 drams | M21 ... | ... | ... | 5 ozs. | 10 drams |
| B33 and M33 ... | | ... | | 8 ozs. | 8 drams | | | | | |

Note :- Service Tool No. 61-3497 should be used on Crankshaft No. 67-1218 which is fitted to the Super Rocket and A10 machines after Eng. No. CA10R-4650 and DA10-101 respectively.

B.S.A. MOTOR CYCLES LIMITED, Service Dept., Birmingham, 11
*(PRINTED IN ENGLAND)*

# BSA SERVICE SHEET No. 805

*Reprinted June, 1960*

## All Models

## BATTERY — LEAD-ACID TYPES

The range of Lucas batteries listed here covers those models fitted to B.S.A. motor cycles in recent years.

PU5E and LVW5E Small capacity batteries for light-weight machines.

PU7E .. .. Standard battery for cradle mounting.

GU11E .. .. Larger capacity battery for sidecar machines.

SC7E .. .. Large capacity lightweight battery for machines fitted with starting motors or two-way radio equipment, e.g. police machines.

All current Lucas motor cycle batteries are 'dry charged', and do not require initial charging. Except that these batteries have porous rubber separators, they are identical with earlier models supplied wet or uncharged and require the same routine maintenance when in service.

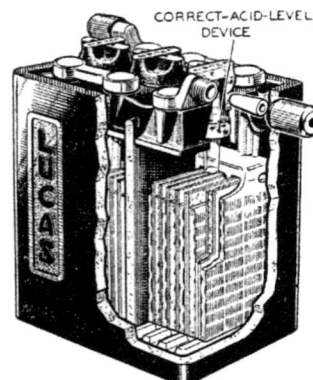

Fig. Y18. Sectioned battery, model PU7E/9

### STORAGE

Used batteries must be fully charged before storing. In temperate climates they should be examined fortnightly, or weekly in the case of model LVW5E and all models when stored in the tropics. If necessary, give them a short refreshing charge.

After a long period of storage, the condition of the battery will often improve if it is put through a 'cycle', as described on page 4.

### MAINTENANCE

Every fortnight, or more frequently in hot climates, examine the condition of the battery. Examine five-plate batteries every week.

Never use a naked light when examining the condition of the cells, as there is a danger of igniting the gas coming from the active materials.

### Cleaning

Remove the battery cover and clean the cell tops. Examine the connections. If they are loose or dirty, remove them and scrape the contact surfaces clean. Coat them with petroleum jelly before replacing.

Remove the filler plugs and check that the vent holes are clear and that the rubber washer fitted under some plugs is in good condition.

### Topping-up

During charging, water is lost by gassing and evaporation. Examine the electrolyte level in each cell and, if necessary, add distilled water to raise the electrolyte level with the top edges of the separators.

SC7E batteries have a woven glass pad fitted in each cell to reduce splashing when the battery is gassing during charging. When 'topping-up' this type of battery it is useful to note that the correct electrolyte level is reached when moisture appears through the porous glass pad.

## The Lucas Battery Filler

The use of a Lucas motor cycle Battery Filler will be found helpful in this 'topping-up' process, as it ensures that the correct electrolyte level is automatically attained and also prevents distilled water from being spilled over the battery top.

## Correct-Acid-Level-Devices

The correct-acid-level-device fitted to some Lucas batteries consists of a central tube with a perforated flange which rests on a ledge in the filling orifice.

Fig Y19. The Lucas battery filler

When 'topping-up' a battery fitted with these devices, pour distilled water round the flange (not down the tube) until no more drains through into the cell. This will happen when the electrolyte level reaches the bottom of the central tube and prevents further escape of air displaced by the 'topping-up' water. Lift the tube slightly to allow the small amount of water in the flange to drain into the cell. The electrolyte level will then be correct.

If a battery requires 'topping-up' too frequently, the voltage regulator (on machines fitted with d.c. generators) may be out of adjustment, i.e. set too high, and should be checked. Conversely, a persistently low state of charge may be due to a regulator being set too low.

If one cell in particular needs 'topping-up' more than another, it is likely the container is cracked, in which event replace the battery and clean the carrier, using a solution of ammonia or bi-carbonate of soda in water. After cleaning and drying, paint the battery carrier and other surfaces affected by the electrolyte with anti-sulphuric paint.

## TABLES OF SPECIFIC GRAVITIES AND CHARGING RATES

| Battery | Plates per cell | Amp. Hr. Capacity | | Electrolyte to fill one two-volt cell | | Home Trade and Climates Ordinarily below 90°F. (32°C.) Specific Gravity of Acid (corrected to 60°F.) | | Climates frequently over 90°F. (32°C.) Specific Gravity of Acid (corrected to 60°F.) | | Initial Charge Current | Re-charge Current |
|---|---|---|---|---|---|---|---|---|---|---|---|
| 1 | 2 | 3 | | 4 | | 5 | 6 | 7 | 8 | 9 | 10 |
| | | At 10 hour rate | At 20 hour rate | Pint | c.c. | Filling | Fully Charged | Filling | Fully Charged | Amp. | Amp. |
| LVW5E | 5 | 5 | 5.7 | 1/8 | 71 | 1.270 | 1.270–1.290 | 1.210 | 1.210–1.230 | 0.3 | 0.5 |
| PU5E | 5 | 8 | 9 | 1/6 | 94 | 1.270 | 1.270–1.290 | 1.210 | 1.210–1.230 | 0.6 | 1.0 |
| PU7E | 7 | 12 | 13.5 | 1/5 | 113 | 1.270 | 1.270–1.290 | 1.210 | 1.210–1.230 | 0.8 | 1.5 |
| GU11E | 11 | 20 | 22.8 | 1/3 | 189 | 1.270 | 1.270–1.290 | 1.210 | 1.210–1.230 | 1.3 | 2.2 |
| SC7E | 7 | 22.5 | 26 | — | 250 | 1.270 | 1.270–1.290 | 1.210 | 1.210–1.230 | 1.5 | 2.5 |

The maximum permissible electrolyte temperature during charging is given below. Should the temperature of the electrolyte exceed this value interrupt the charge and allow the battery temperature to fall at least 10°F. (5.5°C.) before charging is resumed.

| Climates normally below 80°F. (27°C.) | Climates between 80°–100°F. (27°–38°C.) | Climates frequently above 100°F. (38°C.) |
|---|---|---|
| 100°F. (38°C.) | 110°F. (43°C.) | 120°F. (49°C.) |

The specific gravity of the electrolyte varies with temperature. For convenience in comparing specific gravities, they are always corrected to 60°F., which is adopted as the reference temperature. The method of correction is as follows:

For every 5°F. *below* 60°F., *deduct* 0.002 from the observed reading to obtain the true specific gravity at 60°F. For every 5°F. *above* 60°F., *add* 0.002 to the observed reading to obtain the true specific gravity at 60°F.

The temperature must be that indicated by a thermometer having its bulb actually immersed in the electrolyte, and not the ambient temperature.

## SERVICING
### Battery Persists in Low State of Charge

First consider the conditions under which the battery is used. If the battery is subject to continuous discharge, e.g. long periods of night parking with lights on without suitable opportunities for recharging, a low state of charge is inevitable.

A fault in the dynamo or regulator, or neglect during a period out of commission, may also be responsible.

### Vent Plugs

See that the ventilating holes in each vent plug are clear, and that the rubber washer fitted under the plug is in good condition.

### Level of Electrolyte

The surface of the electrolyte should be level with the tops of the separators. If necessary, top-up with distilled water. Any loss of acid from spilling or spraying (as opposed to normal loss of *water* by evaporation) should be made good by dilute acid of the same specific gravity as that already in the cell.

### Cleanliness

See that the top of the battery is free from dirt or moisture which might provide a discharge path. Check that the battery connections are clean and tight.

### Hydrometer Tests

The space between each separator is not wide enough to permit the nozzle of an hydrometer to be inserted. Before taking a sample, tilt the battery to bring sufficient electrolyte above the separators. If the level of the electrolyte is so low that an hydrometer reading cannot be taken, no attempt should be made to take a reading after adding distilled water until the battery has been on charge for at least 30 minutes.

Measure the specific gravity of the acid in each cell in turn. The reading given by each cell should be approximately the same; if one cell differs appreciably from the others, an internal fault in that cell is indicated.

Specific gravity readings and their indications are as follows:

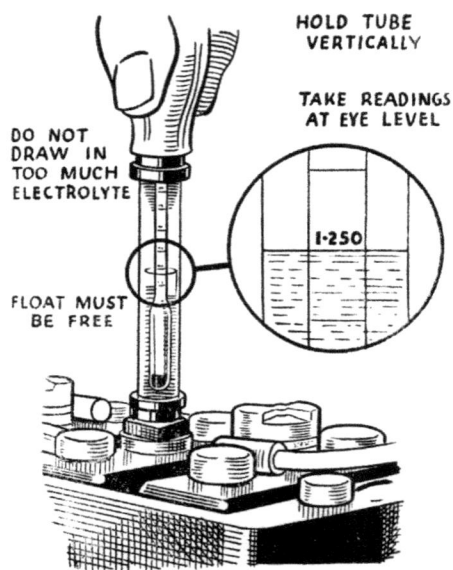

Fig Y20. Taking hydrometer readings

| Climates under 90°F. | | | | Climates over 90°F. |
|---|---|---|---|---|
| 1.270—1.290 | .. | Cell fully charged | .. | 1.210—1.230 |
| 1.190—1.210 | .. | Cell about half discharged | .. | 1.130—1.150 |
| 1.110—1.130 | .. | Cell fully discharged | .. | 1.050—1.070 |

The appearance of the electrolyte drawn into the hydrometer when taking a reading gives a useful indication of the state of the plates: if it is very dirty, or contains small particles in suspension, it is possible that the plates are in a bad condition.

### Discharge Test

Motor-cycle batteries must *not* be subjected to the heavy discharge test, as recommended for motor-car and commercial vehicle batteries.

## RECHARGING FROM AN EXTERNAL SUPPLY

If the hydrometer test indicates that the battery is merely discharged, and is otherwise in a good condition, it should be recharged, either on the motor-cycle by a period of daytime running, or on the bench from an external supply.

If the latter, the battery should be charged at the rate given in the table until the specific gravity and voltage show no increase over three successive hourly readings. During the charge the electrolyte must be kept level with the tops of the separators by the addition of distilled water.

A battery that shows a general falling-off in efficiency, common to all cells, will often respond to the process known as 'cycling'. This process consists of fully charging the battery by passing through it from an external source the appropriate re-charge current given in the table. The battery is then discharged by connecting to a lamp board, or other load, taking a current equal to the normal re-charge current. The battery should be capable of providing this current for at least 7 hours before it is fully discharged, as indicated by the voltage of each cell falling to 1.8. If the battery discharges in a shorter time, repeat the 'cycle' of charge and discharge.

## PREPARING BATTERIES FOR SERVICE

All new batteries are supplied without electrolyte but with the plates in a charged condition. When they are required for service it is only necessary to fill each cell with sulphuric acid of the correct specific gravity. No initial charging is required.

### Preparation of Electrolyte

The electrolyte is prepared by mixing together distilled water and concentrated sulphuric acid. The mixing must be carried out either in a lead-lined tank or in suitable glass or earthenware vessels. Slowly add the acid to the water, stirring with a glass rod. *Never add water to acid*, as the resulting chemical reaction causes violent and dangerous spurting of the concentrated acid. The specific gravity of the filling electrolyte depends on the climate in which the battery is to be used.

The approximate proportions of acid and water are indicated in the following table:

| To obtain Specific Gravity (corrected to 60°F.) of | Add 1 vol. of acid 1.835 S.G. (corrected to 60°F.) to |
|---|---|
| 1.270 | 2.8 vols. of water |
| 1.210 | 4.0 vols. of water |

Heat is produced by the mixture of acid and water, and the electrolyte should be allowed to cool before pouring it into the battery.

The total volume of electrolyte required can be estimated from the figures quoted in the table on page 2.

### Filling the Battery

Carefully break the seals in the cell filling holes and fill each cell with electrolyte to the top of the separators, *in one operation*. The temperature of the filling room, battery and electrolyte should be maintained between 60°F. and 100°F. If the battery has been stored in a cool place, it should be allowed to warm up to room temperature before filling.

### Putting into Use

Batteries filled in this way are 90 per cent charged. If time permits, however, a freshening charge of four hours at the normal recharge rate given in the table would be beneficial.

During the charge the electrolyte must be kept level with the top edge of the separators by the addition of distilled water. Check the specific gravity of the acid at the end of the charge; if 1.270 acid was used to fill the battery, the specific gravity should now be between 1.270 and 1.290; if 1.210, between 1.210 and 1.230.

### Maintenance in Service

After filling, the battery needs only the recommended attention.

B.S.A. MOTOR CYCLES LTD.
Service Dept., Waverley Works,
Birmingham, 10.
Printed in England.

JU/B5029

*Reprinted April, 1960*

## All Models

## LAMPS

### LUCAS LIGHTING

#### Headlamps

Although the headlamps fitted to individual models may vary in detail, they remain similar with regard to the general features described below. All headlamps are fitted with a double filament main bulb and a pilot bulb. One of the double filaments provides the main riding beam while the second, brought into operation by means of the dipper switch, provides the dipped beam.

On some models the headlamp incorporates a panel containing the ammeter and lighting switch but if a cowl is fitted then it carries these components externally to the headlamp shell.

Other headlamps contain wire wound resistances for the purpose of reducing the charging rates under certain conditions and these are described under the appropriate lighting circuit.

#### Setting and Focusing

The best way of checking the setting of the lamp is to park the motor cycle in front of a light coloured wall at a distance of about 25 feet. If necessary, slacken the bolts securing the headlamp and move the lamp until, with the main driving light switched on, the beam is projected straight ahead and parallel with the ground. With the lamp in this position, the height of the beam centre from the ground should be the same as the height of the centre of the headlamp from the ground.

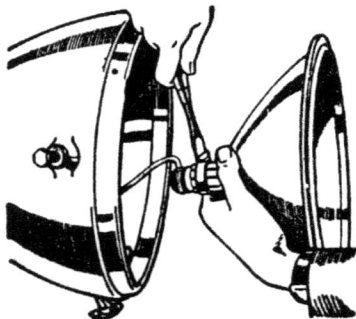

Fig. Y.22 Headlamp Focusing.

The headlamp must be focused so that, when the main driving light is switched on, a uniform beam without any dark centre is given. If the bulb needs adjusting, remove the lamp front and reflector, as described below, and slacken the bulb holder clamping clip at the back of the reflector. Move the bulb holder backwards and forwards until the correct position is obtained, and then tighten the clamping clip.

More sealed beam light units are fitted with the pre-focus type of bulb and therefore no focusing is necessary.

#### Removal of Front and Reflector, pre-1948 models

Press back the fixing clip at the bottom of the lamp. The front and reflector can now be taken off. The bulb holder is secured to the reflector by means of two fixing springs. When replacing the front, locate the top of the rim first, then press on at the bottom and secure with the fixing clip.

## 1948 Models (Fig. Y.23)

Press back the fixing clip at the bottom of the lamp, and remove the lamp front. The reflector is secured to the lamp body by means of a rubber bead. When refitting the rubber bead, locate its thinner lip between the reflector rim and the edge of the lamp body. To replace the front, locate the metal tongue in the slot at the top of the lamp, press the front on, and secure by means of the fixing catch.

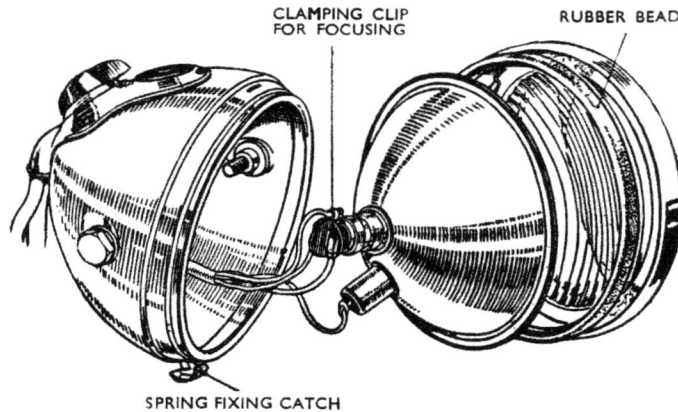

Fig. Y.23.

## Sealed Beam Headlamps

Later models are fitted with a sealed light unit having the reflector and glass sealed together. After slackening the securing screw on the top of the headlamp, the rim, complete with light unit, may be removed. To replace, locate the rim on the lip at the bottom of the lamp body, press the light unit assembly and rim into position and tighten the securing screw. The main headlamp bulb in some of these headlamps is of the pre-focus type and is held in position by a cap with bayonet type fitting. In all cases access to the main or pilot bulbs is obtained by removal of the light unit assembly.

Breakage of the headlamp glass with this type of unit involves replacement of the glass and reflector complete. The light unit may be removed from the headlamp rim after prising out the retaining clips.

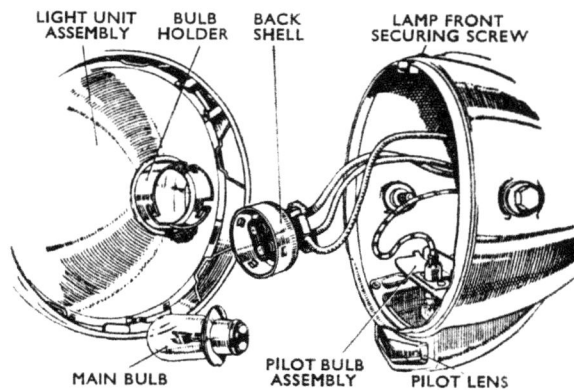

Fig. Y.24 Sealed Beam Unit.

## Replacement of Bulbs

When the replacement of a bulb is necessary, it is important not only that the same size bulb is fitted, but that it has a high efficiency and will focus in the reflector. Cheap and inferior replacement bulbs often have the filament of such a shape that it is impossible to focus correctly; for example, the filament may be to the one side of the axis of the bulb resulting in loss of range and light efficiency.

Lucas Genuine Spare Bulbs are specially tested to check that the filament is in the correct position to give the best results with Lucas lamps. To assist in identification, Lucas bulbs are marked on the metal cap with a number. When fitting a replacement. see that it has the same number as the original bulb.

B.S.A. Service Sheet No. 806 (cont.)

When fitting a main headlamp bulb, care must be taken to insert it the correct way round, i.e. with the dipped beam filament above the centre filament.

The pre-focus type bulb is located by a flange and there is a notch which engages on a raised portion of the bulb holder to ensure correct positioning.

Where the pilot bulb is contained in an underslung cowl, the metal strip on which the bulb is mounted should be pushed to the rear and lifted away in order to provide access to the bulb.

## Tail Lamps

Where the tail lamp is of the metal type the body or back should be removed by pushing it in, rotating to the left, and pulling away, thus providing access to the bulb. The moulded plastic type of rear lamp can be dismantled by unscrewing the two screws in the cover.

When a stop lamp is fitted, a two-filament type of bulb is employed with offset bayonet type fixing pins to ensure that it can only be fitted correctly.

## MAIN BULBS

### Models A7, A10, B31, 32, 33, 34, C12, C15 and M20, M21.

Lucas No. 168, 6v. 24/24w. (with E3H Dynamo). Lucas No. 169, 6v. 30/30w. (with E3L Dynamo). Lucas No. 312, 6v. 30/24w. (Pre-focus type Bulb).

### Models C10 and C11.

Lucas No. 180, 6v., 18/18w. (with E3H Dynamo). Lucas No. 168, 6v. 24/24w. (with E3L Dynamo).

### Models C11G and D1 (early) Lucas

Lucas No. 312, 6v. 30/24w. (Pre-focus type Bulb).

## PILOT

Lucas No. 200, 6v. 3w. Lucas No. 988, 6v. 3w. (with Sealed Beam Light Unit).

## TAIL

Lucas No. 205, 6v. 6w.
Lucas No. 384, 6v. 6/18w. (Stop/Tail Lamp).

B.S.A. MOTOR CYCLES LTD.
Service Dept., Waverley Works,
Birmingham, 10
Printed in England.

JU/B4780

# *BSA* SERVICE SHEET No. 807

*Reprinted June* 1960

**All Models**

## ELECTRIC HORN—HIGH FREQUENCY MODELS

### General

Electric horns are adjusted to give their best performance before leaving the Works, and will give long periods of service without any attention.

### Servicing

If the horn becomes uncertain in action or does not vibrate, it does not follow that the horn has broken down. The trouble may be due to a discharged battery or a loose or broken connection in the horn wiring.

The performance of the horn may be upset by the fixing bolt working loose, or by the vibration of some part adjacent to the horn. To check this, remove the horn from its mounting, hold it firmly in the hand by its bracket and press the push. If the note is still unsatisfactory, the horn may require adjustment, but this should only be necessary after a very long period of service.

### Method of Adjusting

The adjustment of a horn does not alter the characteristics of the note but merely takes up wear of vibrating parts.

If the horn is used repeatedly when badly out of adjustment, due usually to unsuccessful attempts at adjustment, the horn may become damaged, due to the excessive current which it will take. When testing, do not continue to operate the push if the horn does not sound. If, when the push is operated, the horn does not take any current (indicated by an ammeter connected in series with the horn) it is possible that the horn has been adjusted so that its contact breaker is permanently open.

After adjusting, note the current consumption, which must not exceed 3—4 amperes. A horn may give a good note, yet be out of adjustment and taking an excessive current. When adjusting do not attempt to unscrew the nut securing the tone disc or any other screw in the horn.

The adjustment is made by turning the adjustment screw, usually in a clockwise direction. The underside of the screw is serrated, and the screw must not be turned for more than 2 or 3 notches before re-testing. If the adjustment screw is turned too far in a clockwise direction, a point will occur at which the armature pulls in but does not separate the contacts.

ADJUSTING SCREW

Fig. Y26.
Typical electric horn, showing adjustment screw.

**B.S.A. Service Sheet No. 807 (contd.)**

Some models have no adjustment screw at the back of the horn. Adjustment is carried out by means of the grub screw and locking collar which are revealed upon removal of the large domed nut on the front of the horn. Take care that the large nut securing the sounding disc is not disturbed. The locking collar requires a special tool, or a large screwdriver with the blade ground so as to leave two projecting prongs, in order that it may be undone. No attempt should be made to loosen the collar without a proper tool as it is very tight and may become damaged so that it cannot be removed. The adjustment should be carried out in a similar manner to that described for the other type of horn, but the locking collar should be firmly tightened after each adjustment as this affects the note.

B.S.A. MOTOR CYCLES LTD.,
Service Dept., Waverley Works,
Birmingham, 10.
Printed in England.

# *BSA* SERVICE SHEET No. 808J

Revised April 1961.

## Models C15 and B40

### WIRING DIAGRAM.
(Positive Earth System)

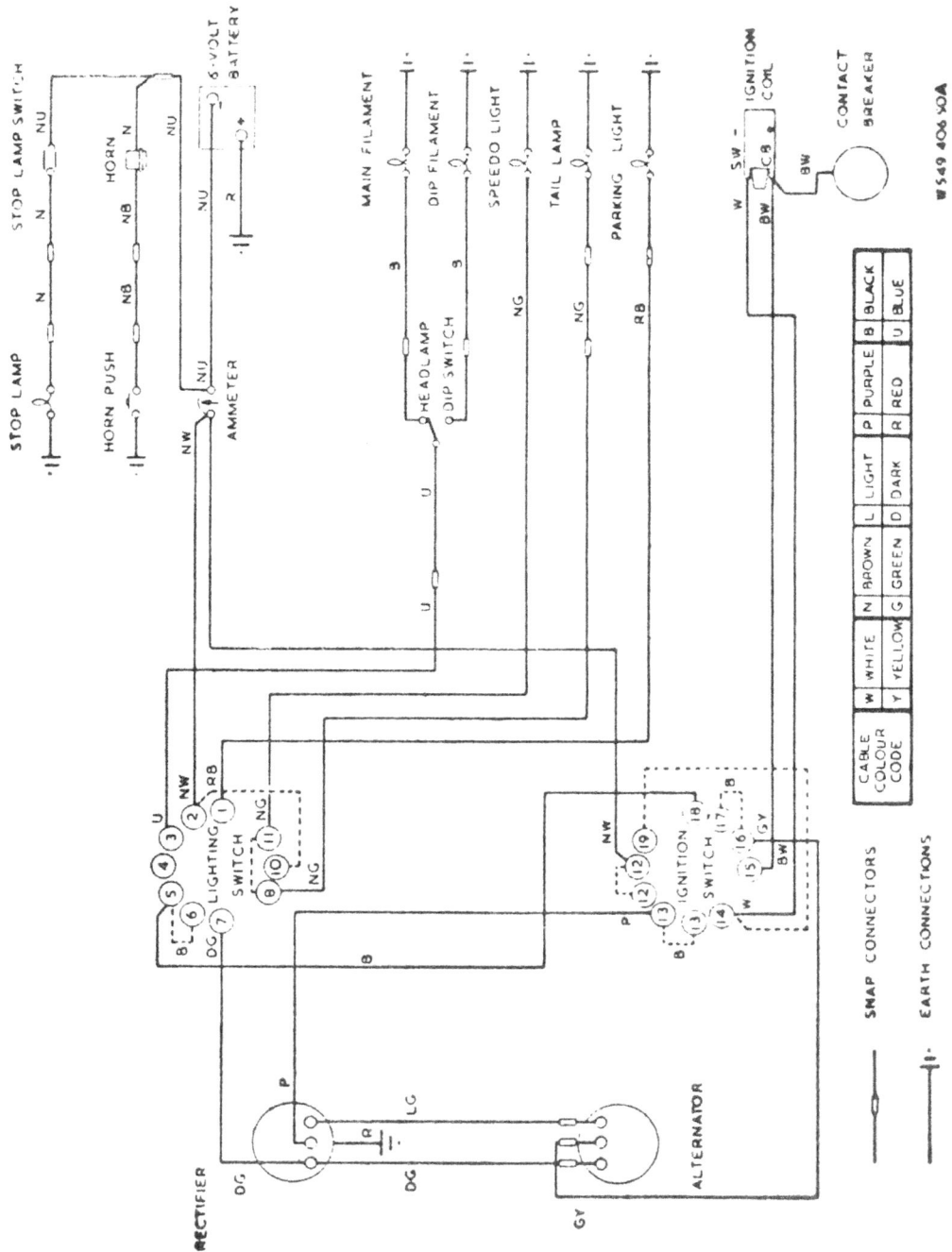

STOP LAMP SWITCH

6-VOLT BATTERY

HORN

MAIN FILAMENT

DIP FILAMENT

SPEEDO LIGHT

TAIL LAMP

PARKING LIGHT

IGNITION COIL

CONTACT BREAKER

W549 406 XOA

STOP LAMP

HORN PUSH

AMMETER

HEADLAMP

DIP SWITCH

LIGHTING SWITCH

IGNITION SWITCH

RECTIFIER

ALTERNATOR

| CABLE COLOUR CODE | | | | |
|---|---|---|---|---|
| W | WHITE | N | BROWN | L | LIGHT | P | PURPLE | B | BLACK |
| Y | YELLOW | G | GREEN | D | DARK | R | RED | U | BLUE |

SNAP CONNECTORS

EARTH CONNECTIONS

133

# Models C15T and C15S

## WIRING DIAGRAM

W549 43594

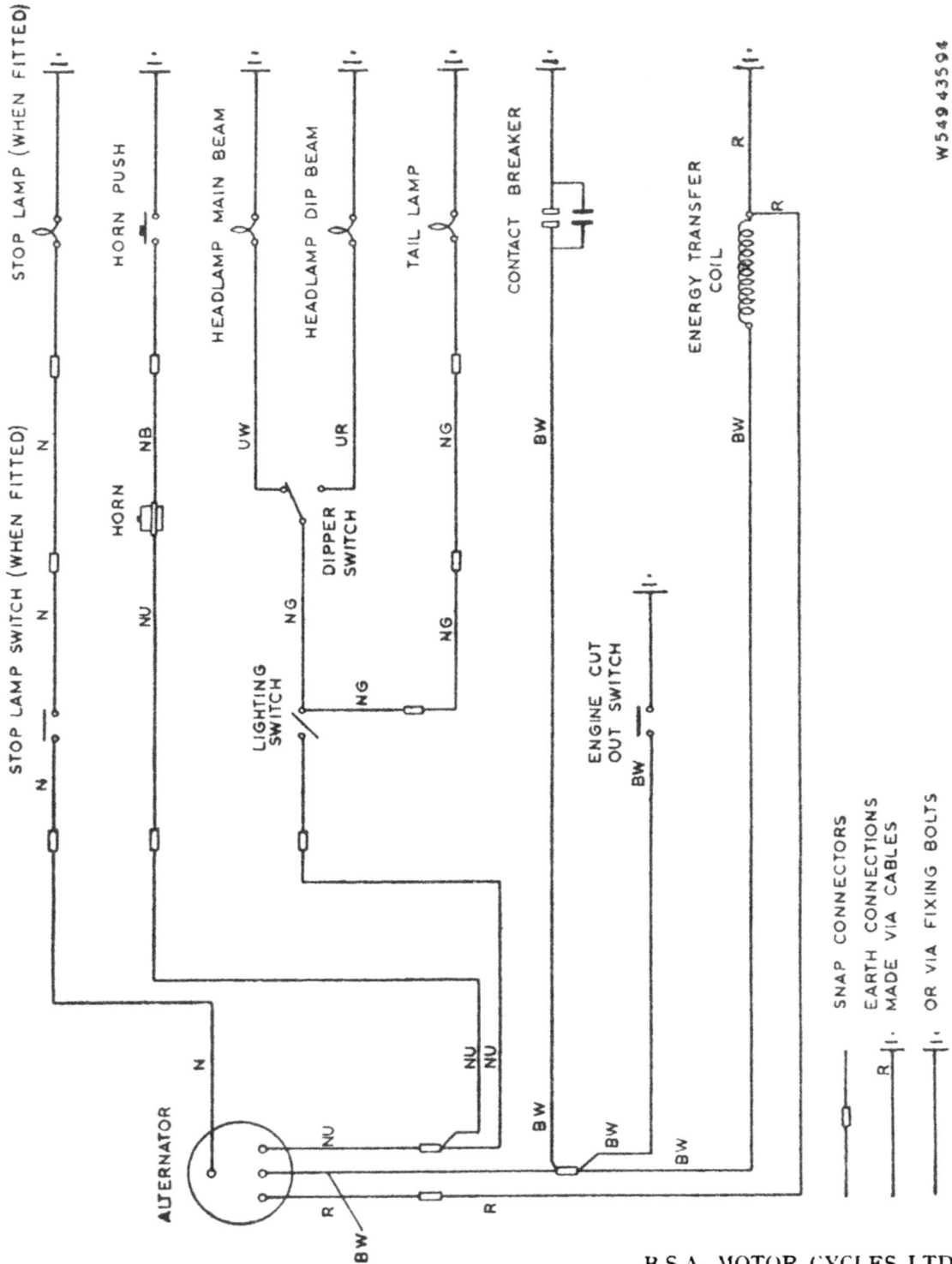

STOP LAMP (WHEN FITTED)

HORN PUSH

HEADLAMP MAIN BEAM

HEADLAMP DIP BEAM

TAIL LAMP

CONTACT BREAKER

ENERGY TRANSFER COIL

STOP LAMP SWITCH (WHEN FITTED)

HORN

LIGHTING SWITCH

DIPPER SWITCH

ENGINE CUT OUT SWITCH

ALTERNATOR

SNAP CONNECTORS

EARTH CONNECTIONS MADE VIA CABLES

OR VIA FIXING BOLTS

B.S.A. MOTOR CYCLES LTD.
Service Dept., Armoury Road, Birmingham, 11.
Printed in England.

# *BSA* SERVICE SHEET No. 813

## "C" AND "B" GROUP MODELS (EXCEPT C15 COMPETITION)
## FITTED WITH CRANKSHAFT MOUNTED ALTERNATORS

### LUCAS LIGHTING

The electrical system used on these models provides D.C. for the battery, ignition coil and lights, by passing the A.C. output of the generator through a bridge type rectifier.

The alternator is connected to a section of the headlamp switch so that the output is automatically matched to the demands of the lighting circuit and the characteristics of the alternator prevent overcharging.

"C" Group except C15

| Cable Colours |
| --- |
| Light Green |
| Dark Green |
| Middle Green or Green/Yellow |

"B" Group & C15

| Cable Colours |
| --- |
| Green/Black or Dark Green |
| Green/Yellow |
| Green/White or Light Green |

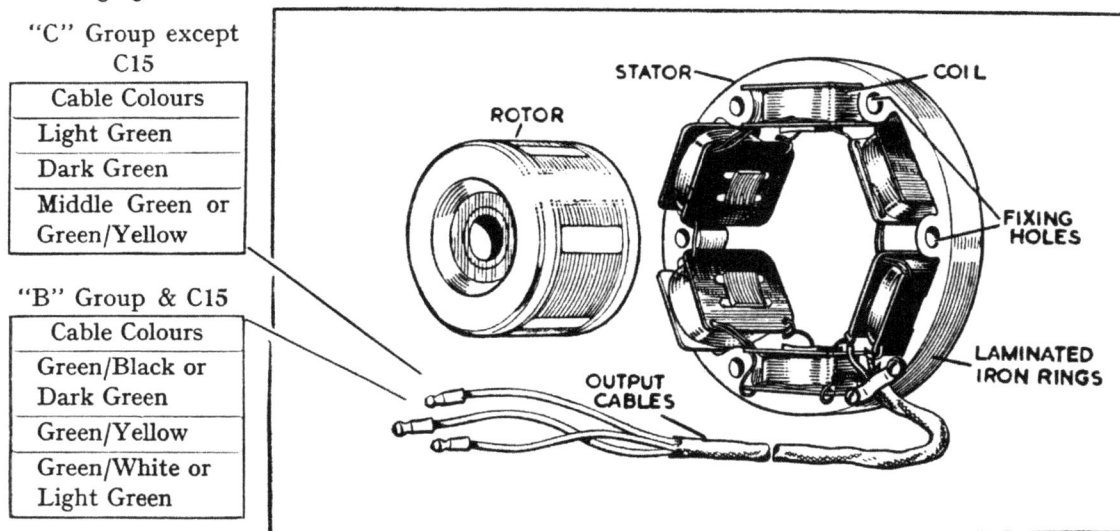

Stator and Rotor of Lucas Motor Cycle Alternator
(RM 13 on C11G and C15, RM 13/15 on C12, and RM 15 on new series "B" group machines)

### Output Control

The standard circuit has the output wires from the generator connected by their snap connectors to similarly coloured wires on the wiring harness and provides the following output control.

### Lighting Switch in "OFF" Position

The output is taken from one pair of coils by means of the Light Green and Dark Green wires, and the remaining coils (Light Green and Middle Green wires) (Light Green and Green/Yellow on "B" group) are open-circuited.

### Lighting Switch in "PILOT" Position

Output taken from one pair of coils by Light Green and Dark Green wires as before and the remaining coils are on open-circuit.

### Lighting Switch in "HEAD" Position

All three pairs of coils are connected in parallel and the maximum output is obtained. Note.—To provide an increased charging rate with the lighting switch in the "OFF" position, some models will be found to have the wire joining terminals 5 and 6 of the headlamp switch removed. This means that no coils are shorted out in this switch position and the charging rate is slightly increased.

In circumstances where a considerable amount of low speed running is necessary or there are long periods of parking with the lights on, it is possible to increase the charging rate with the lighting switch in the "OFF" and "PILOT" positions by connecting the Medium Green alternator cable (Green/Yellow for C15) by its snap connector to the Dark Green harness cable and the Dark Green alternator cable to the Medium Green harness cable (Green/Yellow for C15).

The Light Green cables should not be disturbed. These alternative connections considerably increase the charging rate in these switch positions, and the connections should be returned to standard for normal conditions of use or long runs.

Owing to the effects of the above modifications it is essential that the wiring circuit is returned to standard before checking the charging rates during fault finding.

### Emergency Starting

With the ignition switch in the "EMG" position, the battery is not isolated from the alternator and will, in fact, receive a charge whilst the machine is being run.

This arrangement is also a safeguard against continuous running in the "EMG" position. The back pressure of the battery will increase as it is charged, until it is sufficiently strong to affect the working of the ignition system. When this happens misfiring will occur, resulting in poor engine performance. In view of this, always check that the machine is not being run with the ignition switch continually in the "EMG" position, before testing the system for other faults.

### Motor Cycle Trials Events, etc.

When using the machine for trials riding, the alternator can be used continuously in the "EMG' position without a battery, providing the lead from the main harness to the battery negative terminal is earthed to the machine, but contact breaker points are liable to become badly burned.

### Test Procedure

As the lights and other equipment are operated on a normal D.C. circuit they can be checked by normal continuity tests with a battery and bulb.

The following equipment is required to satisfactorily test the charging circuit. The meters used should be accurate moving coil instruments.

A.C voltmeter scale 0–15 volts.
D.C. ammeter scale 0–15 amps.
D.C. voltmeter scale 0–15 volts.

1 ohm. load resistance.
12 volt battery and 36 watt bulbs.

When checking the alternator output the engine should be run at approximately 3,000 r.p.m.

If the performance of the alternator has proved unsatisfactory, it is advisable to first check the wiring to make sure that good contact is being made at the various connections and that none of the wiring of alternator coils are shorting to the frame.

## CHECKING D.C. INPUT TO BATTERY

**Test 1.** Ammeter connected in series with main lead and battery.

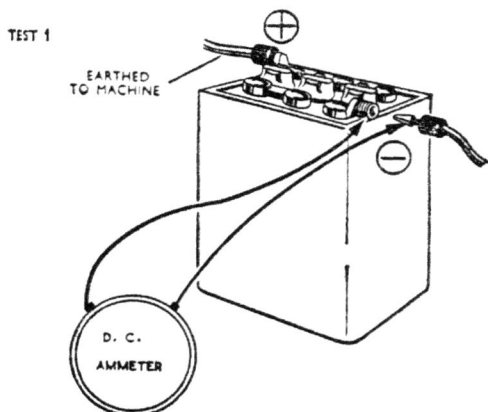

**Test 2.** Disconnect main lead from battery. Connect 1 ohm resistor in place of battery. Feed ignition coil separately from battery. Turn ignition switch to IGN position.

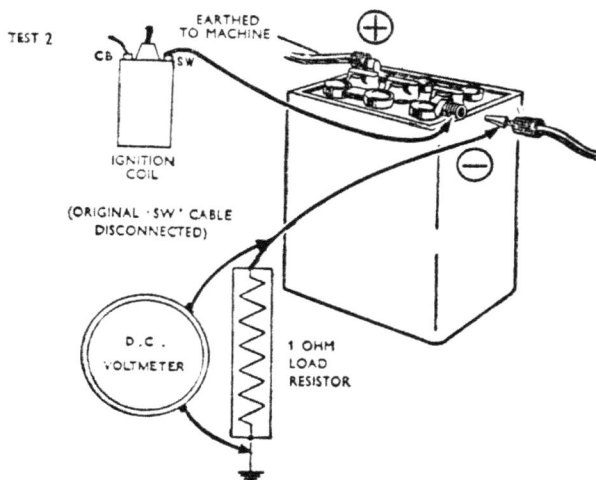

If the battery is in poor condition or low state of charge use Test 2.

| Test | Switch Position | Reading Amps. at 3,000 r.p.m. | | |
|------|-----------------|------|---------|------|
| | | RM13 | RM13/15 | RM15 |
| **1** | OFF | 1.5 (min.) | 1.75 (min.) | 2.5 (min.) |
| | PILOT | 0.5 (min.) | 0.75 (min.) | 1.5 (min.) |
| | HEAD | 0.25 (min.) | 0.5 (min.) | 2.5 (min.) |

| Test | Switch Position | Reading Volts at 3,000 r.p.m. | | |
|------|-----------------|------|---------|------|
| | | RM13 | RM13/15 | RM15 |
| **2** | OFF | 1.5 (min.) | 1.75 (min.) | 2.5 (min.) |
| | PILOT | 1.5 (min.) | 1.75 (min.) | 2.0 (min.) |
| | HEAD | 3.0 (min.) | 3.25 (min.) | 3.0 (min.) |

**Conclusion from these Tests**

**Test 1.** If meter readings are as stated, the charging circuit and alternator are satisfactory.
No reading; check the generator.
A low reading can be caused by a faulty battery.
Proceed with Test 2. If readings still low check battery with hydrometer and discharge tester.

**Test 2.** If meter readings are lower or higher than values stated, check the generator.
No reading on meter; check the rectifier.

**Important**

Inaccurate readings can be due to faulty wiring, bad connections at the snap connectors or poor earths. Make a quick visual check of all connections before proceeding with the tests.

Remember it is no use carrying out Test 1 if the battery is faulty or in a low state of charge; if in doubt proceed with Test 2.

# Testing the RM13 Alternator on the Machine, using an A.C. Voltmeter and 1 Ohm Load Resistor

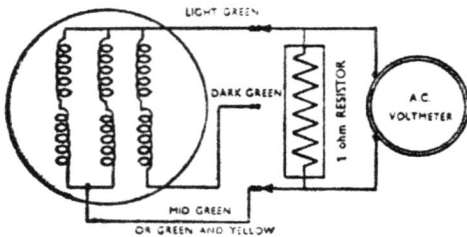

| Test | Voltmeter and Resistor Connected Across | Reading Volts at 3,000 r.p.m. | | |
|---|---|---|---|---|
| | | RM13 | RM13/15 | RM15 |
| 1 | Dark Green and Light Green | 3.0 (min.) | 3.25 (min.) | 4.25 (min.) |
| 2 | Light Green and Mid Green or Green/Yellow | 6.0 (min.) | 6.25 (min.) | 6.75 (min.) |
| 3 | Dark Green and Light Green (with Mid Green or Green/Yellow connected to Dark Green). | 8.5 (min.) | 8.75 (min.) | 9.25 (min.) |
| 4 | Any one lead and Generator Stator (Earth) | No Reading | No Reading | No Reading |

**Conclusions from these Tests.**

Low reading on any group of coils indicates shorted turns.

Zero reading will indicate open circuit coil.

If all coils read low, partial de-magnetisation of rotor may have occured as a result of faulty rectifier. Check rectifier, and battery earth polarity before replacing rotor.

A reading between any one lead and the generator stator indicates an earthed coil. Replace stator or locate earth by isolating and testing individual coils.

**Note.**

With the engine running at 3,000 r.p.m. (approx.) the output voltages are steady, and even if the engine is running a few r.p.m. faster or slower the values stated will be obtained from a good generator.

# Rectifier—Bench Testing

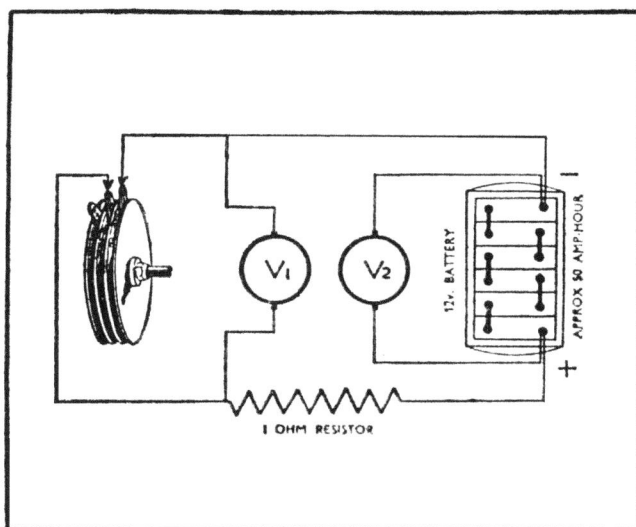

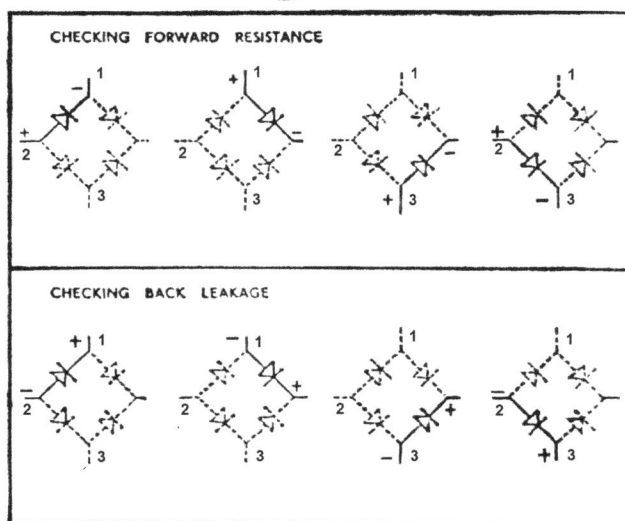

V1—will measure the volt drop across the rectifier plate.

V2—must be checked when testing the rectifier plate, to make certain the supply voltage is the recommended 12 volts on load.

### It is essential that the supply is kept at 12 volts for these Tests.

**Forward Resistance Test**

**Test 1.** Connect test leads in turn to terminals 2 and 1, bolt and 1, bolt and 3, 2 and 3. Reading in all positions should not be greater than 2.5 volts. Keep the testing time as short as possible to avoid overheating the rectifier cell. **Note.**—If the later type of rectifier, which has no terminal markings, is fitted, the same test procedure is followed. The same voltage values also apply.

**Back Leakage Test**

**Test 2.** Proceed as for Test 1, and test each cell in turn, but reverse the test leads. Reading on V1 should not be less than 2 volts below the open-circuit reading on voltmeter No. 2, i.e., 10 volts.

**Conclusion from these Tests**

**Test 1.** If the voltage reading on V1 is more than 2.5 volts, on any cell, it is aged and the rectifier should be replaced.

**Test 2.** If the voltage reading on V1 is less than 10 volts, on any cell, the rectifier is shorted and should be replaced.

**Important**

Before fitting a replacement rectifier check the following points:—

1. Check that battery is correctly connected, **Positive to Earth.**
2. Check rectifier visually for signs of damage.

**Never** disturb the tension of the nut which holds the elements together on the through bolt. The efficiency of the rectifier depends upon the correct tension of the plates. The tension of the nut is set before leaving the works, and cannot be adjusted correctly in service.

# Checking Rectifier in Position on Machine

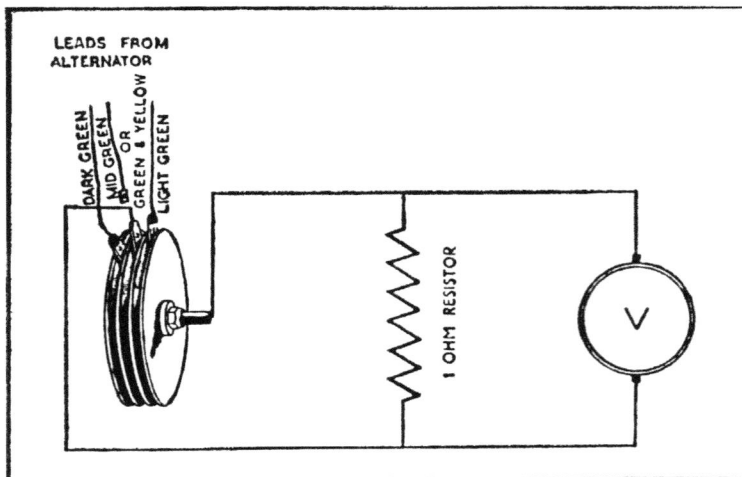

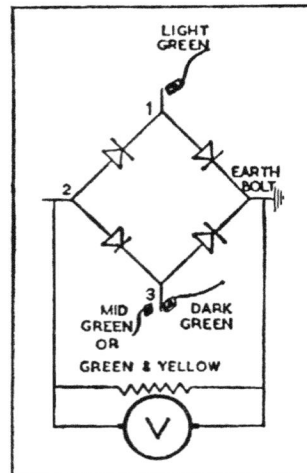

| Voltmeter and Resistor Connected Across | Reading with Leads Connected as Shown |
|---|---|
| Terminal No. 2 (or centre terminal on latest type) and frame of machine | 6.5 (min.) RM13 <br> 7.0 (min.) RM13/15 <br> 7.75 (min.) RM15 |

## Procedure

Connect the alternator leads as detailed direct to the rectifier terminals No. 1 and No. 3.

(**Note.**—On the latest type rectifiers the terminals are not numbered, so connect the alternator leads to the outer cranked terminals).

Connect the test leads which must have a D.C. voltmeter with 1 ohm load shunted across, between earth (frame of machine) and terminal No. 2 (centre terminal on latest type rectifier) when the values stated should be obtained with engine running at 3,000 r.p.m.

## Conclusions from these Tests

If the alternator passes its individual test, but it fails on this test it indicates that either the rectifier is faulty or it is not properly earthed.

Connecting the test leads to the centre bolt will eliminate the possibility of faulty earth connection

# Testing the External Wiring Circuit

### Using D.C. Voltmeter only

1. All cables, including battery, to be connected as normal.
2. Connect voltmeter Red test lead to earth.

### Testing Charging Circuit through Ignition Switch

3. Connect Black test lead to No. 2 terminal on rectifier.
4. Switch ignition to IGN position.
5. Battery volts, i.e., six, should register on voltmeter.
6. If there is zero reading on voltmeter in the above condition, check circuit back through ignition switch, ammeter, etc., to the battery.

### Testing Emergency Start Circuit (Single Cylinder Machine)

7. Connect Red test lead to earth.
8. Connect Black test lead to C.B. terminal on ignition contact breaker.
9. Open ignition contacts.
10. Switch ignition switch to EMG position.
11. Battery volts should register on voltmeter.
12. Transfer Black test lead to alternator Mid-Green lead.
13. Battery volts should register on voltmeter.

### Note

These tests are to be carried out in the case of "No Charge" or "No Emergency Start" if previous tests have been carried out and all is in order.

It is important that both the ignition timing and the rotor timing is correct for efficient operation of Emergency Start.

# Testing the 'Low,' 'Medium' and 'High' Charge Positions

### Using D.C. Voltmeter only

1. Connect Red test lead to earth.
2. The set, including battery connected as normal, with the exception of the alternator Middle Green cable which should be disconnected at the snap connector under the saddle
3. Connect Black test lead to Mid-Green cable coming from headlamp (i.e., not coming from alternator).
4. With ignition switch in IGN position and lighting switch OFF.
5. A low voltage (i.e., 1—2) should register on voltmeter.
6. With lighting switch in PILOT, zero voltage should register on voltmeter.
7. With lighting switch in HEAD position a low voltage should register on voltmeter.

### Note

Incorrect switching of these cables will cause incorrect charging rates, i.e., failure of Mid-Green and Dark Green linking together in HEAD position will result in a low charge rate with headlight switched on.

In the case of incorrect switching it is necessary to check the wiring and the switch for correct connections, etc.

## B.S.A. SERVICE SHEET No. 813 (contd.)

### Headlamp Switch

If both the rectifier and alternator appear satisfactory the wiring and switch contacts must be checked most carefully to eliminate any possible faults. The correct headlamp switch connections are shown in Service Sheets.

| | | |
|---|---|---|
| No. 808D ... | ... | C12 |
| No. 808C ... | ... | C11G |
| No. 808H ... | ... | "B" models |
| No. 808J ... | ... | C15 |

### Alternator Romoval and Replacement

The procedure for removing and replacing the alternator is described in Service Sheets No. 314 for "B" group machines and 409 for C11G and C12, and No. 422 for C15. Note that the stator should be assembled with the clip retaining the output cables on the side of the stator next to the engine on C11G and C12 but on C15 and "B" group machines the clip should be on the side away from the engine

**B.S.A. MOTOR CYCLES LTD.,**
Service Department, Armoury Road, Birmingham, 11
Printed in England.

# *BSA* SERVICE SHEET No. 813B

## C15 COMPETITION MODEL
## ALTERNATOR AND "ENERGY TRANSFER" SYSTEM
## INTRODUCTION AND SERVICE TESTING PROCEDURE

### INTRODUCTION

To cater for special machines such as the C15 Competition, which is a high-performance competition and trials machine, Lucas engineers have developed a special RM13 type alternator and "energy transfer" ignition coil. The alternator windings comprise of two sets of series connected coils, one set for direct lighting when this is required, the other set of coils being connected purely for ignition purposes. The alternator and ignition coil are similar in operation to a magneto whilst retaining the physical characteristics of the conventional coil ignition system namely, separate ignition coil and contact breaker, and are designed for continuous use without a battery in circuit; this is particularly advantageous in competition work.

### 'ENERGY TRANSFER" IGNITION

**Working Principles.**—The main feature of an "energy transfer" ignition system is that the ignition coil primary is connected *in parallel* with the contact breaker points, whereas in the conventional coil ignition circuit the primary winding and contact breaker are connected in series. In practice this means that the current generated in the alternator ignition coils can flow direct to earth through the contact points, when these are closed, but when they are open its alternative path to earth is *via* the ignition coil primary. The sequence of events which, of course, takes place at high speeds, due to the action of the contact breaker, is as follows.

With the contact breaker points closed, the ignition generating coils of the alternator, one end of which is permanently connected to the frame of the machine, are in effect short-circuited causing heavy currents to circulate in them. When the contact breaker points open the short-circuit effect is removed and the built-up energy circulated in the generating coils is rapidly transferred to the primary of the ignition coil. The effect of this "high energy" pulse in the ignition primary is to induce a high voltage in the secondary winding which, in turn, is transmitted through the high-tension cable to the sparking plug. The contact breaker is arranged to open only at peak instants in the A.C. generating cycle, to ensure that maximum energy is available for ignition purposes.

Another feature worth noting is that the "energy transfer" system operates on a rising current in the ignition coil primary, and not as in the conventional coil ignition system, on a falling current in the primary winding.

### GENERAL DESCRIPTION

**Stator.**—Wound with four coils only. Two series connected coils are used for ignition purposes being permanently connected across an "energy transfer" coil model 2E.T. Diametrically opposite are two coils, similarly connected, of a slightly heavier gauge wire, for use when direct lighting is required; these will supply sufficient current for a 6-volt 24/24 watt headlamp bulb together with a 6-volt 3 watt or 6-volt 6 watt tail lamp bulb, i.e. 27/30 watt.

As with previous models of the RM13, three wires are brought out from the stator for connecting to the external circuit. One end of the LIGHT GREEN or RED lead is earthed to the frame of the machine, the other end is connected to both the lighting and ignition coils. The DARK GREEN or BROWN/BLUE lead is connected to the lighting switch, when lighting is used, and the GREEN/YELLOW or BLACK/WHITE lead is connected to the contact breaker and primary of the "energy transfer" coil.

**Rotor.**—The rotor is a standard RM13 unit, but when keyed on to the model C15 Competition crankshaft the magneto timing differs from that of the standard C15.

**Contact Breaker Cam.**—A special short open-period (30°) cam has been designed for use with this alternator to ensure that the maximum of efficiency is obtained from the 2E.T. "energy transfer" ignition coil to give the high performance characteristic required with this type of competition machine.

**2E.T. "Energy Transfer" Ignition Coil.**—The 2E.T. has been specially designed for use in 'energy transfer' ignition systems. It employs a closed iron circuit and a primary winding whose, impedance is closely matched with that of the alternator ignition generating coils, resulting in a high performance characteristic, particularly for starting.

## SERVICE NOTES

**Converting from Standard to Competition Engine.**—The model C15 Competition machine has several engine features which differ from those of the standard machine. A special cylinder head and camshaft, etc., are incorporated in the design. Merely fitting a competition alternator and "engine transfer" ignition coil to a standard machine, and advancing the ignition timing will not bring it up to the competition specification. To achieve this the necessary engine parts will also have to be replaced. Also, advancing the ignition in trying to reach competition performance may seriously damage a standard engine.

If a conversion is contemplated a B.S.A. Agent should be approached for the relevant engine conversion details.

**Timing.**—It is very important that care is taken when timing, for ignition purposes, a machine fitted with this special RM13 and "energy transfer" ignition system. The C15 Competition has been designed as a high performance machine, for use in competition and trials work and therefore the ignition timing, on which the high performance is very dependant, must be accurately set. Remember, it is not only the piston/spark timing relationship which is involved but also the "magneto" performance (spark energy) of the alternator. This will be appreciated more fully when it is remembered that, as the rotor of the alternator is keyed to the engine crankshaft, which in turn is coupled through the connecting rod to the piston, any movement of the piston during the timing procedure will affect the position of the crankshaft and hence the magnetic timing position of the rotor.

In other words the maximum alternator "magneto" performance can only be obtained when the piston is accurately set to the timing position recommended by the manufacturer (12° B.T.D.C.), engine fully retarded.

## SYSTEMATIC FAULT LOCATION

The following notes recommend the procedure to be adopted in the event of trouble developing with the equipment.

**1. Engine Fails to Start**

1. Remove the high-tension lead connected to the sparking plug and hold it approximately $\frac{1}{8}$ in. from the engine cylinder block. The gap should spark at normal "kick-start" speed. If it does check that plug gap is correct to manufacturers recommendation, if plug electrodes are worn or insulation cracked, plug should be replaced. Re-connect high-tension lead to plug and again check for sparking with plug resting on cylinder head. If plug gap sparks refit and proceed to check fuel supply, carburation, etc.

    NOTE:—It is essential that the correct plug gap is maintained—a wider gap will cause difficult starting or perhaps failure to start. Accurate timing is also a critical factor in starting, the correct setting is 12° B.T.D.C., engine fully retarded.

If there is no spark, or if engine still cannot be started, proceed to check ignition system as follows:—

2. Check that contact breaker gap is correctly set, the gap should be maintained at .014—.016 in. Check the capacitor by substitution.

3. Place a piece of dry card between contact breaker points. Disconnect the ignition feed from the harness, and using a 2-volt cell of a 6-volt or 12-volt battery, with an ammeter in series, check the ignition coil primary for continuity. The primary winding has a resistance of approximately 0.5 ohms; the reading on the meter should not be more than 4 amp. An excessive reading indicates shorted turns whilst no reading will indicate open-circuit or earthed turns. In either event a replacement coil should be fitted.

If coil proves to be satisfactory, proceed to check the alternator ignition coils as follows:—
Remove rotor and

4. Connect the 2-volt battery and ammeter across the alternator ignition coil feed and earth (frame of machine). The resistance of the coils is approximately 4 ohms and the meter reading should be approximately 0.5 amp.

An excessive reading indicates shorted turns whilst no reading will indicate open-circuit or earthed turns. In either event a replacement coil or stator is required.

NOTE:—This test must be done as quickly as possible to avoid damage to coils through overheating and misleading readings due to increase in coil resistance with temperature rise. It will be found that two to three seconds duration gives ample time to observe the ammeter readings.

*On no account should this test be made with the rotor in position, otherwise partial demagnetisation will result.*

If after carrying out the above tests the engine will not start even though the stator windings, ignition coil, etc., are satisfactory, remagnetise the rotor or check by substitution as it may have become partially demagnetised, resulting in a low ouput performance.

2. **Engine Difficult to Start or Runs Intermittently**

If after checking as detailed in (1:1) and (1:2), trouble still persists, it will be necessary to proceed as laid down in (1:3) and (1:4).

3. **No Lights with Lighting Switch in Head or Dip Position, and Engine Running**

5. First check for burnt out filaments by substitution.
Check wiring and connections between headlamp and lighting switch, alternator and switch, rectifying as necessary.

Check continuity of lighting switch.

NOTE:—Poor earth connections can be particularly troublesome, and will cause high voltages which reduce bulb life. Burnt-out or blackened bulbs often indicate the existence of bad earths, which should be rectified before fitting new bulbs. This point about earth connections particularly concerns the competition alternator as the earthed side of both the lighting and ignition coils is brought out and connected externally to the frame of the machine. A bad connection at this earth point will, if allowed to persist, result in damage to the contact break points as well as to the bulbs.

If the lights will not work after carrying out the above procedure and bulbs, wiring and switch, etc., have proved satisfactory, check the alternator lighting coils as follows:—

6. With the 2-volt battery and ammeter connected across the lighting coil feed and earth (frame of machine), the meter should reaad pproximately 6½ amps. An excessive reading will indicate shorted turns, no reading will indicate an open-circuit or earthed tuins. In either event a replacement coil or stator is required.

**B.S.A. Service Sheet No. 813B (contd.)**

NOTE:—This test must be done as quickly as possible to avoid damage to coils through over-heating, and misleading readings due to increase in coil resistance with temperature rise. It will be found that two to three seconds duration gives ample time to observe the ammeter readings.

*On no account should this test be made with the rotor in position, otherwise partial demagnetisa tion will result.*

4. **Bench Testing—Alternator and 2E.T. Ignition Coil**
   **2E.T. Ignition Coil**

The 2E.T. ignition coil should be tested similarly to the procedure detailed for the S.R. magneto coils except for the test voltage which must be 12-volts, and no ammeter is required

A four lobe D.K. type contact breaker having closed periods of not less than 42° and having an operating range up to 750 r.p.m. is required. Also, a 12-volt battery, a three-point rotary spark gap and 1 ohm resistor approximately 15 watt.

Proceed to test as follows:—

7. Connect the 12-volt battery, contact breaker, resistor in series with the coil primary winding. Battery polarity should be such that the negative side of battery is connected to the earthed end of the primary.

   Also connect with a jumper lead, the spark gap point that is farthest from the ionising elec-trode, to the negative side of the circuit.

   Connect the high-tension cable from coil to the three-point spark gap to the electrode nearest the ionising point.

   Run the contact breaker at 750 r.p.m. Regular sparking should occur at the spark gap which should be set to 8 mm. (approximately 14 Kv). This test should not be continued for more than 30 seconds because the arcing of the contacts will be fairly heavy, due to the slow run-ning speed and low primary resistance.

**Alternator—Lighting and Ignition Coils.**
**Lighting Coils—D.C. Output Test**

The lighting coil output can be checked by feeding it through a bridge rectifier standard type—into a 6-volt battery. The battery should have a *rheostat connected across it which should be ad-justed as necessary to maintain the 6-volt potential during testing.

Also in parallel with battery, connect voltmeter to measure potential.

The battery and ammeter should then be connected in series with the lighting coils and readings taken at the following alternator speeds.

| Alternator R.P.M. | Output in Amps into 6-volt battery |
|---|---|
| 2,000 | 2.8 (minimum) |
| 5,000 | 5.3 (maximum) |

**Ignition Coils—D.C. Output Test**

Using the same test gear and procedure as detailed for the lighting coil tests, the ignition coil output readings are as follows:—

| Alternator R.P.M. | Output in Amps into 6-volt battery |
|---|---|
| 2,000 | 1.4 (minimum) |
| 5,000 | 1.8 (maximum) |

The stator complete, or individual coils should be replaced if the output readings for either or both the ignition and lighting coils are outisde the figures quoted.

*CAPABLE OF CARRYING 10 AMPS WITHOUT OVERHEATING.

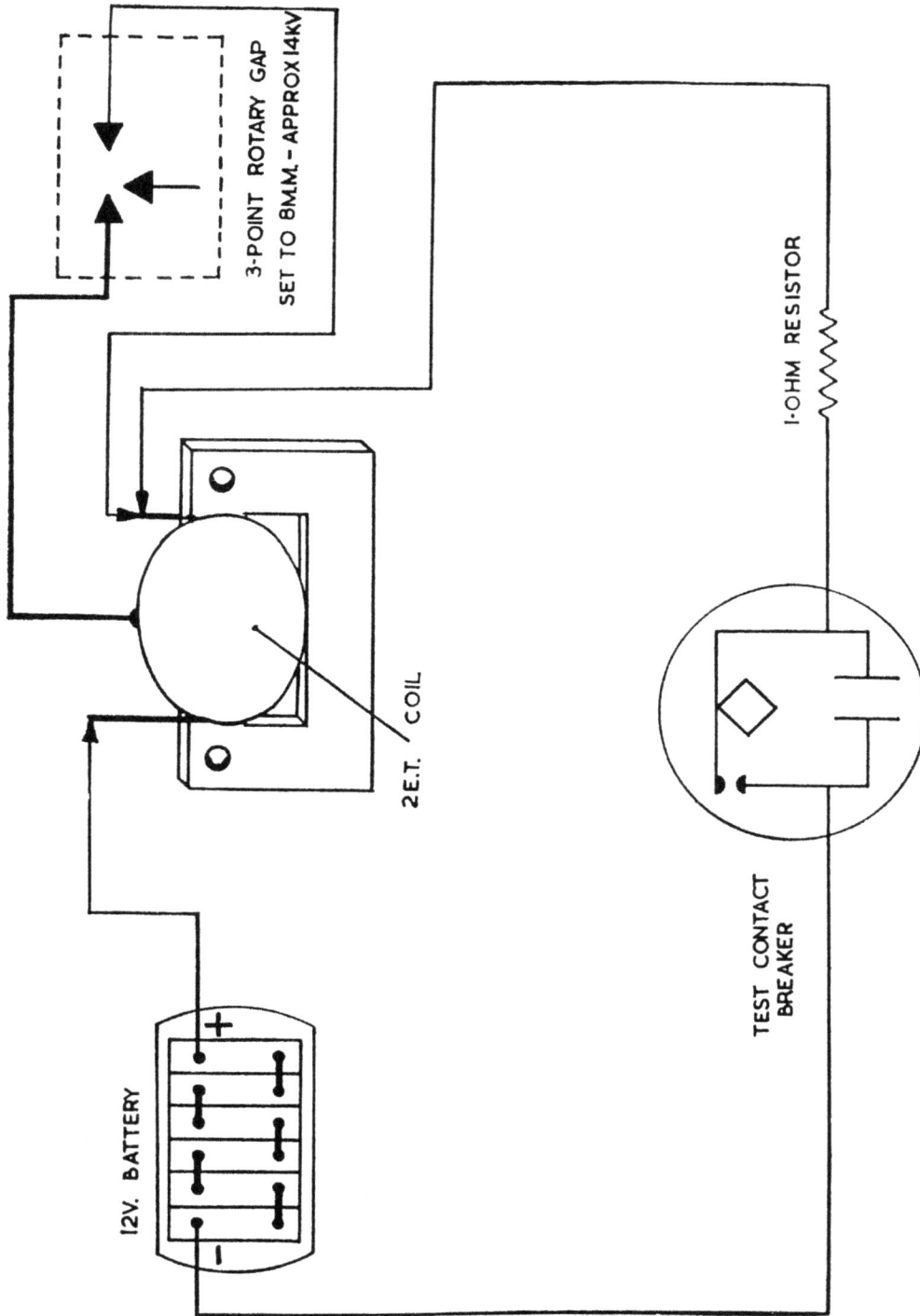

3-POINT ROTARY GAP
SET TO 8MM.-APPROX14KV

2 E.T. COIL

1·OHM RESISTOR

TEST CONTACT BREAKER

12V. BATTERY

2 E.T. "ENERGY TRANSFER" IGNITION COIL
SPARK PERFORMANCE TEST CIRCUIT

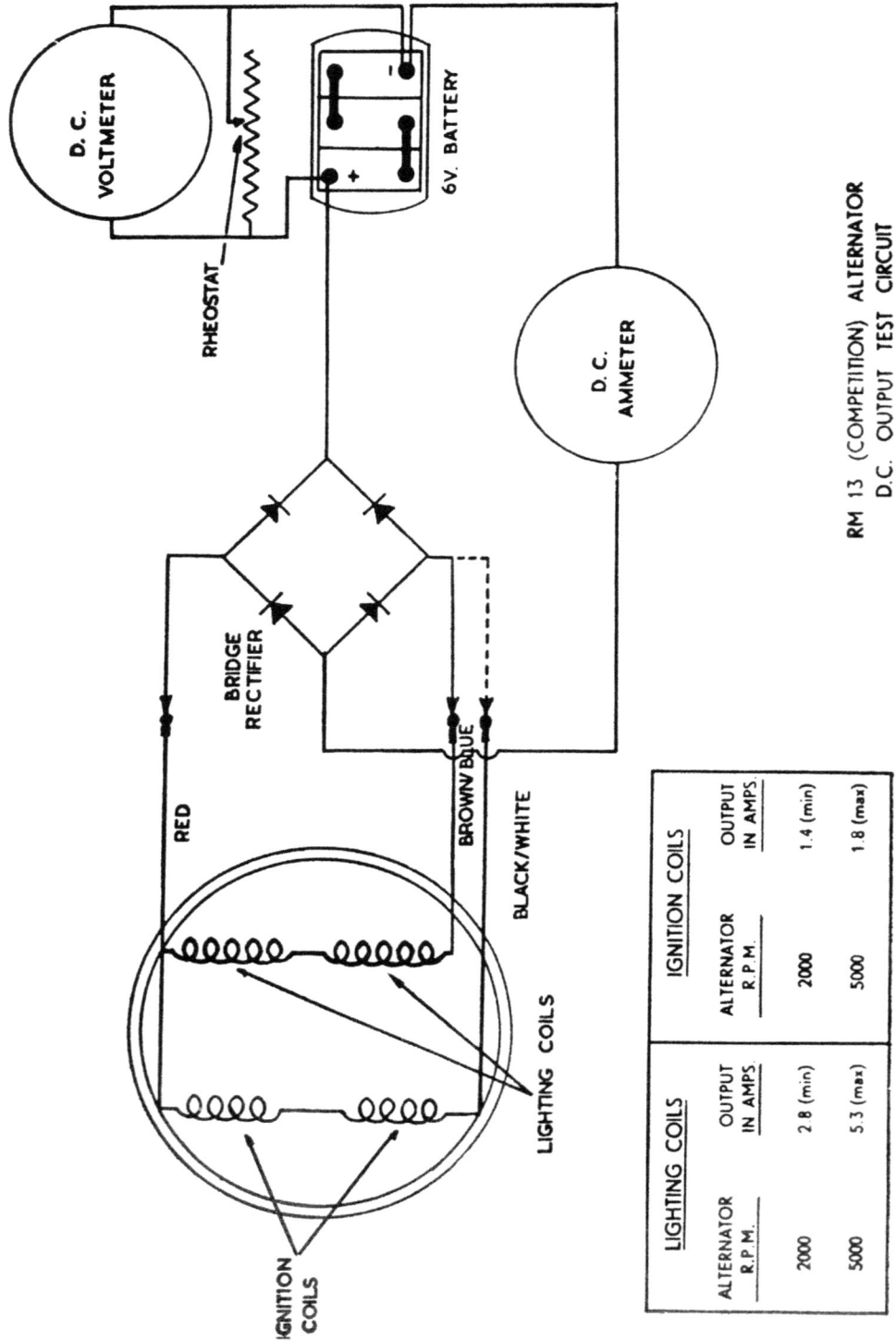

RM 13 (COMPETITION) ALTERNATOR
D.C. OUTPUT TEST CIRCUIT

| LIGHTING COILS | |
| --- | --- |
| ALTERNATOR R.P.M. | OUTPUT IN AMPS. |
| 2000 | 2.8 (min) |
| 5000 | 5.3 (max) |

| IGNITION COILS | |
| --- | --- |
| ALTERNATOR R.P.M. | OUTPUT IN AMPS. |
| 2000 | 1.4 (min) |
| 5000 | 1.8 (max) |

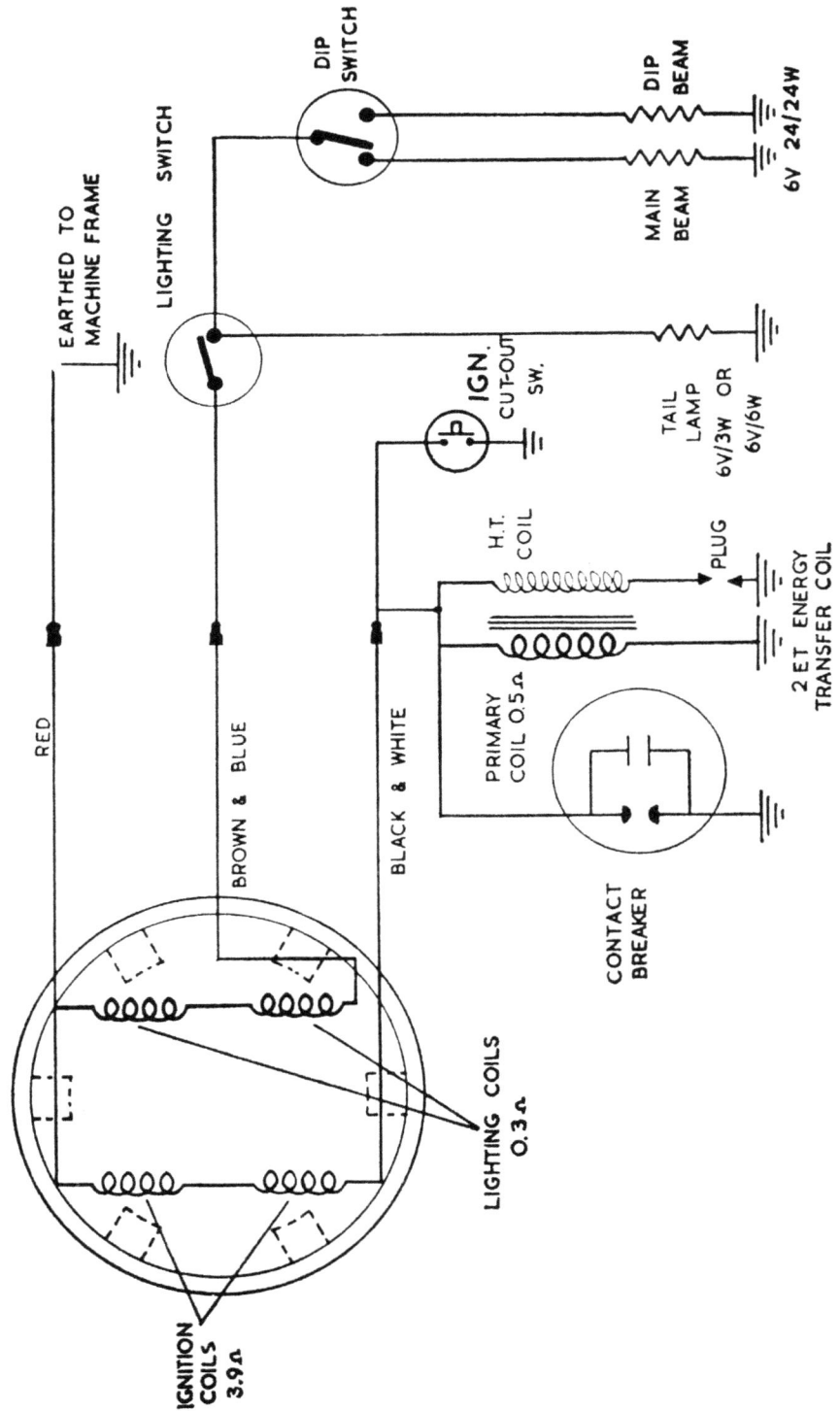

CIRCUIT DIAGRAM OF RM 13 (COMPETITION) ALTERNATOR AND "ENERGY TRANSFER" IGNITION SYSTEM AS FITTED TO C15. COMPETITION MODEL

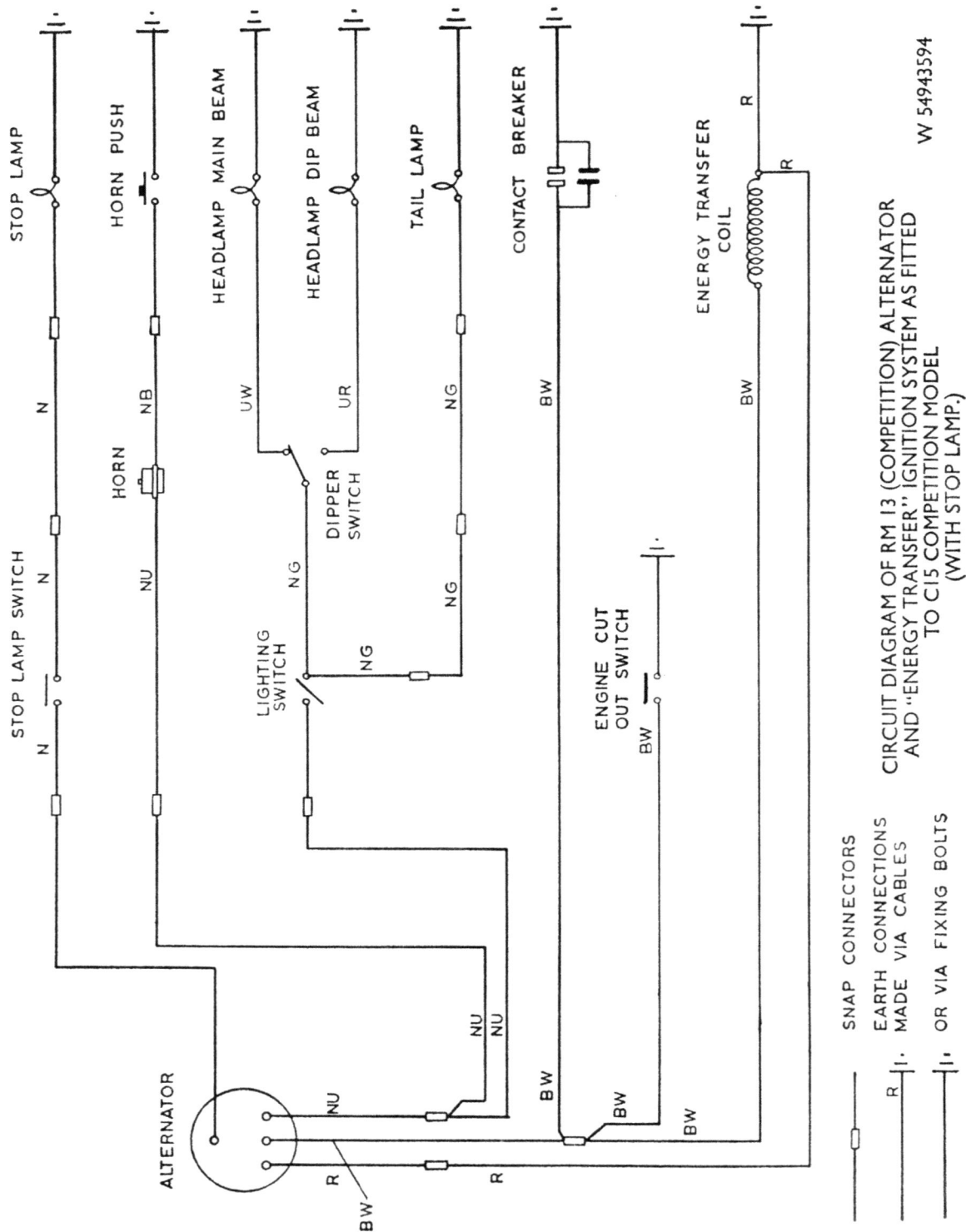

STOP LAMP

HORN PUSH

HEADLAMP MAIN BEAM

HEADLAMP DIP BEAM

TAIL LAMP

CONTACT BREAKER

ENERGY TRANSFER COIL

W 54943594

STOP LAMP SWITCH

HORN

DIPPER SWITCH

LIGHTING SWITCH

ENGINE CUT OUT SWITCH

ALTERNATOR

CIRCUIT DIAGRAM OF RM 13 (COMPETITION) ALTERNATOR AND "ENERGY TRANSFER" IGNITION SYSTEM AS FITTED TO C15 COMPETITION MODEL (WITH STOP LAMP.)

SNAP CONNECTORS

EARTH CONNECTIONS MADE VIA CABLES

OR VIA FIXING BOLTS

**B.S.A. MOTOR CYCLES LTD.**, Service Department, Armoury Road, Birmingham 11.
Printed in England

## VELOCEPRESS MANUALS - MOTORCYCLE

1930'S BRITISH MOTORCYCLE CARBS & ELEC COMPONENTS (BOOK OF)
1930'S BRITISH MOTORCYCLE ENGINES (OVERHAUL & MAINTENANCE)
1930'S BRITISH MOTORCYCLE GEARBOXES & CLUTCHES (BOOK OF)
AJS 1932-1948 SINGLES & TWINS 250cc THRU 1000cc (BOOK OF)
AJS 1945-1960 SINGLES 350cc & 500cc MODELS 16 & 18 (BOOK OF)
AJS 1955-1965 SINGLES 350cc & 500cc (BOOK OF)
ARIEL UP TO 1932 (BOOK OF)
ARIEL 1932-1939 PREWAR MODELS (BOOK OF)
ARIEL 1933-1951 (WORKSHOP MANUAL)
ARIEL 1939-1960 4 STROKE SINGLES (BOOK OF)
ARIEL 1958-1964 LEADER & ARROW (BOOK OF)
BMW R26 R27 (1956-1967) FACTORY WORKSHOP MANUAL
BMW R50 R50S R60 R69S (1955-1969) FACTORY WORKSHOP MANUAL
BRIDGESTONE 90 SERIES FACTORY WSM & PARTS CATALOGUE
BRIDGESTONE 175 SERIES FACTORY WSM & PARTS CATALOGUE
BRIDGESTONE 350 SERIES FACTORY WSM & PARTS CATALOGUES
BSA BANTAM ALL MODELS FROM 1948 ONWARDS (BOOK OF)
BSA SINGLES & V-TWINS UP TO 1927 (BOOK OF)
BSA SINGLES & V-TWINS UP TO 1930 (BOOK OF)
BSA SINGLES & V-TWINS UP TO 1935 (BOOK OF)
BSA SINGLES & V-TWINS 1936-1939 (BOOK OF)
BSA C10, C11 & C12 1945-1958 FACTORY SERVICE SHEETS MANUAL
BSA OHV & SV SINGLES 250-600cc 1945-1959 (BOOK OF)
BSA C15 & B40 1958-1967 FACTORY SERVICE SHEETS MANUAL
BSA OHV & SV SINGLES 250cc (ONLY) 1954-1970 (BOOK OF)
BSA B31, B32, B33 & B34 1945-60 FACTORY SERVICE SHEETS MANUAL
BSA OHV SINGLES 350 & 500cc 1955-1967 (BOOK OF)
BSA M20, M21 & M33 1945-1963 FACTORY SERVICE SHEETS MANUAL
BSA TWINS A7 & A10 1948-1962 FACTORY SERVICE SHEETS MANUAL
BSA TWINS A7 & A10 1948-1962 (BOOK OF)
BSA TWINS A50 & A65 1962-1969 (SECOND BOOK OF)
CYCLEMOTOR (BOOK OF)
DOUGLAS 1929-1939 PREWAR ALL MODELS (BOOK OF)
DOUGLAS 1948-1957 POSTWAR ALL MODELS FACTORY SHOP MANUAL
DUCATI 160cc, 250cc & 350cc OHC MODELS FACTORY SHOP MANUAL
HONDA 50 ALL MODELS UP TO 1970 INC MONKEY & TRAIL (BOOK OF)
HONDA 90 ALL MODELS UP TO 1966 (BOOK OF)
HONDA 125-150cc TWINS C/CS/CB/CA FACTORY WORKSHOP MANUAL
HONDA 250-305 TWINS C/CS/CB FACTORY WORKSHOP MANUAL
HONDA 450 CB/CL 1965-1974 K0 TO K7 WORKSHOP MANUAL
HONDA C100 SUPER CUB FACTORY WORKSHOP MANUAL
HONDA C110 SPORT CUB 1962-1969 FACTORY WORKSHOP MANUAL
HONDA TWINS & SINGLES 50cc THRU 305cc 1960-1966 (BOOK OF)
HONDA TWINS ALL MODELS 125cc THRU 450cc UP TO 1968 (BOOK OF)
INDIAN PONYBIKE, BOY RACER & PAPOOSE ILL PARTS LIST & SALES LIT
J.A.P. ENGINES 1927-1952 & MOTORCYCLES 1934-1952 (BOOK OF)
LAMBRETTA 1947-1957 ALL 125 & 150cc MODELS (BOOK OF)
LAMBRETTA 1957-1970 LI & TV MODELS (SECOND BOOK OF)
MATCHLESS 1931-1939 ALL MODELS 250cc THRU 990cc (BOOK OF)
MATCHLESS 1945-1956 350 & 500cc SINGLES (BOOK OF)
MATCHLESS 1955-1966 350 & 500cc SINGLES (BOOK OF)
NEW IMPERIAL ALL SV & OHV FROM 1935 ONWARDS (BOOK OF)
NORTON 1932-1939 PREWAR MODELS (BOOK OF)
NORTON 1932-1947 (BOOK OF)
NORTON 1938-1956 (BOOK OF)
NORTON 1955-1963 MODELS 19, 50 & ES2 (BOOK OF)
NORTON 1955-1965 DOMINATOR TWINS (BOOK OF)
NORTON 1960-1970 TWIN CYLINDER FACTORY WORKSHOP MANUAL
NORTON 1970-1975 COMMANDO FACTORY WORKSHOP MANUAL
NORTON 1975-1978 MK 3 COMMANDO FACTORY WORKSHOP MANUAL
NSU PRIMA 1956-1964 ALL MODELS (BOOK OF)
NSU QUICKLY 1953-1963 ALL MODELS (BOOK OF)
PANTHER 1932-1958 LIGHTWEIGHT MODELS 250 & 350cc (BOOK OF)
PANTHER 1938-1966 HEAVYWEIGHT MODELS 600 & 650cc (BOOK OF)
RALEIGH MOPEDS 1960-1969 (BOOK OF)
RALEIGH MOTORCYCLES 1919-1933 (BOOK OF)
ROYAL ENFIELD 1934-1946 SINGLES & V TWINS (BOOK OF)
ROYAL ENFIELD 1937-1953 SINGLES & V TWINS (BOOK OF)
ROYAL ENFIELD 1946-1962 SINGLES (BOOK OF)
ROYAL ENFIELD 1958-1966 250cc & 350cc SINGLES (SECOND BOOK OF)
ROYAL ENFIELD 736cc INTERCEPTOR FACTORY WORKSHOP MANUAL
RUDGE 1933-1939 (BOOK OF)
SUNBEAM 1928-1939 (BOOK OF)
SUNBEAM 1946-1957 S7 & S8 (BOOK OF)
SUZUKI 50cc & 80cc UP TO 1966 (BOOK OF)
SUZUKI T10 1963-1967 FACTORY WORKSHOP MANUAL
SUZUKI T20 & T200 1965-1969 FACTORY WORKSHOP MANUAL
SUZUKI TWINS 1962 ONWARDS 125-500cc WORKSHOP MANUAL
TRIUMPH 1935-1939 PREWAR MODELS (BOOK OF)
TRIUMPH 1935-1949 (BOOK OF)
TRIUMPH 1937-1951 (WORKSHOP MANUAL)
TRIUMPH 1945-1955 FACTORY WORKSHOP MANUAL
TRIUMPH 1945-1958 TWINS (BOOK OF)
TRIUMPH 1956-1969 TWINS (BOOK OF)
VELOCETTE 1925-1970 ALL SINGLES & TWINS (BOOK OF)
VESPA 1951-1961 (BOOK OF)
VESPA 1955-1963 125 & 150cc & GS MODELS (SECOND BOOK OF)
VESPA 1955-1968 GS & SS (BOOK OF)
VESPA 1963-1972 90, 125 & 150cc (THIRD BOOK OF)
VILLIERS ENGINE UP TO 1959 INC. 3 WHEELERS (BOOK OF)
VILLIERS ENGINE UP TO 1969 (BOOK OF)
VINCENT 1935-1955 (WORKSHOP MANUAL)
YAMAHA 1961-1967 YA5 & YA6 (WORKSHOP MANUAL & ILL PARTS LIST)
YAMAHA 1971-1972 JT1 & JT2 (WORKSHOP MANUAL & ILL PARTS LIST)

## VELOCEPRESS TECHNICAL BOOKS – MOTORCYCLE

CATALOG OF BRITISH MOTORCYCLES (1951 MODELS)
LUCAS ELECTRONICS BRITISH M/CYCLES REPAIR & PARTS (1950-1977)
MOTORCYCLE ENGINEERING (P.E. Irving)
MOTORCYCLE ROAD TESTS 1949-1953 (Motor Cycle Magazine UK)
SPEED AND HOW TO OBTAIN IT (Motor Cycle Magazine UK)
TUNING FOR SPEED (P.E. Irving)

## VELOCEPRESS MANUALS - THREE WHEELER'S

BSA THREE WHEELER (BOOK OF)
VINTAGE MORGAN THREE WHEELER (BOOK OF)

## VELOCEPRESS MANUALS - AUTOMOBILE

ALFA ROMEO GIULIA WORKSHOP MANUAL 1300 TO 2000cc 1962-1975
ALFA ROMEO GIULIA TECH MANUAL CARBURETED CARS FROM 1962
ALFA ROMEO GIULIA TECH MANUAL FUEL INJECTED CARS FROM 1969
ALFA ROMEO GIULIETTA & GIULIA 750 & 101 SERIES 1955-1965 WSM
AUSTIN-HEALEY SPRITE & MG MIDGET WORKSHOP MANUAL 1958-1971
BMW 600 LIMOUSINE FACTORY WORKSHOP MANUAL
BMW 600 LIMOUSINE OWNERS HAND BOOK & SERVICE MANUAL
BMW 2000 & 2002 1966-1976 WORKSHOP MANUAL
BMW ISETTA FACTORY WORKSHOP MANUAL
CORVAIR 1960-1969 WORKSHOP MANUAL
CORVETTE V8 1955-1962 WORKSHOP MANUAL
FIAT 500 FACTORY WORKSHOP MANUAL 1957-1973
FIAT 600, 600D & MULTIPLA FACTORY WORKSHOP MANUAL 1955-1969
JAGUAR E-TYPE 3.8 & 4.2 SERIES 1 & 2 WORKSHOP MANUAL
JAGUAR MK 7, 8, 9 & XK120, 140, 150 WORKSHOP MANUAL 1948-1961
METROPOLITAN FACTORY WORKSHOP MANUAL
MGA & MGB OWNERS HANDBOOK & WORKSHOP MANUAL
MG MIDGET TC, TD, TF & TF1500 WORKSHOP MANUAL
PORSCHE 356 1948-1965 WORKSHOP MANUAL
PORSCHE 911 2.0, 2.2, 2.4 LITRE 1964-1973 WORKSHOP MANUAL
PORSCHE 911 2.7, 3.0, 3.2 LITRE 1973-1989 WORKSHOP MANUAL
PORSCHE 912 WORKSHOP MANUAL
TRIUMPH TR2, TR3, TR4 1953-1965 WORKSHOP MANUAL
VOLKSWAGEN TRANSPORTER, TRUCKS & WAGONS 1950-1979 WSM
VOLVO 1944-1968 ALL MODELS WORKSHOP MANUAL

## VELOCEPRESS TECHNICAL BOOKS - AUTOMOBILE

FERRARI 250/GT SERVICE AND MAINTENANCE
FERRARI GUIDE TO PERFORMANCE
FERRARI OWNER'S HANDBOOK
FERRARI TUNING TIPS & MAINTENANCE TECHNIQUES
HOW TO BUILD A FIBERGLASS CAR
HOW TO BUILD A RACING CAR
HOW TO RESTORE THE MODEL 'A' FORD
MASERATI OWNER'S HANDBOOK
OBERT'S FIAT GUIDE
PERFORMANCE TUNING THE SUNBEAM TIGER
SOUPING THE VOLKSWAGEN
SOLEX CARBURETORS (EMPHASIS ON UK & EU AUTOMOBILES)
SU CARBURETORS (EMPHASIS ON UK AUTOMOBILES)
WEBER CARBURETORS (EMPHASIS ON ALFA & FIAT)

## VELOCEPRESS BOOKS & GUIDES - AUTOMOBILE

ABARTH BUYERS GUIDE
COMPLETE CATALOG OF JAPANESE MOTOR VEHICLES
FERRARI 308 SERIES BUYER'S & OWNER'S GUIDE
FERRARI BERLINETTA LUSSO
FERRARI BROCHURES AND SALES LITERATURE 1946-1967
FERRARI BROCHURES AND SALES LITERATURE 1968-1989
FERRARI OPP, MAINTENANCE & SERVICE H/BOOKS 1948-1963
FERRARI SERIAL NUMBERS PART I - ODD NUMBERS TO 21399
FERRARI SERIAL NUMBERS PART II - EVEN NUMBERS TO 1050
FERRARI SPYDER CALIFORNIA
HENRY'S FABULOUS MODEL "A" FORD
MASERATI BROCHURES AND SALES LITERATURE

## VELOCEPRESS BOOKS – RACING

CARRERA PANAMERICANA - MEXICAN ROAD RACE (BOOK OF)
DIALED IN - THE JAN OPPERMAN STORY
IF HEMINGWAY HAD WRITTEN A RACING NOVEL
VEDA ORR'S NEW REVISED HOT ROD PICTORIAL

## AUTOBOOKS WORKSHOP MANUALS & BROOKLANDS
## ROAD TEST PORTFOLIOS

FOR A COMPLETE LISTING OF THE AUTOBOOKS & BROOKLANDS TITLES
THAT WE CURRENTLY HAVE AVAILABLE, PLEASE VISIT OUR WEBSITE.
**www.VelocePress.com**

Please check our
website:

**www.VelocePress.com**

for a complete
up-to-date list of
available titles

Milton Keynes UK
Ingram Content Group UK Ltd.
UKHW052103170823
427026UK00005B/319

9 781588 502490